Far Above the Plain

Private Profiles and Admissable Evidence from the First Forty Years of Murree Christian School, Pakistan

1956-1996

Paul Asbury Seaman

and contributing writers

William Carey Library

Pasadena, California

Published by
William Carey Library
P.O. Box 40129
Pasadena, California 91114
(818) 798-0819

Library of Congress Cataloging-in-Publication Data

Far above the plain : private profiles and admissable evidence from
    the first forty years of Murree Christian School, Pakistan / edited
    by Paul Asbury Seaman.
        p.   cm.
    ISBN 0-87808-268-9 (alk. paper)
    1. Murree Christian School (Murree, Pakistan)--History.
    2. Christian education--Pakistan--Murree--History. 1. Seaman,
        Paul Asbury, 1957-
    LG170.M87F37   1996
    377' .8'09549142--dc20   96-19785
                                                            CIP

Cover Art and Design by Karin Tunnéll

Printed in the United States of America

To Beth Haugen Dekkers
and
Wendy Olsen Bates
and
all the others whose lives were shaped by MCS,
whose stories—both precious and painful—
are not celebrated here.

In memory of "Auntie Inger" Gardner
1913-1996
second mother to so many of us,
always with a twinkle in her eyes.
We'll see you in heaven for another round of "kissing fights."

Contents

*The six chapters not otherwise designated
are by Paul Seaman*

Author's Note

What follows is the story of a particular school for missionaries' children, told mostly through the reminiscings of its former staff and students. A smaller portion is devoted to personal evaluations of such an upbringing from the retrospective of adulthood, as well as some historical context. This more holistic approach, does, however, present some challenges to narrative continuity. While each chapter or section is intended to build upon the last, this is an anthology, designed to serve different purposes depending on each reader's needs or interest.

The book is organized into roughly four sections: the early history of Murree Christian School (chapters 2-9); more reminiscings by former students (chapters 10-15); staff sketches and recollections (chapters 16-21); and leaving and looking back (chapters 22-27).

I have preserved the use of certain Urdu words in the text, reflecting the tendency of expatriates everywhere to incorporate elements of the local language even among themselves. Though definitions are usually provided in context, those readers not familiar with Pakistani culture may wish to review the glossary at the back of this book. A map of South Asia appears in the first photo section.

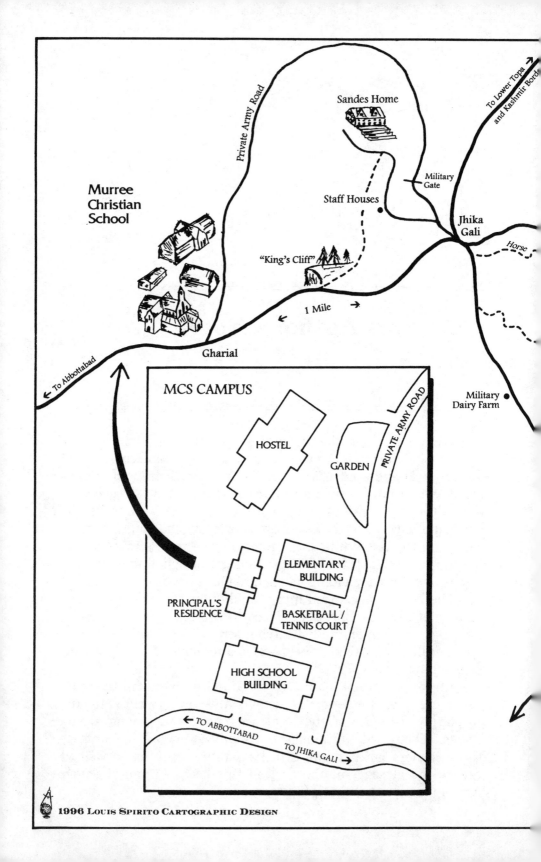

Murree Christian School

Sandes Home

Private Army Road

To Lower Topa and Kashmir Border

Military Gate

Staff Houses

Jhika Gali

Horse

"King's Cliff"

1 Mile

To Abbottabad

Gharial

Military Dairy Farm

MCS CAMPUS

Private Army Road

HOSTEL

GARDEN

ELEMENTARY BUILDING

PRINCIPAL'S RESIDENCE

BASKETBALL / TENNIS COURT

HIGH SCHOOL BUILDING

← TO ABBOTTABAD

TO JHIKA GALI →

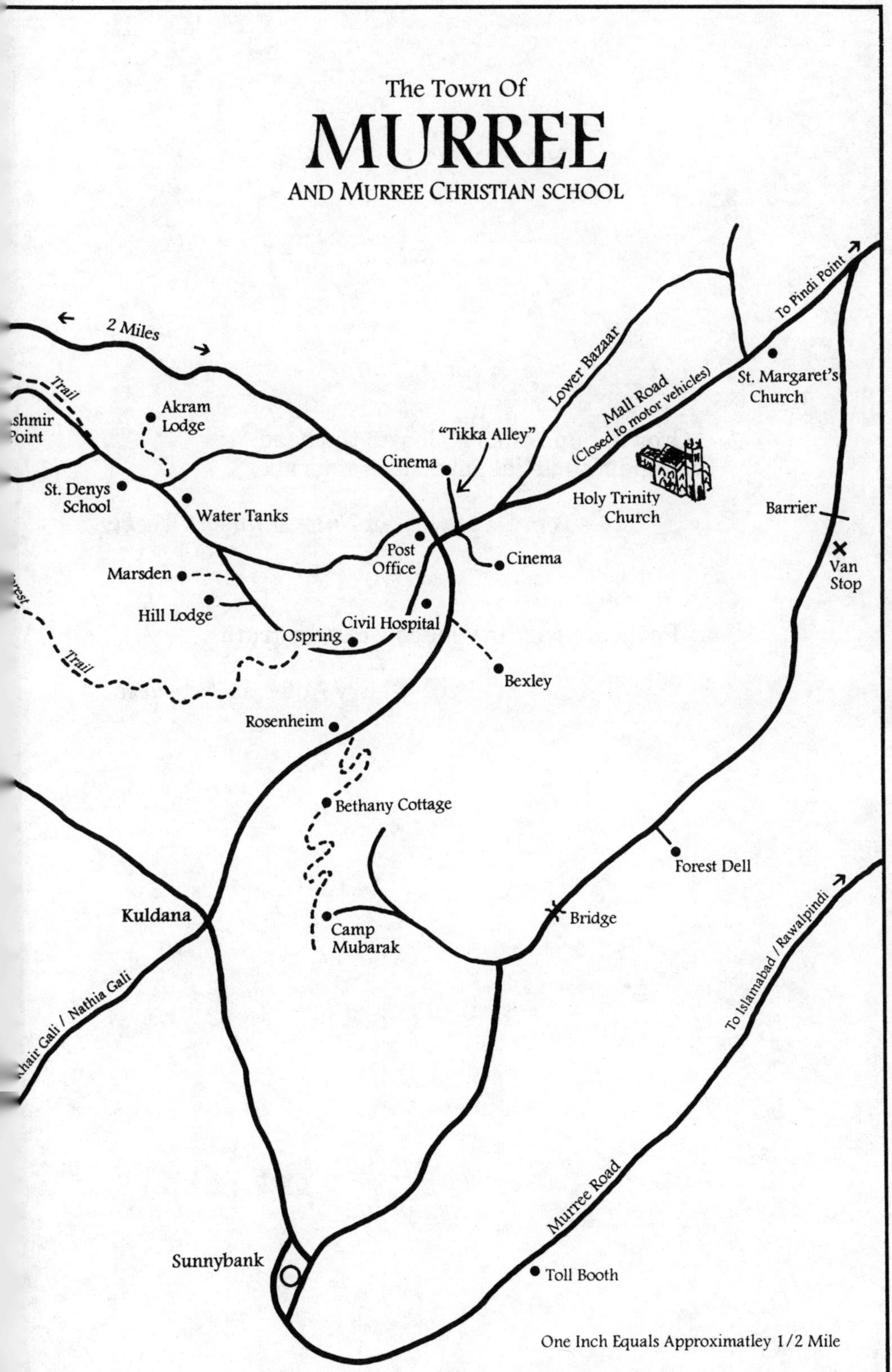

The Town Of
MURREE
AND MURREE CHRISTIAN SCHOOL

2 Miles

Trail

Kashmir Point

Akram Lodge

St. Denys School

Water Tanks

Marsden

Hill Lodge

Ospring

Forest Trail

"Tikka Alley"

Cinema

Post Office

Cinema

Civil Hospital

Bexley

Rosenheim

Bethany Cottage

Kuldana

Khair Gali / Nathia Gali

Camp Mubarak

Bridge

Forest Dell

Lower Bazaar

Mall Road (Closed to motor vehicles)

Holy Trinity Church

To Pindi Point

St. Margaret's Church

Barrier

Van Stop

To Islamabad / Rawalpindi

Sunnybank

Murree Road

Toll Booth

One Inch Equals Approximatley 1/2 Mile

Growing up is like a blow to the head:
It makes partial amnesiacs of us all.

—Tom De Haven, in *Entertainment Weekly*

Facts are only the shadow cast by truth.

—Jerry Adler, in *Newsweek*

Introduction

Our Not-So-Special Uniqueness

I was born the same week the Russians launched into orbit the first artificial satellite, *Sputnik I*, setting off a panic in the Free World and a space race on either side of the Iron Curtain. (The *Sputnik* did this, not me.) Earlier that same year, two art school students from Liverpool, John Lennon and Paul McCartney, met at a church picnic and discovered a common interest in American rock 'n' roll—though it would be another seven years before they had their first hit in the United States ("I Want to Hold Your Hand"). Also in 1957, Murree Christian School officially became a cooperative, interdenominational institution for the education of missionaries' children in Pakistan. While more people may be familiar with the Beatles, their origins are less significant than those of MCS, at least for the purposes of this book.

We can surmise a great deal about the perspective of the school's founders by looking at the times in which they lived. Although many of them had already been in Pakistan for several years, they were aware of and inevitably influenced by the dominant social forces that were shaping the societies from which they came. Most missionaries in the new nation of Paki-

1

stan, founded in 1947, when the British left India, were from the United States. And in the 1950s, conservative Protestant Christian culture was the mainstream cultural myth in America. "Everyone" went to church, lived in nuclear families and, with conscious effort and "right living," had equal access to the American Dream.

In 1957 Billy Graham attracted 100,000 people to an evangelistic crusade in New York City—the largest crowd in Yankee Stadium's history. President Dwight Eisenhower and Vice President Richard Nixon began their second term; Jimmy Hoffa was elected president of the powerful Teamsters labor union. Hula hoops and Marilyn Monroe were all the rage.

In reality, though, by 1957 the Fifties were fast coming unravelled. That year the Ford Motor company introduced the soon-to-be-infamous Edsel, "the best engineered automobile ever designed"—and the biggest flop in automotive history: technology and big business were not necessarily infallible. A discredited Senator Joseph McCarthy ended his ten-year career in the U.S. Senate—though anti-Communist hysteria would continue for several more years, fueled by the stand-off in Korea and the much publicized activities of Soviet Premier Nikita Khrushchev and Chairman Mao Tse-tung.

In 1957, many people had not yet heard of John F. Kennedy, or Vietnam; but the Montgomery, Alabama, bus boycott had begun the year before, triggering nationwide protests against segregation and beginning what would become known as the Civil Rights Movement.

At the same time, Elvis Presley was taking the nation—and the media—by storm. Dick Clark's American Bandstand made its national debut in 1957. Patsy Cline, Sam Cooke, the Everly Brothers, Buddy Holly, Jerry Lee Lewis, Johnny Mathis, Jimmie Rodgers, and Jackie Wilson are just some of the singers who began their careers in 1957. The year began with Harry Belafonte's "Banana Boat (Day-O)" and ended with Jerry Lee Lewis pounding out "Great Balls of Fire." The world would never be the same.

Antique Chevies and my own birth notwithstanding, "57" seems to be an auspicious number. Curiously, this year served as a defining marker, a watershed of changing currents, for the previous two centuries as well. In 1757, at the Battle of Plassey outside Calcutta, the British defeated the native ruler of Bengal, effectively establishing themselves as the dominant power on the Indian subcontinent.

A hundred years later, the privately-owned British East India company had expanded and controlled their territory largely through the use of Indian troops, called Sepoys, under the command of British officers. The Sepoy Mutiny—known to Indian and Pakistani historians as the First War of Independence—began in 1857. While the Rebellion was a failure, its consequences were profound. The following year Queen Victoria abolished the East India Company and India came under the direct administration of the British Crown—thus ending an era and beginning another. European *political* colonialism (not just economic exploitation) would now dominate the globe for the next ninety years.

In 1857 Charles Dickens and Abraham Lincoln were forty-four years old; Dwight L. Moody, one of the century's greatest Christian evangelists, was twenty-one. David Livingstone published his seminal treatise on the exploration and history of southern Africa in 1857, stimulating renewed missionary—and mercantile—interest in that continent. Two years later Charles Darwin published his *Origins of Species.** Wheaton College, a four-year liberal arts school distinguished for its emphasis on international missions, was founded in 1860. (A hundred and thirty-five years later, it is interesting to note that more MCS graduates have enrolled at Wheaton than at any other college.) Woodstock School in Mussoorie, India—the oldest school for MKs (missionary kids) in continuous existence to the present—was three years old in 1857. The Second Great Evangelical Awakening, burning across the United States, crossed the Atlantic that year, revitalizing the missionary movement in Great Britain. As a result, the next several decades saw such a great influx of Protestant missionaries to India, China, and elsewhere that the hundred years preceding World War II have been referred to as "the missionary century."

In the four decades covered by this book, the role of missionaries in Third World countries changed dramatically. Since the 1960s, the Christian understanding of missions has been transformed nearly as much as the social and political con-

---

*I am indebted to Stephen Neill, *A History of Christian Missions*, for these statistics. (For bibliographical data, see For Further Reading at the end of this book).

sciousness of many nations. The new attitudes of East and West toward each other, reflecting better education and changing economic realities, have altered the global dynamic. Yet, missionaries from Western countries are still a significant presence in nations of the *"three-fourths* world."

The care and education of missionaries' children is no quaint enterprise from the past. Today, thousands of MKs still attend special schools "overseas," not even counting Christian academies in North America and Great Britain. No matter where they are located, these schools share a distinct subculture created by the unique combination of isolation and multi-cultural influence: isolated by very specific values and by the circumstances of their presence in a foreign country—yet, influenced by that same foreign context and by the typically international and ecumenical character of the institutions themselves.

* * *

Nestled in the forested foothills of the great Himalayan mountains, Murree Christian School sits 7,500 feet above the plains in northern Pakistan—a developing country that is ninety-seven percent Muslim. The student population of MCS, from more than a dozen countries, has averaged about 130 pupils in twelve grades. The forty-five to fifty faculty and boarding staff, similarly diverse in their nationalites, represent fourteen different mission groups. Some boys and girls came from as far away as the United Arab Emirates, but most of our families were scattered across the plains of Pakistan—on rural mission stations or in Christian hospitals, colleges, and technical schools in larger towns or cities.

Murree is a summer town, a former colonial "hill station" of the British raj. Attending boarding school meant that we moved four times a year, and our schedule was dictated largely by the weather. Like nomads, we moved with the seasons: boarding for three months in the spring; day school in the summer when, like the old colonials, our parents came to Murree for a few months to escape the blistering heat of the plains; back into boarding for the fall; then, before the mountain snows closed in, we left for our family homes and the long winter holidays.

This annual cycle began and ended with a "train party." Each December, forty or fifty of us travelled together in specially designated coaches on a public train, back to our various homes "down the line"—from Rawalpindi at the foot of the mountains, a thousand miles to Karachi on the coast. After the winter break, another train took us away from our families again. Boarding could be lonely, but after three months of separation from our friends, we were usually eager to go back. As with the seasons, with each move we had something to look forward to and something was lost.

So Great a Cloud of Witnesses

Growing up always means leaving some things behind, but when the Final Move, high school graduation or changing family circumstances, brought us back to our "home" countries we lost some of the major reference points that had defined our identity. The sheltered-yet-international environment in which many of us had spent the greater portion of our childhood as "MKs," had also made us "TCKs."

"Third Culture Kids" can usually adapt well to various cross-cultural situations, but no longer feel completely at home anywhere. Returning MKs must not only cope with an abrupt and dramatic transition during an already vulnerable stage of their lives, but must do so while suddenly deprived of the community that shaped and supported them. The result is often a permanent sense of transience and ambiguity about one's social and cultural identity—the loneliness of a restless spirit that no longer knows where it belongs.

Yet, MKs are part of a larger community of "global nomads"—*persons of any nationality who have spent childhood years living in one or more countries outside their passport country because of a parent's occupation.* Whether our parents served with government, voluntary, or missionary agencies, as the offspring of diplomats, international businesspeople, or military personnel, global nomads share a common cultural heritage. Regardless of the number of years or countries involved, or parents' professional affiliation, global nomads to a remarkable degree share similar responses to the benefits and challenges of a childhood abroad. (The definition used here is by Norma McCaig, founder of Global Nomads International, and usually applies synonymously with the term Third Culture Kid. However, others have expanded this description to include those raised at least partially *outside their primary culture,* even if their families remain in the same country. These pre-adult *transcultural experiences* include, for example, U.S. MKs whose parents work with Native Americans on reservations and persons from India brought up in an international/missionary boarding school such as Woodstock.)

The most extensive work on Third Culture Kids has been done by Ruth Hill Useem, who coined the term "TCK" in the late-1960s. "Third Culture" refers to the distinctive expatriate communities that develop in foreign settings (something more than a combination of home culture and host culture), usually distinguished by an international mix yet relatively self-contained. "Kid" emphasizes the particular shaping impact of living in such communities in *childhood* years, as opposed to the experience of adult professionals, parents, exchange students, or Peace Corps volunteers whose core personalities and values are already formed. Thus, someone raised in a missionary boarding school in Asia often will share common traits and perspectives with a person raised on military bases in Europe.

In recent years, much has been written about TCKs and global nomads, analyzing the special skills and insights they have gained as well as the social and emotional consequences of too many goodbyes.* It is sometimes said that global nomads are not rootless—they are rooted horizontally rather than vertically, in relationships rather than a place. This book is not so much a history of an institution as a portrait of a community, providing an example of the distinctive environment in which many global nomads are rooted. It is about the people and relationships that made the place where some of us grew up a memory called home. It is about ordinary life in an extraordinary situation.

---

*See, for example, David Pollock and Ruth E. Van Reken, *Growing Up Among Worlds: The Third Culture Experience*; *Notes from a Traveling Childhood*, ed. Karen Curnow McCluskey; Clyde N. Austin, *Cross-Cultural Reentry: A Book of Readings*; and Ruth E. Van Reken, *Letters Never Sent*, a now-classic, deeply personal account of one MK's struggle with the lifelong impact of childhood cycles of separation and loss.

* * *

We did not hunt lions at MCS; we were not forced to flee native rebellions or face the tides of historic changes often associated with missionary tales from Africa or China. None of us became an astronaut or a senator. None of our parents were martyred and we were only mildly inconvenienced by two short wars between Pakistan and India (in 1965, over Kashmir, and in 1971, related to the civil war in East Pakistan). The worst trauma most of us experienced was schoolyard teasings or adolescent confrontations with authority. Our daily life was dramatic—the way it is for all young children. In most essential ways, we lived a normal life.

So why did MCS have such a lasting impact on all those who passed through it—not just on those of us who grew up there but also on the student who spent only second and third grades there? And why is the short-term missionary who served on staff at MCS for only two years still haunted by the experience two decades later? What makes these memories so compelling, something more than dusty nostalgia for an obscure institution?

Perhaps the answer lies in the series of paradoxes that define the commonality of those who share a similar background:

—the simultaneously disruptive and stabilizing effect of boarding school, taking us from our families yet providing a strong, reliable community we even called home;

—the inter-cultural challenges *within* the insular, evangelical environment of an international and inter-denominational school—and the often limited interaction we had with our host country;

—"feeling at home in several countries or cultures, but not completely at home in any of them" (David Pollock, Director of InterAction, Inc.);

—the tension between the rich experiential education—the global wisdom—of such an upbringing, and the loneliness that often comes with the uprooting, loss, and cultural displacement that are a part of it;

—the conflict between our inner and outer realities—such as dealing with our memories of this experience when feelings are more real than facts yet have less authority.

The community of strangers—our experience of family with other global nomads—is one of the larger and often unrecognized paradoxes of this heritage. Most of us returned to our "home" countries one by one and felt the impact of our uprooting as individuals. Yet, the "unique" background that caused our sense of isolation is shared by a great number of people.

The April 1995 *Evangelical Missions Quarterly* listed 130 schools for missionaries' children in 56 countries. Over half of these have boarding facilities. While several of these schools have less than ten students, 26 of them have over 200. In 1994, Faith Academy in the Philippines had 740 students; Morrison Academy in Taiwan, 690; Academia Los Pinares in Honduras, 604; Kodaikanal International School in South India, 556; Alliance Academy in Ecuador, 503; Rift Valley Academy in Kenya, 470; Woodstock School in Northern India, 460. MCS currently has 112 students.

There are four MK schools on the Indian subcontinent. (Hebron School, run by British missions, has 235 students.) Woodstock and Kodaikanal are among the few schools in the world that are both Christian and truly international in their orientation.* This means not only having MKs from many different countries, but also an intentional policy of keeping the ratio of the student body—in Woodstock's case—one-third MKs, one-third other expatriate children, and one-third Indian nationals. A reunion of Woodstock School held in Harrisonburg, Virginia in July 1995 drew more than 350 alumni.

The report in the *Evangelical Missions Quarterly* indicated over 15,000 students currently attending MK schools around the world. Other recent studies have identified more than 300,000 adult MKs in the United States alone. In *The Absentee American: Repatriates' Perspectives on America*, Carolyn Smith estimates that "nearly a quarter of a million school-age children are currently living overseas and that since the 1940s as many as 700,000 American teenagers have attended high school overseas" (p. 3).

Many books have been written on the transition or reentry experience of global nomads, analyzing their adjustment

---

*Esther Shull Riley, *The Woodstock Quadrangle* (Summer 1988), p. 3.

and development after they come back to their "home" country, and describing the psychological issues that result from this type of upbringing. *Far Above the Plain* focuses on the formative experience itself. While researching the broader context of the MCS experience, I came across several works that chronicled life in MK schools a generation ago.

Sheila Miller's *Pigtails, Petticoats and the Old School Tie* (OMF Books, 1981), for example, chronicles the first one hundred years of Chefoo School in China. Founded in 1881 and run by the Overseas Missionary Fellowship (formerly China Inland Mission), this school had more than its share of high drama: the Boxer Rebellion in 1900; a food poisoning incident the following year in which thirteen people at the school died; in 1911 the Bubonic Plague hit the Port of Chefoo; and in 1935 a ship bringing seventy-four children back to the school after the Christmas holidays was hijacked by Chinese pirates. The Chefoo School experienced World War I, the Sino-Japanese War, and World War II; in 1942 the school actually continued in a Japanese internment camp; and finally, it was expelled from the country in 1951 by the Communist government.

But the alumni of Chefoo School (which still continues in Japan and Malaysia) also remember things familiar to those who attended a missionary boarding school almost anywhere: pillow fights and short-sheeted beds; nightly story time and "crocodile" lines to and from school; little boys eagerly carving roads into the hillside (except their "dinky towns" always included air raid shelters and minimal, overly-supervised contact with the opposite sex.) One woman recalled "midnight picnics in weird places where they were never caught, dangerous ledge-walking on the outside of buildings in their nighties at dead of night. The staff resorted to prayer meetings just for her!" (p. 58). Others remembered severe and humiliating punishments, including canings for the boys, for the most minor infractions of the rules.

Hazel Innes Craig has written a remarkable book about British boarding schools—many of them run by missionaries—in colonial India, from the mid-1850s until Independence in 1947. In *Under the Old School Topee* (BACSA/Chameleon, 1990) she notes, "The 89 schools referred to in the text only represent *some* of the many" (p. 185, italics mine). Her accounts of boarding school life from a hundred years ago are remarkably similar to life at MCS: cold buildings, camp-outs, butterfly and beetle collections, school plays; punishments that included missing tea or weekend privileges, or having to write out lines; Halloweens when the senior high scared the little kids with peeled grapes and cold noodles in a "Ghost Dungeon"; dormitory raids, horseback rides, group outings to a fancy restaurant, roller skating parties, and weekly walks that were the occasion for subtle and nervous flirting.

Hazel Craig's recollections of the religious atmosphere certainly have a familiar ring to them, such as this anecdote:

> [One evening I joined] some of my more devout companions in a visit to a lady missionary's room for a heart-to-heart evangelistic chat. She asked us to cross the bridge and be saved. We readily complied. This was just before supper and we ignored the bell ringing for us to get into line and march into the dining room. We emerged from her room tearful, cheerful and uplifted. What did it matter if we were late for supper? We had been SAVED. The teacher on supper duty was unimpressed (p. 133).

These parallels are further illustrated in Gertrude Sovik and Charlotte Martinson Gronseth's *The Rooster Crows Again: The Story of American School Kikungshan* (private, 1985),* an MK school in China from 1911 to 1949. In this book alumni reminisce about cold baths, love of the beautiful mountain setting, "singspiration"—and enthusiasm at the opportunity to choose hymns--midnight sneaks out of the dorm, secret pets, homesickness, Friday night games, Capture the Flag, Saturday chores and shoe polishing, cups of water over door sills as pranks, seasonal recitals and sports competitions, and Sunday night walks.

Ah, Friday night! No study hall, no baths nor

---

*Both this book and Sheila Miller's *Pigtails, Petticoats and the Old School Tie* are available from the Billy Graham Center Library at Wheaton College, Wheaton, Illinois.

evening prayers, just glorious, wonderful wild
tearing around in the semidarkness playing
games, hoping that the prince or princess would
catch you, even though the games were only little
kids' games . . .

Or this:

To this day I can recite long passages of the New
Testament, learned long ago all for the love of
fudge.

Many other examples could be given from Faith Academy
in the Philippines, Rift Valley Academy in Kenya, or the many
MK schools in Latin America. However, I found the most striking illustration of our similar experiences in *Canadian School
in West China,* edited by Brockman Brace (Hunter Rose, 1974).
One section of this book reports on the results of a questionnaire sent to alumni in 1969 (the school existed from 1909
to 1950). Over *350* alumni responded to the survey, which included a lengthy biographical section on their lives since returning to their home countries. Donald Willmott summarizes
the results thematically, offering a composite, or profile, of the
Canadian School alumni, "responses which by and large characterize many of us and perhaps distinguish us from other people who did not come through the same experience" (p. 130).
Willmott lists internationalism, toleration, anti-materialism,
high standards, activism, faith, and service; he illustrates and
supports these categories with several quotations from the Canadian School survey, including the following (from pp. 130-
137):

(We are) more concerned generally about social
and world issues; more acutely aware of the affluence of the West and the great disparity with
the Third World; more conscious of the World as
a Global Village . . .

We are a bit more tolerant of other ideologies, religions, and races.

The CS gave me a standard of social and communal behavior which I could not escape from now if I wanted to . . . . On the whole, the standards of behavior were very much above those one meets in the "outside world."

I think that the high standards of the Canadian School challenged me to increasing effort at the school and also ultimately in striving for scholastic, church, and social achievement as I progressed in life.

At this point, Willmott perceptively notes that

. . . having high aspirations and high standards does sometimes set the stage for feelings of failure, for feelings of worthlessness, for compulsiveness [a tendency that showed up on the Canadian School survey]. . . .
    Some of this may be a reflection of the fact that many of us experienced very great problems of adjustment when we returned from China to Canada, the United States or England. These difficulties were often mentioned on the questionnaire. This traumatic transplanting may have contributed to our somewhat greater sense of insecurity or self-doubt. But I believe that high standards of achievement are also one of the factors which create this feeling of uneasiness about ourselves.

Willmott mentions the great frequency with which alumni refer to the Canadian School as like a big, happy family, but adds:

from the questionnaire results, and from my memories of some of the Canadian School "kids" I knew, it is clear to me that the school was not a "happy family" for some of us, that there were some who were lonely there, who didn't fit, who felt mistreated or uncared for, or who rebelled. Some of the most insightful assessments of the

positive and negative influences of the Canadian
School have come from such people. (p. 139)

I have deliberately quoted from a somewhat obscure source
whose subject group is more than a generation removed from
our own (Donald Willmott had never heard the term "Third
Culture Kids"). However, these observations could apply equally to a 1993 survey of Murree Christian School alumni, as chapter 25 of this book illustrates. In the past two decades, major
studies of adult Third Culture Kids have, in fact, consistently
shown that TCKs tend to share common characteristics and
similar attitudes, regardless of their parents' occupation or
sponsoring agency. The "TCK profile" is not just a novel theory
of the "self-absorbed, overly-analytical" times we live in.

A recent book by William Nerin is pointedly titled *You
Can't Grow Up Till You Go Back Home* (Crossroad, 1993). Indeed, there are probably no questions more ancient or more
compelling for the human soul than "Where did I come from?"
and "Where do I belong?" Individuals, tribes, and civilizations
have been preoccupied with these questions, stimulating the
greater portion of art, ritual, and mythology throughout history. And they are an integral part of the more modern obsession, "Who am I?" But for missionary kids, the effort to explore
our ethnic and cultural roots presents an enigma. We cannot
just turn to our grandparents and say, "Where did our family
come from?" because, in fact, our family is not the same as
theirs. Our family, our homeland, is in the company of others
with similar experience. Our heritage was not formed by a national tradition, but by a particular situation. And when we left
the artificial communities of our upbringing not only were we
uprooted, so was our family tree. Many of us became cultural
orphans.

In September 1990, I attended a "transition seminar" by
David Pollock, on TCKs and the predictable patterns that often
result from growing up in a country other than the one your
parents call home. It was a cathartic moment in my life—as
memorable as my religious conversion at age fifteen. For the
first time, I didn't feel alone, I didn't have to explain myself,
and I understood that there was nothing wrong with me for being who I was.

Global nomads often overlook, or deny, the accumulated
grief that is also part of our heritage—partly, perhaps, because

we have had no empathetic place in which to express that grief. In his seminar, David Pollock illustrated these several themes with stories that articulated deep feelings that until then I had only dimly comprehended. Many global nomads have found this "naming" of their common heritage to be both liberating and empowering. Again and again, when TCKs come to a meeting of others like themselves their response is, "at last, I feel at home." I hope this book can be a sort of homecoming, the family reunion that many of us were never able to have.

Paul Asbury Seaman
Washington, D.C.
November 1995

1

Opening a Vein

The Blood of Memories

The following recollections are taken from the survey of MCS alumni which I conducted in 1993. If you attended, or worked at, Murree Christian School, these are some of the things you might remember:

• Pinewood fires with that resinous smell[1] . . . fog wafting through the classroom[2] . . . hunting butterflies, particularly the large black ones with tails that floated at what seemed like miles above my head.[3] *Chai* and buns at the tea shop across the road from the school, down in Jhika Gali, or anywhere the bus stopped on a trip—and how they would pour hot milk into a cup and then the tea through a little strainer, holding the smoke-blackened kettle high above the cup to mix it. The sudden roar of pine cones tossed into the wood stove just before cooking a three-egg omelet with lots of red peppers. The clay *chapatti* oven and the metal stick used to turn the bread and pull it out.[4]

• Trips down to Rawalpindi on the MCS bus—on the roof, when the teachers weren't looking. In Middle Boys we used to climb out the back door and up the ladder to the roof rack, and couldn't figure out how Auntie Inger knew we were up there. Years later she told us she could see our shadows on the road, by looking out the bus window![5]

• Camping in high school with Wilder, Brown & company up Mirianjani and finding that the shale we had lined our campfire with explodes when heated.[6]

• "Many hands make light work" --we used to say that every time the electricity went off, hoping the *bijilee* would come back on. We never knew whether it would be off for a minute, an hour, or all night. And of course there were always water shortages. Remember the fire buckets along the big second-floor veranda at Sandes? More than once they got used, not to put out a fire, but to flush a toilet when we couldn't stand the smell any longer.

• Tall "Uncle Paul" Davidson from New Zealand used to organize tug-of-war matches on the field behind Sandes before school started in the mornings, sometimes leaving us with rope-burned hands and bruised egos with which to start the day. Uncle Paul was famous for his big leather slipper which got judiciously applied to our rear ends for misbehavior; but he always hugged us afterwards. Uncle Paul became one of the most influential people in my time at MCS. He took us on wonderful camp-outs—preceded by "long march" hikes that almost killed some of us; organized Capture the Flag contests that spread out over large areas of the woods and occupied several hours on Saturdays; took us skinny dipping in Rawal Lake at night and showed us how to prevent injury to the crown jewels while jumping off the cliff into the water.

At the end of the spring term of ninth grade I stayed home from school one day, thus missing the French examination in Miss Haugen's class. She had to have the results in order to tally grades, so that evening Miss Haugen appeared at Sandes Home to administer the examination there. As she came onto the veranda, Arn Eliasson and Eric Pulliam caught hold of me to give me a pink belly. While keeping me pinned down, flat on the floor, they proceeded to briskly slap my bare stomach whilst Miss Haugen administered an oral French examination to me. Somehow, I never cared very much for learning French.[7]

• I'll never forget Ian and Isabel Murray who smoothed the way for a new bride in foreign parts; or another young staff member, John Unrau, checking for signs of a mustache. And Eddy Brown, trying out his new sense of maturity (at fifteen) by calling Paul by his Christian name, rather than "Unc." I remember with amusement the boys' shower at Sandes Home that gave off electric shocks; the way the *bijilee* went off, and was returned by rattling the wires with a broom. Bicycle trips down to the Kashmir border, with Paul in a truck at the back— picking up the occasional punctures, the misshapen wheels, and bruised boys along the way. The *pani-wallah* carrying hot water—in two kerosene tins attached to a pole slung over his shoulders—up to the houses behind Sandes for the boys' baths (one bucket per boy, in tiny metal tubs). The "slurpers' row" of nursing mothers in the back pew at church.

Rosie Stewart inviting us for a cup of Oxo, which had been stored in a drum in the attic, along with naphthalene, while she had been on furlough, and the strong smell of mothballs as the boiling water was poured over the Oxo. The buzz of the phone off the hook outside our bedroom near midnight, trying to prevent an "Are you responsible for this?!" call from the school, while Arn Eliasson and Co. had sneaked off for a pataka raid [fire-crackers] on the main hostel. Deliberately letting Jim Cameron sleep in, so that his whole house of Junior High boys was late for school (that cured him). Squeezing into Khan Zaman's house to watch the first men landing on the moon on his television.[8]

• The 1964 U.S. elections were a gala event at MCS. Weeks of electioneering and mudslinging went on accompanied by brass bands and bribery. I was in fourth grade at the time and a staunch Johnson supporter (after all, I had good friends by that name) until Ray Tewksbury earnestly and solemnly informed me that, if elected, LBJ would snatch all children from their parents. With propaganda like that, no wonder Goldwater won the school ballot by such a comfortable margin.

In those days, the Pakistani mess hall bearers wore gallant, crisply-starched puggarees, with near-white uniforms— quite a contrast to the jovial, happy-go-lucky crew I remember from high school days, a few years later.

I guess it was by age eight that the predominately negative

feelings for boarding were supplanted by passionately positive ones. That was the age at which one was allowed to own and carry a *chakku,* a jack knife—and be a recognized somebody.[9]

• The worst thing that happened to me was trudging the mile from Jhika Gali to MCS in the snow in sandals because my baggage was caught on the truck. I was lucky not to get frostbite.[10]

• Miss Karen Hicks gave a good start to my academic career. I now know what "pulverize" means. We didn't in those days, and she used to threaten us with it quite frequently, refusing to divulge its meaning.

In Middle Girls, we played Uno and Dutch Blitz (a card game like Skip-Bo) for hours, especially in the early spring and late fall when it was too cold to play outside. Regular playing cards were definitely against the rules in boarding, but any substitutes were fine. My little brother had a pack of cards when he was in fourth grade and was never caught.

One night, on a camp-out with the Middle Kids (fifth and sixth grades), a boy broke a tooth running into a pole during a game of Couple Tag. The result of this was "out of bounds" for the much-preferred dark area out the back. None of the couples ever got "up to anything" out there anyway, but we were aware of the prospects.

• Campouts were of course a highlight for us all, and I think I can remember every one. Then, walking up the hill to Sandes at the end of the weekend feeling very sunburnt and sandy and wondering if there would be anything decent to eat and how much hot water there would be. There was never much.

I remember the time somebody in the bunk above me vomited over the edge into Sunil Lall's slippers! It always amazes me how complex the relationships were in such a small community, and the pool for choosing a girlfriend or boyfriend was pretty small. Friendships changed as people left for and arrived back from furloughs. A person's absence for a year was a normal occurrence. One of the best memories is the camaraderie, the feeling of bravery and defiance, amongst a group of us who used to go down to Jhika after study hall and have a smoke (only cigarettes!) on the back balcony of a tea shop.[11]

• From the start, I feel that I was unfairly picked on; while some of my early childhood habits may not have helped the situation, the negative reactions I got were certainly excessive. And much worse, once you have been "branded" there is no redemption. MCS was kind of a ghetto, insulated from the world-at-large; socially there was really only one "scene." This situation is particularly vulnerable to type-casting, which in my case seemed to build a momentum of its own regardless of my real attitude, behavior, or spiritual growth.

On the other hand, if the label was positive, you were set up in perpetuity, it seemed, as being beyond reproach. Either way, good or bad, you were locked into excessively high or low status, influence and regard, or marginalization and abuse, no matter what the subsequent changes in personal development. Of course this was self-fulfilling, and by junior high, I became more and more concerned that my social and spiritual growth, in a community sense, had been stunted because I was not really allowed any dignified participation. Staff seemed little better than the kids in their susceptibility to playing along with this dynamic.

I wonder how much my subsequent difficulty in finding any assimilation or accommodation with my parents' culture of origin, is due to my negative experience at Murree, which seems to have been sustained, in terms of my basic social adequacy and competence. I have little nostalgia for MCS, and what positive feelings I do have are tangled up in the profound contradiction between my very real and meaningful spiritual experience and bitter memories of my negative social status.

• An implausible, incredible scheme to runaway from boarding together with a friend—only to be foiled by his peanut butter and honey leaking all over the things in his bag before we could get away. . . . Being jumped on by a pet monkey tied to the ladderwork on the back of a bus in the bazaar, resulting in a scratch behind the ear; consequently, I had to endure a full course of fourteen rabies shots, distributed over my arms and legs as well as in my belly, to my considerable physical debilitation for some while.[12]

● I'll never forget the monkeys behind the hostel, our moon-lit nights with *chai* at Charlie's, and the many, many parties we always managed to have in class. One day we decided to have a party in our seventh grade French class. Miss Harms-worth had told us no parties. I think it was Jonny DeHart and Doug Kennedy's idea to go ahead with the party anyway. (It's fun to blame these two anyway, especially as they were Miss Harmsworth's "favorite" pupils!)

We all hid food in our desks. Whenever Miss Harmsworth turned to write something on the board, we quickly opened our desk lids and passed the food along from person to person. I ac-tually don't think Miss Harmsworth found out until the end of class when Jonny and Doug sat there with Cheshire cat smiles. She demanded to know what they were up to. Poor Miss Harmsworth.[13]

● It was difficult to make friends at the beginning because of my shyness, and also because the majority of the other stu-dents had been at MCS for years. I was very homesick. It seemed that these students were not very interested in new-comers. All this changed when someone found out that I had played for the girls' soccer team at the International School of Islamabad and that I intended to play for MCS. Then, of course, I became the talk of the day and everyone wanted to know me.

● I used to sell gospels for a few annas on Saturdays but the Pakistanis often accused me of hurts they harbored about Partition and the British. Even some communist, funda-mentalist Muslims used to harangue me, and once, in a Shia Muslim ceremony, I was set upon by hysterical fundamentalist breast-beaters; they were drawing blood, they were quite fanat-ical.[14]

● One time in the early-70s I was driving the school's VW van, following the school bus up to Murree, and had to stop at the municipal check point near Jhika Gali just as a crowd of angry Pakistani students had gathered for the latest anti-American demonstration. They pulled me out of the car, but one of the students said, "Let this man go. We know him—he has refereed our soccer games."[15]

• I remember the *hot* camping trips on the island on the Indus River. I won't forget Phil Walsh riding his inner tube down the river and getting caught in the current. At that point, he was on his own. As the staff chaperons, we could do nothing: no car, no boat, and the ferry only came out to the island once a day; 110-degree heat. Somehow we stayed calm. Phil showed up several hours later—safe, sheepish—and we were relieved. It was another one of the many ways God cared for all of us, and a reminder of how much was out of our hands.[16]

• I was only seven years old when Pakistan and India went to war in December 1971 [when East Pakistan became Bangladesh]. We all got sent home to our parents' mission stations on the plains so our families would be together. I remember one time when just my big brother and I were at the house and the air raid siren went off. We ran out to the trench in our back yard and he grabbed a card table for cover. Another time our whole family went out to the trench in the middle of the night; Mom made sure that I had my favorite doll.[17]

• At one point, when we all still lived together at Sandes Home, the girls were in one room taking up the hems on their skirts and the boys were in another letting down the hems on their trousers—so they wouldn't have "flood-water pants."

• I was sent to the principal because my skirt was too short, and he wanted to pray w. In fact, I knew my skirts were *not* too short! My mom had carefully measured and hemmed all of them, with the regulation kneeling-on-the-floor check, but I guess I had weird knees or something. Then I went on strike, wearing the same "acceptable" dress all week.

It seemed like I only saw housemothers when it was time for evening devotions or when I was in trouble. I got so mad one day when I passed by the teachers' lounge and heard them praying for me—but they never bothered to say "hi" to me in person, or ask me how I was doing.

• Although I have worked through many of my feelings, it was still like opening Pandora's Box to remember what it was like to be in boarding school! My first term was a harrowing experience. I not only had to cope with leaving home, but also severe culture shock. I was catapulted as a child of eight into a world where people spoke a different language (American), wore different clothes, and came from a completely different culture. I was the only Scot in the school at the time, although there already were some English and Australians. I must have cried most of that first term.

On my first day in boarding I wrote a letter to my parents and left it on my bed. When I came home I found it where I had left it but torn in pieces. I think that the censorship of our mail put an unnecessary barrier between us and our parents. We often had to write them in class in grade two, and because my writing wasn't neat, mine often ended up not being sent as I got sick of rewriting them.

When I was seven, in the spring, I was forgotten at school one day when I went back to fetch something from the classroom. Fortunately, my mother had arrived from the plains to see us kids and came to look for me at the school when she found that no one knew where I was—nor had missed me.

On the positive side, Mrs. Patzold, who looked after us younger girls for a term in boarding, really mothered us. She gave a prize for *trying* to keep my things tidy. She also took us away for a wonderful weekend at the manse in Murree where we had a competition to see who could eat the most pancakes at breakfast.

Jello with sliced bananas on Sundays . . . jam and cream mixed to put on *chapattis* at breakfast . . . canned gooseberries . . . Khan Zaman's donuts. Also, memories of Pass the Spoon, Chinese Whispers, and "magic seats." I once tried to get away with not eating spinach and was forced to consume a whole saucer-full while everyone else watched a movie. But I managed not to eat the very stringy beat greens for a term by claiming an allergy. Woody raw carrots and unripe bananas; watered-down milk was also a real turn off. Obviously it was hard to get fresh food for a school in the wintertime.

Singing on Friday nights started with "The Thousand-Legged Worm." Singspiration on Sundays. Baba Hocha. The long walks home from school turning into the journey from *Pilgrim's Progress*. Camouflage netting on the military trucks across from the school and troops of soldiers high-stepping past us daily. The old blue school bus, an instrument of torture with its long wooden benches and an emergency door that occasionally flew open without warning. Our beautiful surroundings that are completely unparalleled anywhere.[18]

● One afternoon our junior high group was playing "Capture the Flag" on Sandes Hill. Joyce Bavington and I were way up by the water tanks above Sandes Home. We came up over the crest of a hill and Dildar's dog spotted us (remember old Dildar who never "remembered" to turn on the water?). Actually, I think we caught the beast off guard. He let out a snarl, broke his chain and came tearing after us. Joyce went one way, I went the other. I lost my shoes as I threw myself down over brambles, bushes and small cliffs — finally to safety.

When my mom had hepatitis, each evening a bearer from the Sandes kitchen would carry a hot dinner down to our house on a stainless steel covered tray. We learned not to get too excited about what hid beneath the cover. One day we gasped when we lifted the lid. There sat two huge ostrich egg lookalikes. It turned out that they *were* eggs—Scotch Eggs. Inside each "egg" was a hard boiled egg covered with hamburger meat and then a layer of mashed potatoes; all of this was shrouded in corn flake crumbs.[19]

● No true MCSer can forget the beauty of the mountains on a clear morning. Looking across the upper field, one could see range upon range of snow-covered mountains, against the backdrop of a brilliant blue sky, and framed by green pine trees. Whenever I think back to the wonder of this scene, the colors are always vivid in my mind.[20]

SOURCES

(Where no attribution is given, names have been withheld by request, or material is a composite, summarized by the editor. Date listed is year graduated from high school, whether or not at MCS.)

[1]Richard Bingham, '64.

[2]Susan (Arnold) Herbert, '85.

[3]Joe Haas, '67.

[4]Joel Ryther, '72.

[5]Paul Seaman, '76.

[6]Andy Norris, '81.

[7]Steve Rasmussen, '74.

[8]Helen Davidson (boarding staff, 1967–1971).

[9]Roy Montgomery, '73.

[10]Richard Bingham, '64.

[11]Michael Meadowcroft, '76.

[12]Malcolm Bavington, '81.

[13]Ruth (Nygren) Keller, '77.

[14]Richard Bingham, '64.

[15]Don Calderwood (staff, 1956–1987).

[16]Wayne Hildebrand (boarding staff, 1976–1979),

[17]Miriam (Seaman) Mullins, '82.

[18]Janet (Young) Puddy, '72 (at MCS for grades 1–3 only).

[19]Ruth (Nygren) Keller, '77.

[20]Amy Jo Inniger, '89.

2

The Bone Structure

Painting by Numbers

The previous chapter suggests the kind of reminiscing that might occur at an alumni reunion, the random quality typical of conversations. These memories, still close to the surface after twenty or thirty years, are colored, of course, by perception and interpretation and the biases we all bring when looking at the past: the justifications of our present identity, the weight of old wounds, or a "witnessing" agenda—the need to defend God.

I remember an adult confirmation class I attended once in which we talked about the different *windows to faith*—how people come to experience "salvation" or spiritual understanding through a wide variety of means, from dramatic altar calls in huge revival halls to the methodical process of Christian education, or simply through the still, small voice that slowly guides and convicts until without any conscious moment of "crossing over" one finds his or her allegiance has changed.

Similarly, there is no one objective truth about history, about a person, or about Murree Christian School. In presenting my version, I have tried at least to be fair, thorough and honest. For the most part, I have let participants speak in their own words—as many of them as possible, students and staff and an equal number of men and women, staff and students. While most of these narratives are written in retrospect, chapters three and five reproduce contemporary staff correspondence from the school's early years, offering the slightly-guilty pleasure of reading other people's mail.

A chronology of major events is like a child's connect-the-dots game compared to the Russian novel of real life, but it does provide convenient reference points, a skeleton around which to fix the pulse and pulp of more personal stories. Listed below, then, are some of the most significant dates in the first forty years of Murree Christian School.

1951-55: Committee meetings in Murree and elsewhere discuss the need for a school for missionaries' children in West Pakistan. After much discussion, and for lack of agreement on how to begin the school, the United Presbyterian mission is asked to set up and start the school (with other missions to later join in), largely because they have the most students—and own suitable property. Around this time the Lahore Diocesan Trust Association (Anglican) gives its consent for MCS to use the Gharial Church property for the location of a school. The LDTA charged MCS ten rupees per year for the use of the property.

1956: In March, the United Presbyterian Mission opens school and boarding at Sandes Home with eight children. Paul Pulliam is the first principal. That summer classes are held for the first time in the old British garrison church at Gharial, one mile away.

1957: The Evangelical Alliance Mission (TEAM) closes their MK school in Abbottabad to join MCS. In July, the school's constitution is approved, establishing a board of directors representing nine cooperating missions.

1959-60: With a rapidly growing student body, school officials explore sites in Abbottabad, Khaira Gali, St. Denys, and several other places in and around Murree where there are either more adequate facilities or more room to expand. After much consideration, and an architect's feasibility study of the Gharial property, the decision is made not to relocate the school, but to build on the present site.

1963: First library built; the PTA decides on the school emblem; and the first yearbook is published (the first student council met in 1962).

1964: MCS holds its first graduation ceremonies. While there are only three seniors to receive diplomas, eight years after opening, the school's enrollment is now up to 157 students.

1965: New four-story hostel opens on school property; staff housing below Sandes Home built at this time.

1969: New elementary classroom block completed, with apartments for single women teachers on the second floor (these become the senior high girls dorm in the late-eighties).

1973: MCS joins the South Asia Inter-School Association (SAISA), and is the only *Christian* school cooperating with eight other expatriate schools for sports competitions and cultural events.

1981: The twenty-fifth anniversary of Murree Christian School is celebrated that summer.

1982: School gets its first computers.

1985: Sandes Home is renovated. Chuck Roub retires after twenty-five years as principal of MCS. Stewart Georgia becomes the new chief administrator, with a principal of the high school, a principal of the elementary school, and the boarding superintendent under him.

1987: The girls basketball team wins SAISA tournament for the first time—and for the next two years in a row.

1992: Ashe Wing behind Sandes Home is razed and rebuilt as a modern, six-unit apartment complex for staff. A large underground water storage tank is constructed next to the main school, in an attempt—one of several—to relieve the school's perennial water shortages.

1993: Phil Billing becomes the new "director" of MCS, following Stewart Georgia's resignation. The stage area of the high school is completely renovated, creating a storage basement below the stage and a new library and classrooms above it. In another historic statistic, 1993 produces only one graduate, Joshua Bartlotti.

1996: A record number of MCS alumni return to Pakistan in July for the school's fortieth anniversary celebrations.

*   *   *

Asked to list what he felt were ten of the most significant developments in the life of MCS, Chuck Roub came up with some very different entries. While building the new hostel and the decision to join SAISA are mentioned, here is the rest of his list (not necessarily in order of importance):
— The decision of the school board to accept only certified, qualified, experienced Christian teachers.
—The decision that teaching staff (faculty) and boarding staff would be two separate entities—with close cooperation between the two groups being the ultimate aim.
—The decision of the United Presbyterians to turn over ever-increasing facilities at Sandes Home to MCS on a permanent basis.
—The decision (made around 1961) to run a dual education curriculum, providing British children with O-level and Scottish Highers (exams) so they could be prepared for re-entering their own education systems back in Britain. This enriched the American system's offerings considerably as well and, though sometimes difficult to implement, it is one of our strengths when we compare ourselves to other missionary children's schools.
—The early formation of the Parent Teachers Association at Murree Christian School, and the gradual development of a philosophy of a parent-run school—often

through the board, often with individual parent participation.

—The decision by the board and the administration to make every possible provision for the special educational needs of students returning to other countries, especially in Europe (such as Germany, Holland, and Finland).

—The early commitment of participating missions to give the school high priority in recruiting, and in helping out when it became necessary.

—The rapid expansion of the school's governing base (most of which took place in the late-60s and early-70s) from five affiliated missions when it started to more than twenty in the 1980s.

*   *   *

An equally revealing—though diplomatically risky—compilation might list the staff who have been most influential in shaping the life of Murree Christian School (see chapter seven). Such a list must include the magnificently mustachioed Khan Zaman, the school's chief cook for many years, and also Paul Pulliam who worked at MCS for less than a year, but is, in fact, the man who got it all started.

3

A Cold, Windy Old Barn

Paul R. Pulliam

"Enclosed herewith are copies of contemporary correspondence to family, friends, or churches back home in the States, between 1954 and 1956. The first entry was written from the church manse at Gharial, which was run by the Church Missionary Society (CMS) of England at the time. For all the weighty matters that would later require so much earnest struggle, Murree Christian School in fact began with a picnic."

July 12, 1954. Lots of vacationers are arriving at Sandes Home these days. It is just a mile from here so we often walk up. Most of our mission *miss-sahibas* (single ladies) have arrived so nearly every afternoon someone strolls by for a visit. Tomorrow a couple of young couples will come for a picnic lunch. These days all of us young folks are pulling hard to get a school for missionary children here in Murree. Our home board is ready to back it. But to acquire property and to build facilities in a land like this is absolutely a heart-breaking job. One mission has worked for more than three years to get land to build a hospital. People inherit land out here, and because they respect the family inheritance very highly, they are loathe to sell even at a profit. And in Murree things are sky high because now that India is closing her doors, this hill station is more crowded than ever.

Just now history is being made in Murree. A constituent assembly is meeting here to draw up a constitution for Pakistan. Until now it has been administered by a legislative assembly and Governor General appointed by Britain when she withdrew. I hope that they are successful in their efforts. It is certainly a tremendous task. Their coming has been attended with elaborate preparations—among other things the prices of milk and eggs doubled!

December 7, 1955. Now the mission has given us a new assignment—temporarily—to set up a school for missionaries' children in Pakistan. We have as assets one old building to remodel for boarding arrangements, one large stone church to convert into classrooms, and a generous scarcity of cash. Furniture for boarding and for classrooms must be designed, ordered, and installed; a fee schedule must be drawn up; a prospectus prepared and sent to all missions; enrollments accepted; additional staff procured; the remodeling overseen—and all of this by March! Then comes the ticklish job of negotiating with about twelve other missions interested in co-operating in the school, and developing a basis of cooperation (theologically, financially, and educationally) acceptable to all. . . .

February 9, 1956. Snow is lying about in deep drifts wherever there is shade. Yesterday I brought a very heavily loaded trailer up and in spite of my fears, the car pulled it up the hill beautifully. I did have to go twenty miles in second gear. The road for the last half mile from the highway to Sandes is very steep and dirt. In good weather only an empty car can get up it. So all the trailer load of my furniture and baggage had to come up on the backs of coolies. Eight men did it in an hour, though, which I thought was excellent. Afterward they pushed the trailer up and by chipping ice off a bad corner, they pushed me a bit and I got the car up. . . . Now I am rattling around alone in this huge building. I am getting my room fixed up as comfortably as possible. The day is clear and sunny and in the sun it is warm, but the temperatures are below freezing at night. Just now the watchman's wife walked across the front yard bare-footed, wading through snowdrifts without noticing. These poor hill people lead a miserable life. They simply must not feel the cold!

February 27, 1956. Ardella Reetz, one of our young teachers from the Lutheran mission, has been here for about a week. The white-washers had finished her room so she had moved from temporary quarters into her own room today—and how very nicely she has it fixed up. Tomorrow Gene Purdy our other teacher (and a United Presbyterian) arrives. Then we have about a week to get things in shape for the boarders' arrival and the opening of school. I am setting up the bookkeeping system for the school now and getting accounts in order.

We drove up in rain today. The snow has all melted and the rain continues. It is sorely needed. Murree is so short on water that we haven't had enough pressure to get any water for five days. We have been using melted snow and rain water— just pouring buckets of water down the commodes to flush them. Most places in Murree do not have a flush system but use pots which are emptied twice daily by sweepers. It really is a better system when water is in short supply, but Americans all abominate the sweeper system and think they must have flush toilets no matter what. . . .

You would be a bit shocked to see this cold, windy old barn of a building and to try to imagine it serving as a boarding school. Still it has its comforts and conveniences when you stop to look for them. And it is in a most beautiful setting. I never tire of these hills.

March 13, 1956. This is the first night in two weeks that I will have been in bed before midnight. But at last the rush is over and the school has started. . . . If I do brag on my own work, I never thought Sandes Home could be made so attractive. We painted, had furniture made—even had to varnish some last minute furniture ourselves. The classroom compares favorably with any classroom in America—except that I had to design and have made every stick in it, including desks, blackboards, bulletin boards, etc. Starting a school out here isn't simply ordering stuff out of a catalogue like at home. Also I have to keep the books and act as sergeant-at-arms when needed. Now that school is going my job will become more routine and less pressing. I will make up for lost sleep these nights.

April 16, 1956. I have been wearing the tie pin you got me and find it very satisfactory. I like the design very much. My tastes run to simple but rich-looking things. I always joke and say that I am one of the few obvious cases where the Lord got mixed up in His Providence—He gave me the nature of a playboy and the salary of a missionary! Things are going very smoothly in the school just now. It keeps me stepping because I am roughly the following: house engineer (every commode in the building leaks, many roofs leak; water system has to be watched like a hawk because we get city water only twice a day for an hour each time and we store the surplus in a big tank to use in between times), treasurer, secretary, accountant, Bible teacher, and general manager. I am getting a huge lot of fun out of the job, but it has such variety I sometimes wonder whether I am getting at loose ends or not. The school is going very nicely and everyone seems pleased so I can rejoice in that. Now this month the building work must be done at Gharial (pronounced "GARD-ee-all"). Then after that I will start negotiations with all the missions to try to work out a constitution which will be acceptable to everyone.

April 23, 1956. [My preschool children] Kerry and Eric are with me here in our one-room-and-bath apartment. We eat with the school. I have thoroughly enjoyed the two little mischiefs after a three-month separation. Baby Anne is still with the Glassmans. I have seen her once since January 1. She, of course, didn't recognize me but allowed me to hold her. I go once a month to Sheikhupura to keep the district work going and to handle the accounts there. Nap time for the children is almost over so must say goodbye.

April 28, 1956. I am beginning to get a little desperate on the building here. The work hasn't begun yet but has to be completed in May. However, it should be started now within a couple of weeks and once it starts it will go fast. Everything has to be approved by the property committee of the mission. That is right and should be, but it is time-consuming.

Have just now come up from church. It requires a good bit of ingenuity to preach to an audience that consists almost entirely of first through fourth graders. The kids are doing real well on their memory work. Also every morning after breakfast we sing hymns for a few minutes. Each week we select one hymn and learn it. Thus far they have learned "Holy, Holy, Holy" and "Guide Me O Great Jehovah" along with a lot of choruses that kids like. . . .

Another interruption—morning coffee. The cook here always puts on a lot of flourishes. Every morning at ten he takes a tray of coffee around to the staff. This morning all the mothers gathered in the yard in the sun and we sipped coffee and talked. Finally the sun was so hot we had to move into the shade. Harreitte and Chase sent us a long-play record of the Mormon Tabernacle Choir singing familiar hymns, so I put that on the phonograph and we had lovely music floating out across the yard. . . .

The Board has found a young couple to come out and take over this school. They will arrive on the field this fall. I'll stay here until November and help them learn all the routines.

May 1956. After two uninterrupted weeks of rain, sleet, snow and bitter cold [in late-March], the weather man has been making up to us ever since. April and May have been beautiful and just about everything else in Murree has been in keeping with the weather. For those interested in statistics, we have twenty children attending class at the moment with thirty enrolled and a small waiting list of hopefuls wanting to join in June. The twenty now here come from eight different missions with one ICA boy thrown in for good measure. When parents began arriving in the hills early this year, we anticipated a mass exodus from our boarding department, but apparently our baby sitting is cheap at the price, because we still have almost as many as we started with. [One mother and father] have asked us to start beating their boy so he will come home willingly on weekends. Another family reports their scion asking "to go home"—back to boarding, that is! Ardella Reetz gets about 100 percent of the credit for the smooth and happy boarding arrangements. When I have sometimes wondered if she wasn't ready to collapse from the confinements and heavy load, she develops peculiar cases of homesickness when her kids go home for weekends. Gene Purdy has exhibited a master touch in the classroom. With the room already bursting at the seams, I get fearful with the arrival of each new child. But when I carefully throw my hat in ahead of me, Gene calmly emerges, escorts the new pupil to his desk and accepts him into the brood as though a new grade, a new desk, and a bundle of new problems make no difference at all.

On May Day we had a gala celebration when about thirty parents came for the program and tea. Another program is on the drawing board, with a life-size television set just about completed in the classroom, and will likely be the kick off for a Murree PTA. Although some people are hard to convince, we, at least, think that we have kept busy up here. Gharial building work has been delayed as a result. . . .

The Calderwoods are a most unexpected answer to prayer. We need prayer for help in the boarding department—and are looking hopefully to the New Zealand CMS who know a qualified girl interested in such work. I admit my lack of faith when I still wake up pinching myself to make sure things here are actually real and not simply the dreams of a committee which will suddenly evaporate with the words, "Let us adjourn."

May 22, 1956 (on letterhead of "Gharial Christian School," with a photo-offset of Sandes Home in the top left corner). Yesterday two of our senior ladies who had stopped in for a breath of cool hill air had to go to Taxila to audit building accounts. I couldn't possibly miss the chance to go when most of the gas bill would be paid, so piled Eric and Kerry in the car and we drove down the hill to Taxila for the day. What a grand day it was. It is the first time our family has all been together since November 22. Anne was as sweet and cute as could be. Kerry and Eric about smothered her with love. They all played together so excitedly and had such fun. I filled a big tin tub with water and let them play on the porch for a while. Kids normally have to stay in the house most of the day on the plains because it is hitting 110 to 114 degrees now-a-days, which means that it is about 140 in the sun and too hot for little heads. . . .

A week from tomorrow boarding closes. Then our days will be less confined here. I will push like anything to get the building at Gharial completed. Everything out here from a nail to a stone requires a permit from some officer. All of these things are a nuisance and consume a lot of time and patience. However, I hope the building work will be finished up by the middle of July. After that, getting an agreeable constitution that all the missions will accept so this school can become cooperative will take the diplomacy of a Churchill. The gamut between the Church of England and the Conservative Baptist [from the U.S.A.], for example, shows you what divergencies exist—and yet there is a splendid feeling of fellowship and unity among all the missions out here. Everyone—even the faith missions—observe comity and work together in conventions and conferences.

June 13, 1956. The remodeling of Gharial church is almost complete. With good luck we may get to move in out there next week and get the school kids out of Sandes. A few souls have already arrived here for vacation—and when the kids storm in and out of the school room it doesn't make for a very restful vacation. Mr. Sutherland is able to oversee the work at Gharial which has saved me infinite labor. We brought up cement blocks from Taxila and are filling in the partitions with them. People are eagerly watching because to my knowledge it is the first time cement blocks have been used in Murree. Everything here is made of local stone which takes an infinite time to dress and lay.

June 23, 1956. Tomorrow I'll spend the day getting cleaned up after the builders. I was very much fearful about electricity. The main line runs nearby, but it would require a transformer to effect a 220-volt connection. The military has power which they could give us—but quite rightfully balked at supplying a civilian installation. It seems that things are cleared now and that maybe by the end of the week we'll have lights burning in our new classrooms. We depend on artificial lights during most of the monsoon season when it stays overcast and rains daily.

Friday there is a PTA meeting at which time we will have a service of dedication for the school rooms. Things look so nice at Gharial—we haven't really disfigured the building at all so no one can complain. It is an old Anglican garrison church. Being consecrated we have had to move a bit carefully. The English people are quite in favor of our using it for a school, but the national brethren are of the strictest sect of Pharisees and we have to be pretty careful. They would, for example, prefer to see a church fall into ruin and collapse rather than be used for some other purpose. That is the custom of the land. . . . [The United Presbyterians] are still financially carrying the school—

but it must be gotten onto a cooperative basis before next year. That is the next big task now that the building work is about finished. Oh yes, we still have to install toilets. That involves building a nice outhouse. . . . The scruples of the Anglicans keeps us from putting toilets inside the church itself.

August 15, 1956. Yesterday was a big day. We had a PTA meeting at which the problem of a constitution for the school was discussed. I felt it was a very great victory because all the missions but one seemed eager to come in and help out. TEAM [The Evangelical Alliance Mission] has been balking from the first, bringing up all sorts of questions—most of which point to only one fact in their philosophy: "What we can't run we won't join!" Why are fundamentalists always so blooming bull-headed? Ha ha. Some of the missions felt that our proposals were too expensive. However, that is a detail that can be thrashed out in the small committee that meets tomorrow to work out details. . . . It looks to me as though the missions that want this thing to succeed will just have to kick in—and those that don't will have to sit on the sidelines and be bypassed. One older, experienced man from another mission whispered to me yesterday—"You have made a good beginning. Don't worry about a few recalcitrants. When the band wagon gets going and starts to pass them by, they will be only too glad to hop aboard." I think he is right.

. . . . After I started this letter the old contractor who has been doing some building work in connection with the school came. The bills that he presented were so ridiculously high all I could do was laugh. When I dug out receipts from some of my last year's building work in Sheikhupura he began to squirm and plead, "Oh, sahib, don't go to that trouble—just cut my bill down a little!" These fellows are amazing in the lengths they will go in cheating. What amazes me is that they think I am so stupid as to swallow some of their wild stories.

September, 1956. [I am] going around bleary-eyed these days from the delightful task of welcoming new staff members to Pakistan. Eloise James arrived on the third in the middle of the night with a group of Sandes-ites to meet her. Audrey Jennings came on the eleventh—also in the middle of the night. Boarding has re-opened with twelve youngsters keeping things lively about us. Within two weeks our boarding department will climb to twenty-one and keep us humming at that level until November 30. The children live at Sandes and walk both ways to Gharial each day. Incidentally, for all those who got soaked in July and August, we have had only one rain in September and that has come at night!

The big news is that Ruth and the children are back with me after nine months of separation. We have fitted ourselves up luxuriously in Angel's Wing and find it very comfortable except that the floor plan is much like that of a trailer house. The children are well and happy. Ruth is continuing to make gratifying progress for which we rejoice. She is out of bed a good part of each day and seems thus far to be standing the strain of the youngsters very well. . . .

[In the same in-country newsletter for UP missionaries, Gene Purdy writes:] School's back in full swing again after a three week holiday. Our boarders are back, so once again Sandes Home echoes with the sound of children's laughter, and the hillside is dotted during free time with imaginary cowboys or young potential scientists waving butterfly nets! You former summer residents of Sandes would hardly recognize your rooms now, with the gay chintz curtains, the children's pictures on the wall, the newly painted floors and woodwork, and the bunkbeds in each room. . . .

A PTA was organized during the summer, and was very well attended, both by parents, teachers and many interested friends. We've discovered a new meaning for the "A" in PTA—Parents, Teachers, and Aunties!

September 30, 1956. Ardella Reetz, our boarding matron, is down flat today. She had a Pakistani dentist do some work on her this summer and he evidently banged up a nerve in her cheek somehow. At any rate she gets severe neuritis with pain that is so severe that even Code-pyrine tablets give no relief. Part of it may be just nerves and fatigue. We have her in bed today with strong doses of pain killer and sleeping pills. Maybe a good rest will give her some relief. She was unable to close her eyes from twelve midnight on last night because of pain. We are reorganizing staff duties to take a bit of the load off her shoulders. Twenty-two kids is a big responsibility, especially when most of them are younger than eight years. Ardella is far more conscientious than most girls, too, and thinks she has to give the kids a real home-like atmosphere here. As a result, she does everything for twenty-two kids that a mother might do for two or three, and the job is just too big. I am pulling one of the teachers out of the classroom and putting her in the dorms (the teachers are willing) and that will tide us over through the end of November.

I must get busy and start getting concession railway tickets. We can get special rates for a school party. Classes end on November 28 and we ship the children off the next day. One of the teachers will take a train party 200 miles to Lahore; there one of the parents will pick it up and take it on south, dropping a child here and there as they go. Some of the children will have to travel a thousand miles and ride for more than twenty-four hours on the train.

November 20, 1956. Thoroughly enjoyed your recent letters. I have been a little slack in writing, but since we are nearly homeward bound haven't felt the need to write quite so often. My, the beautiful weather we have been having here is enough to make one shout. I take the kids on frequent and long hikes for purely selfish reasons—I just thoroughly enjoy hiking about in these mountains. It is crisp and cold at night. However, during the day the sun is quite warm. We eat and sit out in the sun all day—have a bit of heat from an oil stove in the house at night....

The new couple who are taking over from me are certainly grand. They are from Kansas. Don Calderwood is a quiet chap but full of fun and we have gotten along together very well. I have really enjoyed having someone here to share in the work. Often in the evening we play ball with the boys. He has gotten into the work quickly. I am turning things over to him as fast as I can because he will learn much quicker by doing the work and bumping into the problems than by just listening to me tell him things.

A few nights ago we had a welcome dinner for all the new staff. Ruth and I cooked it and gave it. After the boarders had all eaten and been tucked away to bed, we went into one of the teachers' rooms and had a real feed. Ruth and I decided to eat some of our rabbits, but the crazy things had hidden in the bushes so that I was only able to catch one of them. We ended up with two chickens and one rabbit. We browned the meat first and then put it in the pressure cooker to make it tender. Well, it was supposed to cook for fourteen minutes. But we allowed for the altitude here and also for Pakistani chicken (pure iron) and cooked it for half an hour. When we opened the pressure cooker we were disappointed to find that we had got hold of the only tender chicken in the country and that it was cooked to death—the meat had all fallen off the bones and was just a stew. However, it tasted okay. We had Harvard beets, mashed potatoes and real chicken gravy, apple pie with cheese, coffee, homemade marshmallows and chocolate fudge and roasted nuts.

The water man is calling me for my bath and is about to have nervous prostration because he is afraid the water (which he has heated over an open wood fire) will get cold before I get into it. So I'll close and write more later. Much love to all. *Paul*

Two weeks later the Pulliam family left for an extended furlough in the United States.

4

Moving from Floor to Knee

Getting Started . . . :Looking Back

Paul R. Pulliam

When the *S.S. Dewey Beagle* sailed from San Francisco in the spring of 1946 it was still configured much like a troop ship. The sailing was widely reported across the U.S. because the passenger list consisted almost entirely of missionaries returning to their posts throughout Asia after the end of World War II. Dr. and Mrs. William Sutherland, my parents-in-law, were among those aboard this historic voyage (that almost ended in disaster when a storm of typhoon proportions very nearly caused the ship to capsize). Most of those missionaries were unaware of how profoundly the world had changed during their absence from their respective fields. Within the next few years the number of foreign missionaries would increase dramatically.

One result of this sudden escalation, not apparent to the older missionaries at the time, was the fifteen-year gap in age between the veteran missionaries and the new arrivals. In 1947 few of the mission agencies so prominent a few years later were then serving in Pakistan. Included among these were TEAM, the Conservative Baptists, the World Mission Prayer League, and the Pakistan Mission of Missions International.

By the mid-1950s, however, more than 600 missionaries had arrived in Pakistan. It was not long before questions about the education of their children became an urgent topic of discussion.

For almost a hundred years, the missionaries in India had all sent their children to Woodstock School in Landour, Mussoorie, a hill station now on the other side of the border; a few, to Kodai Kanal, in southern India. After independence in 1947, the schooling of missionary families in Pakistan became a pressing problem. Members of the older missionary community took it for granted that younger missionaries would continue to send their children to Woodstock School in Northern India and to spend their vacations in that hill station. Newcomers who knew nothing of Woodstock and Landour were considered naive. An ominous new factor appeared by 1950. The anti-missionary posture of both governments, but especially India, made it increasingly difficult for people to cross the border between India and Pakistan. Parents of a child studying in Landour experienced more and more red tape and delays in securing permits to cross the border. And some of them had scary experiences trying to get back into Pakistan. A child could fall ill and die before the parents could obtain permission to make the trip from Pakistan to India. Younger parents with no loyalty toward Woodstock, faced with the formidable barriers now posed by the international border, began to agitate for a school in Pakistan where their children could be educated.

An additional motivation for such a school arose as mission families began leaving the field because there were no provisions for the education of their children. All of us lamented the departure of experienced missionaries—a loss both to the kingdom of God and to the cause of missions in Pakistan.

A group from the United Presbyterian (UP) Mission, of which I was a part, and from the World Mission Prayer League—"Wimple," to us—began discussing this problem in earnest during the summer of 1954. Our first meeting took place on the lawn behind the manse at Gharial, which later became the principal's house. (What a beautiful spot that was—a spacious expanse of green sloping upward from a badminton court toward the pine and deodar forests above. Though I rejoice in the lovely hostel that now occupies that site, I still feel a certain sadness at the loss of such a peaceful, green meadow.)

These preliminary discussions climaxed that fall at the annual meeting of the Sialkot Mission—the United Presbyterian Church's organizational body in Pakistan--when the mission appointed a small committee to investigate the possibility of starting a school in Murree.

The Sialkot Mission Minutes show that the idea of starting a school in cooperation with other missions began as early as 1951—and that the Presbyterians, too, were divided and confused. (At that same meeting a special Anti-Communist Committee was appointed to deal with the problem of Pakistan's growing interest in—and continued ignorance about—Communism.) In the beginning, it was assumed that the Murree School would be only a primary school and that the high school students would continue to go to Woodstock.

During the summer of 1955, as missionaries arrived in Murree for language school or to vacation, I met frequently with representatives from approximately sixteen different mission groups. We enjoyed wonderful fellowship at our meetings but didn't agree on much of anything except that a school was desirable. These were not angry disagreements but simply the voicing of sixteen opinions on every issue. One of the key struggles pertained to theological beliefs. Members of TEAM mission insisted that any school in which they participated must be founded on a doctrinal statement which all staff members would sign. The Scottish Mission said that if they had to sign anything they would not join. (The latter were in no way reluctant to express their beliefs but, like Scots everywhere who stand on principles, took the position that their home board in Scotland did an adequate job of screening mission candidates.) Though the issue of a doctrinal standard was a sticky one, the mission community in Pakistan generally experienced a unity of spirit that was quite unusual. There had not been the divisive tensions between "conservatives" and "liberals" that have sometimes plagued relationships among missionaries in other countries.

Another major issue concerned the capital investment needed to get the school started. In fact, it became quickly apparent that the question of how missions would participate financially in the school was not an easy one to answer. Inevitably, discussions about how the school would be financed led to concern about how the school would be controlled. Presumably, a board of directors would decide all policy matters. But who would be represented on such a board and what would be the basis for their participation? Would missions be represented on the governing board according to the number of students they sent to the school? Or would their financial contribution to the capital and operating costs of the school determine their representation? A few of the missions found it difficult to recruit personnel but could donate cash to the school, while others had difficulty raising cash for such an institution but could obtain people who usually raised their own support. It was obvious that support for the school would come in two forms: cash or staff.

Throughout 1955 we wrestled with these issues without coming to a satisfactory conclusion—which may have simply meant that nobody agreed with me! I recall a meeting in Murree in which I had been pressing the point that missions who invested money had a right to direct school policy. A representative of another mission interrupted me explosively by saying, "That's the trouble with your mission—you think if you pay the bill you have a right to control the policies!" Just how much influence those missions should have whose children made up a majority of the student body (and who, therefore, were paying substantial sums in fees) compared to those who sent fewer students but supplied generous grants was not an easy question to answer.

The previous summer TEAM missionaries Rosie Stewart, her sister Marjorie, and Rachel Steeves taught some of the TEAM children in the apartment of Dr. and Mrs. Kaarsgard at Sandes Home. Other missionaries were invited in 1955 to send their children to TEAM's "school" at Bexley Cottage in Murree. About twenty-five children were involved. Meanwhile, at the UP Mission annual meeting in September 1955 the issue was once again hotly debated.

Gene Glassman presented a lengthy paper outlining the importance of the education of missionary children. Gene was a gifted linguist who would later guide Bible translation projects in such diverse places as Iran, Hong Kong, Nepal, Pakistan, and Afghanistan. The burden of Gene's presentation to the UP Mission was that we should take the initiative in establishing a school in Murree and afterward invite others to join. The people who were in favor of organizing a school in Pakistan pointed out how the mothers didn't get to go with their kids that summer, and the ones that were opposed to starting a school kept saying, "Oh, but there is such a crisis. We don't want to organize something else at the time of crisis." (The Prime Minister of Pakistan had been murdered that summer, so it was an anxious time.) Then Mrs. Sutherland, my mother-in-law, who was a short, heavy woman at retirement age, got up from the back row. In a very slow voice she said, "We have been going from crisis to crisis all these forty years of our service. If we wait until there is no crisis, we'll never get anything done." And that wisdom turned the tide in favor of starting a school.

As one of the newer missionaries on the field at a time when district evangelism was undergoing many changes, I was in a sense the low man on the totem pole. I was relatively inexperienced, hence expendable, so the mission assigned me for one year to the task of opening a school in Murree.

The first thing I did was appeal to the home church for a volunteer experienced in educational matters to come to Pakistan as soon as possible to take over as principal of the school. The next priority was to obtain equipment for the school and, as soon as the weather permitted, to get started on renovations to the church in Gharial which would ultimately become our classroom block.

The old garrison church at Gharial had once reverberated to the skirl of bagpipes and the voices of Scottish troops clad in kilts. But since the British withdrawal when Pakistan obtained independence in 1947, the church had remained empty and unused. The person with the clearest claim to the property was the Anglican Bishop of Lahore, Lawrence Woolmer. However, the lovely church had not escaped the eye of the Roman Catholic bishop of Rawalpindi, who saw in it an opportunity. He compelled the watchman to unlock the church door, placed some furniture in the church hoping to establish a basis for a later claim to jurisdiction over the property. Since the government of Pakistan was careful to respect the ownership of former British religious properties, a religious leader's claim of possession carried considerable weight in establishing who rightfully controlled the property. Fortunately, the Bishop of Lahore prevailed and the Bishop of Rawalpindi lost a couch and a few chairs which had become home to a colony of presumably irreligious mice. Bishop Woolmer then formally gave the right to use the church to Murree School, after conducting a service in which the altar area was deconsecrated.

During the winter months of 1955-56 my father-in-law, Dr. William Sutherland, was a great help. He served for forty years as an evangelistic missionary to Muslim peoples in the North-west Frontier Province. The UP board had permitted him to return to Pakistan only on the condition that he live near a mission hospital where help would be readily available should his less-than-robust heart give trouble. He had moved into a bungalow at the Christian hospital in Taxila where he served as a chaplain and superintended a number of building projects. He had discovered a Muslim contractor whose initiative and integrity were great assets. He loaned this man to me for the refurbishing of Gharial Church into school rooms. In those days lumber was purchased literally "by the log." With his help we examined dozens of logs (squared up on a band saw) looking for specimens with the fewest visible knot holes and splits. These were loaded onto hand carts and transported through the Rawalpindi bazaar to a saw mill where a noisy, rickety band saw—vibrating threateningly—sliced board after board from each log. The cut boards were then trucked to Gharial.

The arches in Gharial Church ran parallel to the length of the sanctuary supporting the flying buttresses of the building. These were to be filled in with large cement blocks to make walls for additional rooms. The center of the former sanctuary would be left intact for use as an assembly hall and gymnasium; the flying buttresses would provide classroom space. Cement blocks were virtually unknown to local construction people at that time. So we had to make our own and, as the weather was too cold and damp in Murree, they were made at the Christian hospital in Taxila, under the supervision of my father-in-law, and then trucked up the hill. The blocks were made a few hundred at a time by mixing the concrete, pouring it into metal forms until the concrete had firmed up, then allowing the blocks to cure for several days. While the blocks were being readied I lived in Taxila with my son Eric, then about three-and-a-half. One afternoon he spotted a line of blocks just removed from their metal forms drying in the sun. Stepping carefully from block to block, he managed to proudly walk the entire line without falling—in the process destroying the day's output of the block makers. His grandfather was not amused!

The previous fall I had placed an order with the Boy's Industrial Home (BIH) in Gujranwala—later known as the Christian Technical School—for the beds, desks, and chairs that the school would need. I recall carrying a tape measure in my pocket and at every opportunity compelling mission children to permit me to measure them. The length from floor to knee, from knee to bottom, and from bottom to chest became important figures. This research determined the height of the chairs and desks we ordered as well as the dimensions of the chair seats. Three sizes of chairs and desks were finally manufactured. Irv Lotze (of the UP Mission), who then headed the BIH, provided indispensable help in designing and making the furniture. The bunk beds used in the boarding hostel were made from an original design by Irv.

A few days before school opened in March 1956 a truck arrived from Gujranwala piled high with the yet to be assembled furniture. Irv had sent two boys from the BIH to assemble the pieces and finish them on site—a brilliant idea which saved us from beginning school with scratched or damaged equipment. (The typical finish used in Pakistan at that time was known as "lac polish"—a name for shellac made from granules of shellac dissolved in methylated spirits.) The truck arrived in Jhika Gali late one afternoon, but was unable to get up the steep driveway to Sandes Home. Momentarily, however, it seemed that virtually every man within a mile radius of Jhika Gali (most of whom are unemployed throughout the winter) had flocked around the truck wanting to act as coolies to transport the furniture up the hill. With only an hour of daylight left, I concluded that whatever we did had to be done quickly. Grabbing a pocketful of business cards from my desk, I had the BIH boys unload the truck, giving to each coolie a fair and equal load. As each coolie in turn started up the hill with a load, I handed him a business card. The agreement was that each man would be paid a set price per trip times the number of cards he was able to give me in return. With this system the truck was unloaded in jig time.

*   *   *

It was something of a miracle that we had available to us such commodious facilities as we found at Sandes Home. The property had enjoyed a rich history before the UP Mission obtained it for a summer residence for missionaries. During the British Raj when large numbers of homesick, poorly paid British Tommies were posted in India, some Christian women saw the need for a place where such rootless young men could enjoy a healthful, restful vacation. Thus was born the string of Sandes Soldiers Homes across Asia—hill resorts offering English soldiers inexpensive accommodations in a Christian environment. After Partition (when the British left India in 1947), the family who had initiated the idea were only too glad to have their properties continue in the service of Christ. Mr. Charles Stewart, the treasurer of the UP Mission, negotiated the purchase of the Sandes property and managed to persuade a reluctant UP Mission to approve the terms. He was able to obtain the unexpired time on a ninety-nine year lease at a cost ridiculously low by any reasonable standards. But to missionaries who thought of language school, missionary children's school, and summer vacation as something one did in Landour, India, purchasing an extensive property a difficult three-mile walk from Murree (to which no one went anyway) seemed the height of folly. However, the acquisition of Sandes Home proved to be a major Godsend. Even before Murree School was established, Pakistan missionaries had begun to make regular use of Sandes as a holiday residence and as quarters for newer missionaries attending the Murree Language School. By the time we asked to use Sandes property for Murree school, a number of UP missionaries were hesitant to relinquish their exclusive use of what had become their regular summer home. What had once been bemoaned as a folly had become an indispensable necessity!

Over the years as the school increased in size and the UP Mission shrank drastically, the school occupied more and more of the premises for a longer season of the year. As could be expected this created a perpetual source of friction between the school and the UP Mission.

* * *

We opened Sandes Home to boarders and for classes on March 8, 1956, with eight students: Marty Christy, Kathy and Patty Hamm, Don Lotze, and Mary Louise Selby (United Presbyterian); Marilyn and Margie Kane (World Mission Prayer

League); and Billy Harmon, from a USAID family. We had admitted Billy as an experiment to see how a non-missionary expatriate child would meld into a group of mission kids. He and his family arrived in a large Buick automobile one afternoon. Poor Billy was at first like a fish out of water. He was at Sandes hardly fifteen minutes before he had gotten into a fight with the son of Chowkidar Ashraf. Thus, I was able to demonstrate my fierce authority as principal. (Billy's father had taught agriculture at a high school in Casa Grande, Arizona. In Pakistan he was responsible for setting up facilities for repairing tractors throughout the northern areas and had built a huge maintenance shop. I was amazed at the time because I wondered whether there were more than three or four tractors in the entire region!) Billy ultimately fit in well after this initial incident, which was simply a classic case of cultural misunderstanding.

That spring, the school boasted three expatriate staff: Miss Gene Purdy (UP), a gifted teacher whose contribution in that first year was incalculable even though she had some misgivings about coming all the way to Pakistan to teach *American* children; Miss Ardella Reetz (WMPL), a Scandinavian nurse from Minnesota with a rare capacity to make a crude and chilly boarding hostel seem like a warm, loving home; and myself, serving as principal. With all the students between seven and nine years old, Ardella was the perfect housemother. Firm as necessary, she also played fairy-godmother, putting money under the kids' pillows when they lost their teeth.

Complimenting the expatriate staff were Pakistani assistants whose helpfulness cannot be overstated. Khan Zaman had been a cook in the UP Mission for years and for several summers had operated the food service arrangements for summer boarders at Sandes. He was a natural for school cook—a job that eventually turned out to be much bigger and lasted far longer than any of us could have foreseen at that time. The Sandes watchman, Ashraf, and the watchman at Gharial, Lal Khan, provided extremely useful links to the local population and lore. The loyalty and devotion of these men was of immense value to the school.

In preparation for opening day I had varnished the floor in the large bedroom that was to be used for classes. In the cold, humid climate of Murree the varnish failed to dry. So the night before school opened, Gene Purdy, Ardella Reetz, and I were on our hands and knees washing the floor with turpentine to remove the gummy varnish. We were still afraid that the next day children might stick to the floor! I shall be eternally grateful to those women. That task turned out to be a harbinger of many similar ones to follow.

Our first attempt at operating a boarding hostel turned out to be a fairly cozy experience. Each evening Ardella brought her boarders clad in pajamas and bathrobes into the large parlor (now the Charles Roub Recreation Room) where everyone gathered before a crackling fire for devotions and some stories. One evening during this time a child was heard to pray, "Dear Lord, help Auntie Gene be a good teacher; and help Auntie Ardella to be a good housemother; and help Uncle Paul to be a good . . . a good . . . uh, father." It was clear the youngsters had very little idea what I did or why I was there.

My wife and I lived in Ash Wing (which was razed in 1990 and replaced by a new building). The first classroom was the large rear bedroom upstairs on the left side of the building, overlooking the garage and the hairpin turn of the driveway going up behind Sandes. The Lotze family lived underneath the classroom, Irv having come to Sandes in order to superintend construction. After Ardella had tucked in all "her" children, she and Gene Purdy would go downstairs to join Irv and Marion for such goodies as coffee, tuna sandwiches, and dill pickles.

Our beginnings were small, but within two weeks—having added Dewey Christy, Ruth Dobra, Mary Beth Lotze, Tim and John Philbrick, Frank and Roy Rutherford, and Don Price—we were up to sixteen pupils. By the end of May we had twenty-two—quite enough for a lone teacher coping with three grade levels in one room! The children came from a variety of backgrounds. As well as those from the UP mission and WMPL, others came from the Afghan Border Crusade, the American [Reformed] Presbyterian Church, the Methodist Church, and the New Zealand Church Missionary Society.

I will always remember watching young mothers leaving a child in boarding for the first time. They managed to put up a brave front as they waved goodbye, until they got passed the big tree in the parking lot below Sandes and were hidden from view. At that point they burst into tears, weeping copiously till they reached the bottom of Sandes hill.

While we tried to be worthy substitute parents, some details inevitably fell through the cracks. Dewey Christy came into boarding that first year with fourteen brand new pairs of underwear; at the end of the term, his parents discovered with some chagrin, he came home with thirteen brand new pairs of underwear.

Several weeks into the term, one of the Methodist boys threw a stone which lacerated the scalp of another boy badly enough that Ardella thought stitches might be required. Dr. Christy, fortunately in Murree at the time, was summoned. He cleansed the wound, then "sewed" it up by tying together clumps of hair on either side of the cut. It healed without incident—except perhaps for the teasing the boy must have endured for a time over his odd hair-do!

The Lord graciously spared us innumerable tragedies which could have resulted from the flammable, poorly wired structure in which we all lived. A few days before school opened Marion Lotze and Ila Mae Selby arrived somewhat earlier than usual to occupy the apartments they had reserved at Sandes for the summer. One evening a thunder storm of majestic proportions rocked the hillside. Blinding flashes of lightning repeatedly illumined the entire area. Suddenly Ila May Selby and Marion Lotze appeared at my door, fright written all over their faces. We were barely able to talk above the crashing thunder and the din of hail pelting the tin roof. Knowing that they were both sensible, hardy women, I was surprised at their fear and teased them about being afraid of a little thunder. They then related to me how as each bolt of lightning shook the old wooden structure we were in they had watched sparks crackle back and forth along the exposed electrical wiring in the hallway. They had visions of Sandes going up in flames at any moment! It was to be many years, however, before the electrical wiring at Sandes was upgraded to an acceptable standard.

Another time, Khan Zaman, the school's head chef, came to me in a state of great agitation. He blurted out, "I quit!" Trying to calm him I asked what was troubling him. "I keep getting shocked in this kitchen," he replied, his bushy gray eyebrows and big handlebar moustache all twitching at once; "and I am afraid I will be electrocuted." I summoned Irv Lotze, an engineer by training, who immediately pooh-poohed Khan Zaman's fears. Khan Zaman led us into the kitchen which was at the back of Sandes next to the hillside. The tin roof had been continued down the back of Sandes forming the kitchen wall. Khan Zaman, standing barefooted on the damp cement floor, asked Irv to jiggle the water faucet which came through a round hole cut through the tin. Irv, wearing thick rubber soled shoes did so. As the water pipe jiggled against the tin, sparks flew in every direction! The problem was solved when Irv discovered that when the main electrical service had been installed, the electricians had grounded the system by tying a wire into the tin roof. It was, indeed, a miracle that Khan Zaman or someone else had not been electrocuted.

One of my primary tasks was to secure enough water for the hostel. The municipal water was on only two hours each day. This was adequate as long as the resident population remained small. With the advent of boarding and the earlier arrival of families from the plains, however, our existing storage facilities proved woefully inadequate. Furthermore, our aged water closets and their worn valves were no match for the pressure we encountered when the municipal system was turned on. The water tanks on the walls above the toilets filled quickly when the water was on, then sprayed great showers of water all over the bathrooms. One of my morning chores was to race through the building flushing commodes to prevent a flood, at the same time begrudging every drop of water wasted in that process. Somehow by storing as much water as we could in tubs and buckets everyone managed an occasional bath. It is quite likely that the boarders developed helpful immunities by dipping their tooth brushes into buckets of questionable water. Looking back we veterans view with amazement the comparative luxuries enjoyed in the hostel today.

In addition to acute water shortages and potentially lethal electrical wiring, we had to cope with lice, bed bugs and sometimes larger varmints. The only netting on the windows was chicken wire. It was designed to keep out the flying squirrels and monkeys but cicadas could and did come into the building making an awful racket. Our only source of heat, apart from a few fireplaces, was a couple of small oil heaters. However, we had to run about the building so much that we kept comfortably warm. And in the cold weather few of us felt any great urgency to bathe too often, getting cold, as it were, all over at once! Daily shampooing of hair had not in those days become common place even in the West.

In mid-summer 1956 our school building was ready for occupancy. Four classrooms had been completed along the sides of the Gharial church sanctuary. More teaching staff began to arrive. Don and Evelyn Calderwood reached Murree in the fall, giving me an opportunity to turn over gradually the principal's responsibilities. As Don increasingly took administrative control, Evelyn began serving as our math teacher—a great blessing as upper grades were quickly added in subsequent years. It was also heartwarming to see the school move quickly from being a UP institution to a cooperative effort involving many missions. The school started by TEAM continued in Abbottabad during Murree School's first year. (See Karen Pietsch's valuable history, *The Mosaic of TEAM in Pakistan*, published by TEAM in 1992.) By March of 1957, however, an inter-mission conference approved a constitution for Murree Christian School bringing five mission groups into a cooperative venture. These were the Church Missionary Society (CMS) of Great Britain, the Conservative Baptist Foreign Mission Society (CBFMS), the Pakistan Mission (of Missions International), TEAM, and the United Presbyterian Church.

The question of a doctrinal statement as part of the school's constitution proved to be one of the most difficult hurtles. Some groups—especially TEAM—were so set on protecting the "purity" of the school that they did not trust the boards of some of the denominations that they perceived to be too liberal to send the right type of staff members. So they insisted that each staff member had to sign the statement of faith as written in the constitution of the school. There were at least three denominations which questioned this practice, and some would not join in sponsoring the school. The Methodists had difficulty with this requirement, and at one point the United Presbyterians voted *not* to join the school which they had started! However, because they were more interested in keeping the momentum going during this crucial early period, in spite of reservations, we sometimes acquiesced to the more vehement voices on the board rather than arguing over what seemed to be fastidious matters.

While they may at times have seemed intransigent to other participants in the process, there is no doubt that TEAM wanted to join forces—and resources—to create a cooperative school with other mission groups. The TEAM school in Abbottabad already had kindergarten through seventh grade. They quickly realized it would be impossible to continue adding a grade level each year. Expanding into a high school would require more personnel than could be justified for a small group of children. But the strict independent evangelical/fundamentalist structure of their organization made it difficult for them to affiliate with mainline denominational churches. They finally were able to work out an arrangement with the home office to join the MCS as the "Hazara Christian Fellowship" (not TEAM), skirting the separatist concerns of many of their sponsoring churches.

*   *   *

From the beginning we had planned to open the school with two or three grades, adding one grade each year as needed. By 1962—just six years from its inception—that time table had been long superseded. That year Ian and Isabel Murray arrived from Scotland to a school boasting eleven grades, and in 1964 the first MCS students graduated from high school. In that class were Dave Davis, Skip Lundgren, and Robert Tebbe.

In 1992 my wife Ruth and I had the supreme privilege of returning to Pakistan for three months. To visit MCS thirty years after our simple beginnings was a deeply satisfying experience. Discovering the number and quality of young people who have passed through MCS, many of whom have gone on to engage in significant Christian ministries, touched us profoundly. I remember one evening, while sharing devotions in the little boys hostel, I had to fight back tears of joy. Among the children in the room were three grandchildren of missionaries who had been my contemporaries. Through our own children we have been aware of the esprit de corps that exists among alumni of the school and reflects their appreciation for what it did for them. Meeting the current staff at MCS was an experience best described by C.S. Lewis—"surprised by joy." From the beginning Ruth and I have considered an assignment to Murree Christian School to be among the most difficult mission tasks. The boarding staff have to become parents to and provide a home for young people who are not in Pakistan of their own will, children who have become aliens twice over—

residing in a land to which they do not belong, and studying in a school which they did not choose. How can students be encouraged to respect what their parents are doing, to appreciate the calling their parents feel, while at the same time be prepared for a world very different from the world in which they are brought up? That this has been done so well is no small tribute to the commitment and sensitivity of the staff. I believe and hope that most mission kids appreciate their parents work and come to MCS happily. But saying that does not mean that I underestimate the difficulties involved.

I believe the staff is the essential foundation upon which the school fails or succeeds, and I marvel at how well the school has been able to keep up with the changing physical, cultural, and academic needs of the students while providing the continuity so vital to their emotional and spiritual well being. When we opened MCS the vast majority of our students were Americans. Now they are in a minority. It amazes me how MCS has been able to assist the wide diversity of nationalities now serving in Pakistan. Indeed, what a testimony to what is possible, when those called by God, sent and surrounded by prayer, are willing and steadfast. I praise God for those who have responded and remain at MCS, and keep you—even now more fervrently—in my prayers.

This is an amended version of a talk on Murree Christian School presented in Rodney Simmons' staff apartment at Sandes on June 27, 1992; with additional research by Paul Seaman.

5

Letters From the Front

God is in the Details

Evelyn Calderwood (1956–1987)*

The following excerpts are culled from letters to my parents, 1956-1960. We arrived in Pakistan in October 1956 for Don to take over as school principal. We were both twenty-five years old and had been married less than four months.

October 28, 1956. One of the first things we will have to do is to have a long bed made. None of the ones here are quite long enough for Don.

November 4, 1956. The electrical wires that run from Sandes Home to Murree cross some other electrical wires, and every time we have a storm or a wind, the lines short out. Paul (Pulliam) says that he has called the company as many as two times in one week and they always come right out and fix it. . . . To add to the excitement, this morning the water pressure was unusually high and all the toilets on the second floor ran over, all at once, and showered the people on the first floor. . . . We

---

*Indicates years at MCS, if staff; year of high school graduation (not necessarily at MCS), if alumni.

57

started language study this week. It will be imperative to learn at least enough to talk to the servants, because next March when school starts everyone here will be new, and nobody will know how to speak Urdu.

December 9, 1956. We received word this week that TEAM mission has voted to come into Murree School (they have had a school of their own). So it looks as though we'll have well over fifty in March. We have ordered more bunk beds, desks, etc. . . . We are going to have to build a dormitory in another year or so. . . .

Last Tuesday the staff ate at Fircos, the only restaurant in Murree where it is safe to eat.

January 1957. [We spent the winter with other Presbyterian missionaries in Gujranwala.] The *dhersi* (tailor) is coming today to do some sewing for the school. He will make some bearers' coats, some kitchen aprons, hem eight dozen napkins, and make some curtains. He charges the equivalent of about 65 cents a day and will work two or three days. Everything is lining up pretty well for the re-opening of school, except that we don't have a nurse. How we wish we had a car at the school. Without one it is a walk two miles each way just to go to the bank. We've ordered a big set of plastic dishes for the school. The Boontonware factory in New Jersey gives a fifty-percent discount to church groups. We wish they would arrive before school begins, but they won't.

February 1957. Don is trying to schedule a meeting to organize the Board of Directors for the school before school starts. There are lots of decisions that should be made right away, and we don't want the responsibility of making them ourselves. . . .

This morning Don is head over heels in red tape. Some of the school textbooks we ordered have arrived in Karachi and we have to get an import permit before we can get them, because the value is more than 150 rupees. The New York office hasn't sent the invoices yet, and we can't get the import permit without them, so we're wondering what will be the fate of the books. If they aren't cleared in thirty days they can be confiscated, and it was over a week before we received the notice that they had arrived. This is not unusual. Things like this happen all the time. Very frustrating!

March 1957. [We were returning to Murree for the opening of school; Eloise James, one of the original teachers at MCS, traveled with us.] We had so much baggage it was really funny. We thought for a while that one of us would have to stay behind in Pindi and take the next bus with the rest of the stuff, but we finally got it all on. The bus was two hours and twenty minutes late leaving Pindi, and when we got to Murree it broke down. We don't get off at Murree, but go to the next stop, Jhika Gali, which is right at the bottom of the hill from Sandes. So when the bus broke down in Murree two miles away from our destination, and already several hours late, the driver was very accommodating. He said they had phoned for another bus from Pindi and it would be here in two and a half hours! A bus from another company, seeing our predicament, offered to take us and all our stuff to Jhika Gali for eight rupees, which is almost as much as it had cost us clear from Pindi, so we told him nothing doing, and Don walked up to Rockedge where the Conservative Baptists live and borrowed their jeep and we loaded our stuff and took off. No cars had yet been up the driveway to Sandes and it had snowed several inches deep, and even the jeep couldn't make it, so we had to hire coolies to carry the stuff the rest of the way. Just a few minutes after we arrived, Audrey Jennings and Joan Larsen, the two other teachers came. Five minutes later, Khan Zaman the cook came, so we were all set. The next day, Rosemary Stewart, the matron, and Dawn Bursma, the nurse, came, so now our staff is complete. . . .

When we got here, of course, the water and electricity were shut off. The electricity was turned on the next day, but there is water only on the first floor, and we live on the second. Don had some of the servants dig up the pipes, and found that there was a break, so sent for the plumber. After waiting a day and a half to come, he didn't bring his tools with him, so we hope he comes back again tomorrow.

April 1957. We're on the trail of a school bus which is badly needed, especially during the summer time when the families are scattered all over Murree. We sent out a letter to the Board of Directors today to get permission to buy the used bus. The Church of Scotland mission is selling it.

We finally received the books we ordered from Scott/ Foresman. They have been in Karachi since February 14, and they arrived on the 6th of April. Customs is still holding a large order of books from Rand McNally.

May 1957. We have so many kids in school now that we don't have enough desks or books for them. It's kind of disgusting because last winter the plea went out to missions to let us know how many and who was coming so that we could be prepared for them. We are going to make the parents pay the airmail postage on the textbooks for the ones who didn't pre-enroll. . . . The "new" bus finally arrived May 31st. It's been nice having it. Only one trouble—we've already outgrown it!

July 1957. The school board met Wednesday and they really made some changes! We've already outgrown Sandes for boarding, so there will be another hostel (dorm) in Murree for the older boys. . . . The Board also decided to buy Norval Christy's Chevy Carry-all ('51) for the school. *[One decision made at the first Board of Directors meeting, held in March, 1957, was to change the name to Murree Christian School, because it seemed Westerners would have difficulty pronouncing "Gharial."]*

August 1957. The set of plastic dishes for the school arrived. They were ordered in January. There are seventy-two place settings, which we hope will be enough for awhile.

October 1957. Today we took all the Sandes kids over to Hill Lodge (our other boarding hostel) for a picnic. We were supposed to leave at 11:00. Don went out at 7:30 this morning to see if the bus would start. It wouldn't, so he and three Army mechanics from across the road worked on it until twelve noon and finally got it fixed. Needless to say, we were late for the picnic. Last Sunday we all got to church just in time for the sermon because the battery was dead and Don had to borrow one from the Army. The generator isn't working right, and doesn't charge the battery.

Sugar is still rationed, one half cup per person per week.

November 1957. School closed early because of a flu epidemic. Before it finished, all but two of the students and all but three of the staff and most of the servants had had it, some more than once. Most parents came to get their children. Dr. Norval Christy (from Taxila) accompanied the final thirteen children all by himself by train clear to Karachi, armed with his black bag containing a good supply of aspirin and sleeping pills.

June 1958. The school board meeting went off nicely on Wednesday—it was calmer than most of them are. They OK'd the plans for 40,000 rupees to be spent in building additional classrooms. Enrollment is over 100 now.

July 1958. We had dinner with the Roubs today. They are the Conservative Baptist folks who are going home next month. He will get his master's in education and come back to start our high school for us in the summer of 1960. They will be assigned permanently to the school by their mission. We are very glad.

. . . The boarding situation is getting tense again. Each mission sits and wait for the other missions to contribute somebody for houseparents. Nearly every term we have to threaten not to have boarding at all and then someone finally gets on the ball and digs up someone for the job. That happened this week. The executive committee of the board met and decided that each mission would have to have its own boarding hostel and furnish its own personnel. After hearing that, the CMS got excited and furnished us with the Binghams—just about the best people we can think of for the job.

September 1958. We're using Marsden Cottages as well as Sandes Home for boarding because of the great number of kids.
. . .

Don has a secretary one day a week now, to do the accounts, letters, etc. This is so that Don can do more teaching. The teachers have very heavy loads, especially the upper grade teacher. Don is teaching math and science to the older kids, and also has more time to play ball with them.

November 1958. We had some disappointing news today. Our school board had been negotiating with CMS mission to buy the St. Denys property and move our school there. It is a beautiful large campus with nice buildings and would have solved our housing problems. But it seems that the government has some strings on the property and if the St. Denys folk give it up, the government gets it. So we're right back where we started—bursting at the seams and no solution in sight. We still don't have the title to this property and can't build until we do.

July 1959. The title for the property has finally been cleared, after two years of sitting in offices, so we can go ahead with plans to build a dormitory. . . .

Our first annual sports day was scheduled but was rained out and has been postponed indefinitely. Finally held after three postponements. Don Calderwood won the men's race and Ruth Butterfield won the women's. Thirty women entered because the prize was a can of coffee! (Very expensive and hard to get out here.) School board meeting held to get started on plans, and also plead for more staff. Trying to rent property for boarding in Murree, but nothing suitable that we can afford. . . . Friday was another PTA meeting. It was a musical program put on by Ken Butterfield. He had a good program, but a lengthy one. In one way I was glad it was long. It kept the PTA from discussing the controversial subject of boarding in Murree.

We have decided to build some temporary classrooms because we need them immediately. We are building them of brick with lime mortar, so that the bricks can be reused. (Cement is unavailable at the present time.) With the capital being moved from Karachi to Islamabad, we will probably be unable to purchase cement for some time.

August 1959. The Board has appointed a building committee to draw up plans for a hostel to house eighty children. The plan is to construct the hostel on the pre-sent school property. The title is clear now so it is up to us to draw up a trust deed that will allow us to use the property as long as the school is needed in Pakistan.

Most of the children and staff had to have chest x-rays because of three cases of TB [tuberculosis] among missionary kids this summer.

November 1959. The architect came to look over the site that had been selected for the new dorm if we ever get around to building it, and he said that it was the most expensive site we could have chosen because a lot of excavation will have to be done, and he's not sure how solid the ground is underneath. The fact remains that it's the only site we have to build on.

We still can't go ahead with the building, but now that Don has the power of attorney he can apply for permits to build. It may take as long as a year to get them, and we don't have enough money for the dorm yet. However, we do hope to have some classrooms built by June.

July 1960. Thursday there was a PTA meeting in which the staff tried to inform the parents of some of the things that the school is doing, and how we are doing them. The staff rather dreaded the meeting, but it went very well.

We're still working on an import permit for a VW microbus. Just because it was refused twice doesn't mean we can't try again.

August 1960. Yesterday a car-full of us went to a place about ten miles from here where there is an empty army camp that might be available for a possible site for the school. We are still thinking that it might be better in the long run to move the whole thing than to try to expand any more in our present location. Anyway, this place has a lot of buildings and ground but would need quite a lot of repair.

The school bus has been out of commission for six weeks, due to inability to get parts. Six cars were used to transport students.

6

Outpost Cadets

The Early Years—For Students

Tim Philbrick, '65

My first memory of MCS is a cold, wet Easter Sunday in 1956—which happened to fall on April Fools' Day that year—just a few weeks after the school had opened. The few students and staff gathered in the drawing room of the lower level of Sandes Home for the service. Gene Purdy, our teacher, liked singing and programs to include the appropriate props and costumes, so we young charges found ourselves outfitted in make-shift construction paper choir collars, standing before the small assemblage, singing the two Easter songs that had been taught to us in a hurried pre-service practice session.

We lived on the second story of Sandes, girls on the left and boys to the right. Our regular meals were taken in the middle room, near the outside stairs and above the latter day dining room, with everyone seated around no more than two large tables. Khan Zaman was the cook and we ate like kings. I particularly remember breakfast—we consumed prodigious amounts of *suji* in huge, basin-like bowls, topping it off with generous portions of whipped cream and sugar. To be sure there was *dahlia* too (a coarser, lentil-like cereal), and occa-

64

sionally *savian,* sweetened with the oddly-bitter syrup of unrefined sugar. The cereals were of course followed by eggs and toast, accompanied by tea. No one went hungry. Equally memorable are the afternoon teas, which were sometimes served in the large cobblestoned dining room on the main floor. The tables were filled with cakes, doughnuts, cookies—you name it— and we obliged Khan Zaman (who was revered by all hungry urchins and had not yet acquired the "KZ" moniker) by dutifully eating everything in sight.

After supper everyone joined in singing, with considerable gusto, songs like "I've Been Working on the Railroad," "The Bear Went Over the Mountain," and "She'll Be Comin' Round the Mountain When She Comes." The only boarding parent in those very early days was Ardella Reetz, a very young woman from North Dakota, who read all of us bedtime stories from Laura Ingalls Wilder's *Little House in the Big Woods* and *Little House on the Prairie.*

Sandes was home, school, and church that first spring. We seldom left its environs except for regular Saturday hikes, weather permitting. After the usual hearty breakfast and chores we'd all assemble, and following an enthusiastic Paul Pulliam, walk through the woods for what seemed like hours. We'd stop for a well-deserved picnic lunch and rest, then find our way home, eager to hear our leader's estimate of the number of miles traveled.

When school resumed in March of 1957 Murree was still in the grip of winter. It was cold, and everything was under a foot or two of snow. We wore multiple layers of clothing, especially shirts, to stay warm; some slept in their coats on occasion. Enrollment at MCS increased dramatically, due in part to the addition of students from the TEAM-operated school at Abbottabad. By summer, the school was pushing into junior high. Gone were the informal days; now we had competitions, inspections, and rules galore. We even had names for our bedroom groups: members of the corner room were "Irish Setters"; those in the adjoining room were "Bulldogs." The room names were undoubtedly meant to give us some group identity and spur competition for inspection points, but not surprisingly, the early result was rivalry and ridicule. Almost immediately, some talented Bulldog writer/composer came up with a short ditty which went: "The Irish Setters are big bed wetters, and big bed wetters are they, ey, ey!" Not to be outdone, the Setters retorted with: "The Bulldogs are no good. We'll chop them up for firewood. And when we've done all that, we'll feed them to the old tom cat."

The days of great eating were also a thing of the past. Now we were assigned places on benches at long tables in the big dining room, where staff members, one at each end of the table, kept us quiet and enforced table etiquette. The food wasn't as fancy or plentiful—whipped cream for cereal got scarce and then disappeared, there was no longer an endless supply of *suji*. In fact, someone in authority must have loved *dahlia*, because we seemed to have it all too often. Worst of all, the great teas with cakes, doughnuts, and *samosas* were now the exclusive privilege of the staff—we kids got tea in enameled tin mugs and a couple cookies. Finally, we no longer enjoyed our informal walks to and from school. Now we were assigned a walking partner, and a place in the "crocodile line" from which we dared not deviate. "Guards" at the front and rear of the formation blew whistles when vehicles approached from their direction. All in all, boarding had become a real drag.

When it rained—as it would for days on end during the monsoons—we had to stay indoors. The "gym," or central part of the church building was the only playground on those occasions, and roller skating was a favorite activity. Most kids had skates—not the kind with rubber wheels and permanent boots attached as is common today, but the 100-percent metal kind that attached to the soles of shoes by means of clamps and a strap. When twenty or more kids were skating on the concrete floor the din was unbelievable. Much of the time the skaters rolled singly around the outside of the gym and through the two arches near the entrance door; counter-clockwise seemed to be the preferred direction. Sometimes energetic shoe-clad friends pulled individual skaters around with ropes, chariot-style, the length of such encounters dictated by the stamina of the runner. Sooner or later someone would start a "train," which might have twenty skaters hanging onto each other behind one struggling locomotive who seldom had the strength to go more than a couple rounds. Inevitably, trains turned into a couple "crack the whip" games, after which everyone went back to singles skating.

There were several cardboard boxes in the gym area containing jump ropes, bean bags, and various types of balls. One rainy day, someone discovered that by tying one end of a jump rope around the middle of a bean bag a person could twirl the bean bag slingshot style, and propel it into the uppermost regions of the building. This was great fun, winding these creations up, sending them aloft and watching the rope trail behind. But alas, it wasn't long before one, and then more, of these critters tangled in the wires stretched across the building just beneath the ceiling. The manufacture and operation of these bean-bag comets was soon banned, but not before a half dozen or so found their way to the wires, where they hung helplessly for the next twenty or thirty years.

More than balls, bean bags, and jump ropes found their way into the cardboard boxes in the gym. One morning, I was one of the first students to enter the building and headed for the nearest box. Skip Lundgren beat me to the box and as he grabbed a basketball a flying squirrel jumped out. Foolishly, we gave chase and cornered the squirrel, which bit Skip when he tried to catch it. I don't remember the fate of the squirrel, but I do recall that Skip had to have a series of rabies shots, in the stomach, administered by the school nurse. I saw the syringe and needle one night, and was glad I hadn't caught up with the squirrel.

Flying squirrels made periodic appearances inside the old school building. I remember the year one disrupted the awards assembly the day before graduation. Someone caught it under a trash can, but not before the squirrel and its pursuers raised quite a commotion.

* * *

In the spring of 1958 boarding arrangements for the "older" boys (grades four through six) moved to Hill Lodge above Murree, with John and Monica Meadowcroft as the boarding parents. We lived on the second floor of the building, where there was a row of small cubicle "rooms," all with a common view of rafters and ceiling. Anyone with a mischievous bent could toss an item—someone else's underwear, for example— over the cubicle wall and cause it to hang up on one of the girders or fall into another room. After-lights-out whispering was possible even between non-roommates, but was also easily discovered and dampened by an eavesdropping staff member.

On Saturday mornings after breakfast and the ritual clean-up and inspection, "Crofty" would head down Bank Road to the National Bank of Pakistan in Murree and return a short time later with our allowance in change, carried in one of those very British gray wool socks. He would set up shop on the front porch or in the drawing room and, using the familiar students' copy book for record purposes, dispense our weekly stipends. Fifth and sixth graders recieved twelve annas (an old form of coins, the equivalent of 75 paisa—or about ten U.S. cents, in those days); younger colleagues got six or eight annas.

Our pockets jingling, we headed for Murree in small groups (mandated to be two or more for safety) where we practiced the fine art of bargaining in the Lower Bazaar, or succumbed to more "fixed price" shopping on the Mall—in Esajee's, or in the Corner Store, where we bought numerous copy books and leaky pens. We usually returned to Hill Lodge before lunch, but on occasion bought buns in the bazaar or arranged for take-out lunches, which we ate with a companion or two somewhere in the woods, usually on or near the path known as Forest Trail that went all the way down to Sunny Bank.

When we weren't exploring the woods we played with our cars. Everyone had a small collection of "Dinky" or "Matchbox" toys, virtually indestructible and amazingly accurate die-cast metal reproductions of mainly British vehicles of the day. We drove these cars on the ever-expanding road systems that we carved out of any hillside *kud* (steep embankment) with every young civil engineer's tool, the *chaku,* or pocket knife.

Every kid loves to hear stories, and we "boarding brats" were no exception. Most of the stories we listened to came from books, some more interesting than others. I especially remember gathering in the big drawing room in the evenings to hear Uncle John read "tiger stories," riveting accounts by the British adventurer, Colonel Jim Corbett, who had hunted man-eating tigers on the Indian subcontinent in the 1930s and 1940s.

But the very best stories I heard during all my years at MCS came straight from the lips of two of the best storytellers that ever lived: One, a Mr. Cecil Johnston, an absolutely delightful British gentleman based somewhere in India; he worked for Scripture Union and visited MCS occasionally. He had two trademarks: a natural knack for communicating with children, and a well-worn attaché case which accompanied him everywhere. When he came to Murree he would speak at the morning chapel service and in Bible classes, but we kids couldn't wait until evening storytime. He had been a chaplain in the British Army during World War II and was assigned to a unit which operated behind Japanese lines in Burma. His experiences, needless to say, were fascinating and unique, and when told with his flair, coupled with intriguing British accent and humor, we were spellbound and couldn't hear enough.

The other storyteller extraordinaire was Ken Old, who in the late '50s had responsibility for the Sandes property for the UP Mission, so at times visited the area during boarding. I can still see our crowd of kids, in pajamas and bathrobes, gathered around the barrel stove in the dining room, listening to Ken's chronicle, which he made up as he told it, and which continued from night to night and visit to visit. The details escape me now, some thirty-five years later, but I remember that the characters invariably included members of the audience. This never ending saga had us taking shrinking pills, falling into cracks in the floor which led to underground caverns, dealing with mysterious characters, and the like. When "Uncle Ken" would try to end an episode we would plead for more, because like any good storyteller he would leave us in some precarious situation that demanded solution. But we would have to wait—until the next evening, or another visit, or possibly the next boarding term.

For all its variations, this same story, basically a parable about good and evil, managed to continue seamlessly from one generaton of kids to the next without ever running out of steam. And I suspect Uncle Ken was always as curious as his audience to find out what would happen next.

* * *

On Sunday, October 8, 1961, I returned to MCS from two years in the States and was placed in a room with two old friends, fellow ninth graders Don Lotze and Jim Glassman. A third roommate, Mark Halter, was an eighth grader whose father was a U.S. Army major stationed in Rawalpindi. That day changed MCS history, for I brought a transistor shortwave radio, and that same afternoon Mark's dad drove up to see his son, and left an electric 45-RPM phonograph with a stack of single records. By the end of the day we were spinning disks and listening to recent pop hits, including "Kathy's Clown" by the Everly Brothers and "Rubber Ball" by Bobby Vee; "Every Little Star," and "Hot Rod Lincoln"; Chubby Checkers' "The Twist" and others by Brenda Lee, The Drifters, and maybe some Elvis, though I don't think we really had a sense of who he was then. Almost all of the older students (eighth, ninth and tenth graders) had been to the States during the previous two years and were somewhat familiar with these tunes. The music revived memories of "neat" times in the U.S., and gave everyone a chance to feel "cool." During the next couple weeks, the phonograph found itself the center of attention at one or two mixed group informal listening sessions but for the most part stayed in our room in the top house on the Sandes property. Among students the music was an occasional topic of conversation, but hardly a sensation.

It must have alarmed some among the staff a fair bit more, because within two weeks of its arrival we returned from school one afternoon to find our boarding master, John Greenslade, listening to the records. He explained that there was some concern by certain unnamed staff members, and that he had been asked to listen to all of the records. We were relieved when he told us that he found only one selection objectionable, an instrumental with a stronger beat, called "Bongo Rock." But his report must have met with some disbelief from certain quarters of the staff, for after further review and discussion we got the word: this "music" was unsuitable. Shortly thereafter Mark Halter left the school, along with his phonograph and records; for the moment, the issue was dead. His father made a brief early-morning visit some months later during which, unknown to us, he donated the phonograph to the school. It found its way to a cluttered corner of the *godown* and gathered dust, out of sight and mind, until discovered two years later by a couple students conducting an inventory of school property.

One must remember that this was long before the days of boom boxes and cassette tapes, and until then the only musical recordings belonged to staff members, and only a few of them at that. For the most part, these selections were limited to religious or classical music. The school's music expert was Mr. Kenneth H. T. Butterfield, a Welsh man from Swansea, who joined the faculty in the spring of 1959.

Mr. Butterfield was a thin, wiry man with a Hitler mustache, round dark-rimmed spectacles, formal manner and se-

rious disposition. The most hilarious situation would only make
him sniff and snort in suppressed laughter. He taught high
school math, English and phys ed, but his forte was music, specifically piano. Rumor had it that he had earned the second-
highest degree or rating in classical piano, and if you saw him
play, you could believe it. Mr. Butterfield was devoted to religious and classical music—in his view there was little value in
other varieties, although he did include what one might call
"ordinary" songs in his music classes, occasionally even permitting a rousing rendition of "What Should We Do With The
Drunken Sailor?" But any jazz or rock and roll was out of the
question, considered downright decadent. In 1961 and '62, following Sunday night singspirations, he and his wife, Ruth,
hosted an hour or so of "music appreciation" for high schoolers
in the Butterfields' Ashe Wing flat. Most of the boys attended
because it afforded an opportunity to be with the girls; presumably at least a few of the girls went for the music. During these
sessions everyone sat in silence, listening to and then cri-
tiquing various symphonies. I attended a few times, but withdrew when it became obvious my frank written analyses (which
included comments such as "little evidence of any tune in this
piece," or "no beat or rhythm") were not appreciated.

Mr. Butterfield was easily, and understandably, the school's
strongest proponent of classical music, but he was far from the
only staff member opposed to anything resembling jazz. On
that point there was little if any public disagreement by staff
members, although there were certainly a few who privately
enjoyed music which would not have received the MCS seal of
approval. The problem, undoubtedly, was one of where to draw
the line. There were numerous discussions by various interested parties, and none came to any definitive conclusion. In
the spring of 1962 we were told there would be a staff committee which would listen to any students' records and decide
whether they were acceptable. I submitted two Sousa march
records, someone else had a couple Blackwood Brothers Quar-
tet records, but essentially that was it. The committee took all
term to pass judgment—my march records made the grade, but
(I believe) not so the Blackwoods. For all practical purposes,
the point was moot, because there was no equipment available
to play our records on. We took them home, and while we continued to disagree with the staff on the merits of various types

of music, there was little or nothing concrete for any committee to rule on for several years.

We may not have had records, but I had a shortwave radio, and with luck we could tune in Radio Ceylon and Radio Australia. The latter was the station of choice, but it was very difficult to get a good signal, even with an extensive antenna strung in the trees outside our dorm house. Radio Ceylon was more reliable; late in the afternoon on weekdays they played half an hour of pop music, complete with dedications ("to my darling, Rosebud" was a favorite). Saturday mornings we would hurry to finish breakfast by 8:30 so we could run up the hill and listen to the "Benaca Hit Parade," sponsored by a South Asia toothpaste. Some of the songs we heard included "Take Good Care of My Baby," "Good Luck Charm," "I'm a Travelin' Man," "Listen to the Rhythm of the Falling Rain," "Lipstick on Your Collar," and "Soldier Boy." The radio's music was hardly popular with the staff, but no one ever tried to censor its use, possibly because good reception was far from guaranteed, the volume and fidelity were limited, and also because we listened to other types of programming as well, including news, and—believe it or not!—classical music from Radio Moscow. When we discovered Mark Halter's phonograph languishing in the *go-down* one of our enterprising students borrowed it (ostensibly to fix it), brought it to our dorm house, put it in the closet and ran wiring up through the attic and down to the radio, so it resembled the antenna lead. He then did a minor rewiring to the radio, so it could act as the phonograph's speaker. The only problem was we only had one or two 45-RPM records. When the novelty wore off we reverted back to conventional radio listening.

MCS students were a pretty musical lot, and when we were not readily able to listen to the music of our choice we made our own. Admittedly of amateur quality, it was nonetheless pleasing to our ears, and singularly satisfying when it got the goat of particular staff members. On trumpet and trombone, piano, accordion and Pakistani drum, as well as voice, we boys replicated popular songs of the day and even added a little syncopation and beat to hymns.

*   *   *

In the spring of the year, as soon as the snow melted and the temperatures began to warm, our athletic attention turned to track and field, culminating in the great Sports Day competition which effectively closed out the school year and boarding term. For high school boys (seventh grade and up) a major event was the cross-country race, held about a week before Sports Day but included in the overall competition. This grueling run started at school and went up the hill through the pine trees to Upper Topa. When you thought you couldn't run up hill any longer the road plunged downward toward Jhika. Your gait lengthened as feet made loud clop—clop—clop noises and your guts were thrown about, sometimes necessitating a walk to recover. Once down the hill and through Jhika, you had to keep a steady pace on the final leg while passing younger kids and girls walking home to Sandes—after all, you didn't want to come this far only to look like a wimp to younger admirers and members of the fairer sex. A couple curves before school you called up every bit of reserve for the final sprint and nearly stumbled across the finish line, totally exhausted. We generally practiced for this event once a week in phys ed, but as the race date approached and runners got psyched up it was not uncommon for a number of them to get up at 5:30 in the morning and run essentially the same route, starting and ending at Sandes. It was invigorating to run in the cool, crisp air, just after dawn, with a clear head and amazingly light feet, and without the normal distractions and the pressure of a stopwatch. I sometimes wonder if the times would have been better had the actual race been run in the early morning rather than late afternoon.

Appreciation of the early morning calm prompted some of us—with permission—to occasionally get up early on Saturday mornings and take a walk through the woods or along some deserted road. There was something special about witnessing the beginning of a new, undefiled day while listening to water running in a mountain stream and a constantly changing choir of birds—even the laziest sleepyheads had to experience it at least once a term. We ended our strolls in Jhika, just as its residents were beginning to stir. An old man with a stubbly beard in a small tea shop would be nursing a smoky fire, heating water for his first batch of tea. We'd stoop into the small hovel, sit on old rickety benches at a dirty, wobbly table, make small talk with the proprietor, and delight in a breakfast of raisin buns and tea. This was living, and no one who had this experience would trade it for anything today.

Judy (Haas) McKeehan, '65

My parents were short-term missionaries, teaching at Gordon College in Rawalpindi between 1959 and 1961. My brother, Joe, and I went to MCS for those three years. Going to a boarding school seemed like a great adventure but I know my brother was more apprehensive. During our first term, the girls lived at Marsden cottage in Murree and the boys were at Sandes Home. My brother and I could only see each other during the day at school. I loved Marsden and the lush green woods and meadows. As one of the older girls, I lived in a curtained-off area of the hall on the top floor. Auntie Joanie Larsen was our boarding parent. I remember that Geoff Bingham and his wife were in charge at least one term and I remember the Australian folktales he taught us about the Bunyip. I also remember Uncle Ken Old visiting and telling us about the fairies that lived in the wood. Who could forget his exciting stories about Jock and Georgie and the Snugglewump, and the Wizard of Woggle and the elephant's tooth? And if somehow these characters weren't compelling enough, Uncle Ken's little listeners always seemed to find their way into his stories, assuring our rapt attention.

The Sunday afternoon picnics were another highlight. The bus ride to school from Marsden was always filled with gospel songs. I also remember that we were given a noxious pink mix to put in our milk to kill some of the water buffalo taste. The UK kids were all excited one day because we were going to have "blanc mange" for dinner, but it failed to live up to my expectations. While at Marsden I caught hepatitis and had to spend one whole boarding term with my parents in Pindi.

When I was well enough to return, the girls had moved to Sandes Home, the boys lived in the houses farther up the hill, but we had many more opportunities to see them. There were, however, strict rules about not being in mixed company without an adult supervisor. I remember being made to eat everything, including gooseberries that tasted like vinegar. I also remember Marilee Kane being required to eat her eggs every morning, even though she always threw up. The trick was to eat quickly and get out of the dining room before that happened.

My favorite lunch was tandoori *roti* and bowls of pungent *budjia*. I remember *pakordas* for Sunday tea, and spilling jars of Ovaltine (purchased in another vain attempt to make buffalo milk palatable) in our desks where it turned into a sticky mass. I remember pouring my lunch milk between the cracks of the rock wall around the school, all flavorings having failed. I remember helping to collect enough chestnuts to fill the floor of our classroom and being assigned a copying of the first 200 lines of "The Ancient Mariner."

I roomed with Janet Miller most terms, but Judy Dial at least one; Kathy Hamm and Nonie Lundgren were the other older girls. Marty Christy was close behind. I remember memorizing all the words to "My Fair Lady" with Janet and elaborately rearranging our tiny room to create a "sitting room," where our trunks served as seats. I remember singing "Men of Harlech" and putting on the play "Jean Val Jean" from *Les Miserables*.

Mr. Butterfield—who, in appearance only, was a dead-ringer for Groucho Marx—was our music and religion teacher. We used to try to keep up with his brisk walk from Sandes to school, but couldn't. I remember his sweet wife, Ruth, and their baby, Ardith. I remember that Auntie Rosie Stewart would attend to those little girls who were sick during the night. As they threw up in one side of the basin, Auntie Rosie threw up in the other. I remember sitting in a circle during night devotions and having to pray out loud. I didn't hear anything anyone said up to my turn, due to anxiety, nor anything after, because of relief. I remember the walk from Sandes Home to school through the woods and along the dirt road. I remember walking into Murree on Saturday to spend our allowance. I almost always spent mine on yarn. We would pool our colors and knit brightly striped sweaters for the servants' children, a skill which I still enjoy. I also always got "monkey nuts" freshly roasted, in a hand-made paper sack.

I remember a hike the older girls took with Auntie Joanie

and Auntie Rae. We bought cucumbers from a village we passed through and washed our faces with the insides of the peels. We stayed in a small building on a promontory that pointed out over a sheer drop to the plains. In the morning we got up to hike around the bluff to watch the sunrise. As we turned a corner, a black panther dropped onto the path in front of us. We scattered and ran back to the village where we were told the panther had carried off a small child the day before.

*   *   *

I remember being taught narrow and judgmental religious doctrine. I became skilled at guilt, and examined my soul carefully for signs of vanity. I remember sitting in the "magic seat" one dinner and being chastised for some minor infraction of table etiquette, singly and in front of the rest of the diners. On another occasion I became the subject of a night devotional diatribe after I had reached across one bowl to take the larger bowl of ice cream—the only ice cream I remember in my three years of boarding. When I came back from a vacation with my parents with a tube of pale pink lipstick and shaved legs I was called a "paint and powder box." I remember when Steve and Jimmy Glassman returned from furlough with rolled up sleeves and duck tail hair styles. Skippy Lundgren rushed to imitate them and they were all three sent to comb out their hair. I remember being taught to play baseball via ridicule by Mr. Esden.

It is not possible to tell all that I remember. I remember playing "Flashlight Beckon" and "Kick the Can" around Sandes Home on summer evenings. I remember holding hands with Skippy Lundgren. I remember Donny Lotze and Robbie Tebbe putting centipedes and scorpions in a jar to fight it out, and tying string to cicadas' wings to swing them around and hear them buzz. I remember watching the "four o'clocks" close at night and watching the fog come up from the plains to surround Sandes. I remember a British teacher telling us the story of Dunkirk and the tears in her eyes at the telling. I remember reading every Elsie Dinsmore book in our small library.

I remember crying when we left; I know I would not trade my time at MCS for anything. The aunties whom I loved and who loved me will always be a part of who I have become. I always told Auntie Joanie that I would be a teacher. Then I thought it would be at the first or second grade level because she let me come into her classroom and teach songs and help with lessons. Many of the things I learned from Mr. Butterfield have continued to enrich my music and my life. Eloise James and Rae Steeves gave me a firm academic foundation and Auntie Rosie helped with the hugs I needed. There are many things, especially in my relationship to God, that I have had to work through. For a time I resented the kind of indoctrination I received, but that is behind me and the part of my life that I spent at MCS is very important to me. I'd love to go back, but the people are gone. And, if I can't room with Janet and talk to Nonie and Kathy and Jimmy, it will only make me sad.

7

Firm Foundation . . . Leaky Roof

God is in the Details, Part Two

When the Calderwoods were appointed to Pakistan, the United Presbyterian Board of Missions assured them that the school in Murree would always be a small school, and would never have more than forty or fifty students. Nobody dreamed of the way in which missionaries would arrive in Pakistan during the 1960s. And in those days, the average missionary family had four or five children. Toward the end of that decade, enrollment at MCS was close to 200.

The frustrations of living in a barely-modernized country and under mission bodies with limited financial resources remained pretty constant throughout the years: shortages of staff, vehicles, space, and water.

One problem was the need to close boarding for the summer months so that the UP mission could use Sandes Home for its vacationing missionaries. All the school furniture had to be moved from Sandes to be stored in the school at Gharial. Coolies were hired to carry the bunk beds on their heads to the school. A system had to be worked out so the impoverished hill people, carrying the beds along the desolate, mile-long road through the woods to the school, would not be tempted to steal them.

In the early days, water was heated in a big *hammam* in a shack behind Sandes. It was often said that the only hot running water in Murree was what Mara, the *bhishti,* or water carrier, ran with as he brought it to your bathroom.

"Auntie Rosie" Stewart's bedroom was the only heated room in the girls' department, so on cold days the girls often used her room as a play area. On bath days, once a week, five small tin tubs were hauled into her room and the *bhishti* filled them with buckets of hot water. The girls first took a basin full of water out of the tub; then they washed their hair in the tub, using the basin water for rinsing. Then they got in the tub and bathed. The tub had to be hauled to the bathroom for emptying. One time the staff were having tea in Sandes dining room when water from the tubs above in Rosie's room started leaking down on to the dining room table.

One evening three fourth-grade boys failed to show up for Sunday supper. When they didn't appear after much bell-ringing, some of the staff went looking for them with some anxiety. The boys—Sammy McMillan, Dougie Thompson, and Eric Pulliam—were found, halfway to the school in a sort of cave area along the road, scooping scorpions into one of Eric's socks. They had bagged nine up to that point.

In the early days, lunch was prepared in the kitchen at Sandes and carried down to school in large *degchis* (steel pots) on the heads of the bearers.

Until 1963, the school bathrooms were housed behind the church building in a small red corrugated tin structure, affectionately known as "the Pulliam," after the man who designed it and supervised its construction. There were girls' and boys' sides, each with a hand-washing section and four commodes in two small cubicles. No running water graced this facility, which featured buckets, basins and regular attention from a Pakistani sweeper. Interior decor was vertical pine board, which withstood the wear and tear of thousands of visits with hardly a blemish.

However, Tim Philbrick remembers, one summer day shortly before the new bathrooms were completed, an artist and humorist on an unhurried solitary visit pulled out his ball-point pen and drew, on the wall beside his seat, a handle with the accompanying instruction: "In Case of Emergency, Hold Here." Seeing this, other would-be artists felt compelled to contribute, either in the form of original works or modifications to existing pieces. For example, someone drew a simple frame, and called it a "Mirror." Moments or hours later someone else added a face to the inside of the rectangle. A third person, recognizing irresistible opportunity, added round glasses and a Hitler-style mustache to the face, and "Butterfield's" to the now off-center nameplate, in honor of a "favorite" teacher. Once spawned, the graffiti multiplied quickly—in two or three days there were probably twenty or twenty-five entries; none were "dirty," and several were truly hilarious.

As school adjourned on Friday afternoon the principal suddenly called a meeting for all older boys, and everyone knew the fat was in the fire. Somehow managing to maintain the most serious demeanor—while the boys were all dying with internal laughter—Mr. Roub expressed his disappointment and displeasure with the recent prolificacy in the bathroom. The caricature of a staff member was bad enough, he said, but— referring to the inscription accompanying a large strategically placed arrow—most disturbing were the words "Piss Pot." At the mention of these magic words one of the boys lost his composure and let out a loud, uncontrollable sputter, while everyone else practically bit off their tongues. Without flinching, Mr. Roub continued his lecture concluding with a call for all who made any contribution to show up Saturday morning and help remove the graffiti. Almost everyone came to the cleanup party, and using sandpaper and carpenters' planes, disposed of the offending items in short order.

Transportation has always been a difficult issue at the school. Tim Philbrick remembers riding in Price's Plymouth station wagon, Rutherford's Chevy carryall, and a variety of Jeeps and Land-Rovers belonging to Roubs, Schlorholtzes and Dobras. That all changed when MCS acquired its own bus, a British-built Commer, which had already seen years of previous service—starting *before* World War II, was the consensus among its hapless passengers.

"I well remember viewing it for the first time," Tim recalls, "as it came around the corner on a rainy morning and squeaked to a stop at Rosenheim estate on Kuldana Road. It was painted deep blue (repainted gray and green in the spring of '62), with 'MURREE CHRISTIAN SCHOOL' in white lettering on each side, and 'SCHOOL' listed as the destination above the small windshield. The pronounced front fenders, rounded but slender hood, bulging headlights and small horizontally-striped chrome grill gave it a rather distinguished look. Without a doubt, there were few like it in the country. But I was deeply disappointed to find that it didn't have ordinary bus seats—instead, there were bare wooden benches which ran around the sides of the passenger compartment and in two rows, back-to-back, down the center. And the windows were the *kutcha* lift-up type that offered little view unless they were open. It heaved on the corners and made certain we felt every bump; but in time we grew to love it, even as we longed for a more luxurious replacement.

"In addition to his duties as principal, Mr. Calderwood was the bus driver in those early years. I'll always remember his strong arms wrestling the steering wheel into submission on Kuldana Road's hairpin curves, his alertness and concentration while driving, and his frequent use of the electric horn, which was applied using a large button to the right of the windshield.

"Occasionally some school-bus passengers—usually several of the older boys—engaged in some *shararit,* or mischief. Normally it took one of two forms; in both, the perpetrators almost always sat in the rear corners of the bus. In the first instance they were armed with containers filled with water, which when squeezed would expel a steady stream of the liquid at any intended target. More than one unsuspecting pedestrian woke up to a morning face splash delivered in this manner. At other times the miscreants would have sticks, sometimes with pins attached to the end, and would either knock or lift the hats off passing pedestrians."

On rainy days kids used their umbrellas *inside* the school bus to avoid the drips from the leaky roof. But that old bus was used for the next eight years, until the new hostel was completed in the fall of 1965. At that time, the school had a bus body built onto the Dodge truck chassis that had been used during the hostel's construction. The long-suffering students thought the Cadillac of busses had been delivered to them: it had a beautiful modern exterior with large windows, and inside—*padded* plastic seats in nicely spaced rows.

That first second-hand bus was purchased from the Church of Scotland for Rs.12,000 ($2,500); when MCS purchased it third bus in 1983, it cost Rs.240,000 (about $24,000): a good indicator of inflation!

For a couple of years Don Calderwood, who was a very handsome man—like an airplane pilot—was the only male staff member at MCS and he sometimes felt self-conscious when the whole staff would walk in to Murree together. One time Mary Pegors, who didn't realize he was married, saw him with Evelyn and said, "My, Don sure is getting fresh with that one staff member." Driving the *miss-sahibs* around in the school's borrowed VW microbus, sometimes he would stop at the police checkpoints and the Pakistanis would look inside and wink at him and make some exclamation, impressed that he could handle so many wives.

Driving the bus was not so glamorous. The old clunker was extremely hard to maneuver—like driving an old tank, Don used to say. (The driver's seat did have padding, however: it was stuffed with coconut hair.) Don tried out a series of Pakistani drivers who turned out to be bad drivers as soon as he turned his back. He finally was able to hire a Christian driver, but he didn't last long either. So Don continued to do most of the driving.

One time, after stopping at the petrol pump near Forest Dell, the bus wouldn't start again. The bus was on a slight slope and Don turned to Mara, the *bhishti,* and said, *"Dhuka dena"*—"Please push." Don was sitting in the driver's seat and nothing happened. After a minute or two Don turned and there was Mara, sitting on the floor behind the driver's seat, with his hands on the back of the seat, pushing for all he was worth. Don had neglected to say, "Push the *bus.*"

Miscommunication due to language barriers and other cross-cultural blunders were not limited to communication with Pakistanis. In second-grade Bible class one day, Kathy Hamm was summarizing the story of Caleb and Joshua's journey into Canaan and said they went up to have a *deko.* A little snicker prompted her to say, "Isn't that English?"

One Friday night when Kathy Nichol from Scotland was Little Boys' housemother, she passed around the evening treat after the games--American popcorn. As the boys lined up their eager faces quickly took on puzzled expressions: "Auntie, this isn't popped!" they hollered. How was she supposed to know?

When the school was beginning, none of the staff had had experience in a boarding school. During the three-week summer break in 1957, Don and Evelyn Calderwood, two teachers (Audrey Jennings, Eloise James), and the new boarding matron

(Joan Larsen) went to India for a week to visit Woodstock School, to observe the workings of a well-established school. Woodstock, located in Mussoorie, another, older hill station of the British raj, at about the same 7,000-foot elevation as Murree, had been established in 1854. (Today it remains the oldest school for missionaries' children in continuous operation anywhere in the world.)

The main impression they got was how large and extensive Woodstock was: the school property contained 300 acres--at an elevation of 7,000 feet or 8,000 feet, depending on where on the campus you stood! Enrollment was nearly 400 students. There were several school buildings for grade school, middle school, and high school, and there were numerous dormitories spread across the steep countryside. Because there were no motorable roads on the sprawling campus, or even to the campus from town, the distances seemed even greater. You had to walk everywhere, and all supplies had to be carried by coolies. And they had thought transportation in Murree was difficult!

Each of the dormitories—which seemed like barracks—had a missionary housemother, but she was in charge of fifty to seventy-five children, and was assisted in her work and responsibility by several *ayahs*—Indian women helpers. This is one of the main reasons for the emphasis at Murree on having a housemother for about every twenty to twenty-five students, and even less in the younger boarding groups, if possible. When they returned to Murree they insisted on redesigning the plans for the new hostel to create a more home-like layout for each department.

* * *

In the summer of 1962, MCS held a contest to see if someone could come up with a school hymn. At the time, Ralph Brown was living at Alpine with his family and the other Conservative Baptist families who had come up to Murree for the summer. Alpine was one of the many rustic formerly-British estates now owned or rented by missionaries for vacation homes, but was not exactly on the five-star list: the back of the house constantly looked like it was going down the mountain. The Browns lived in one of the front apartments.

Ralph Brown had four children at MCS (soon to be five) and was on the board of directors, so it was natural that he should feel a certain investment in the guiding rituals of the school. Ralph enjoyed scribbling out poems as a hobby and when he got in the mood it didn't take long to write a little rhyme or a song. He had always enjoyed the tune of the Gordon College song (his alma mater), which was the same tune as Cornell University's song, "Far Above Cayuga's Waters." So it was these majestic strains that floated through his head as he sat down at the table in the tiny, damp kitchen at Alpine to try his hand at a school hymn for MCS.

When the song committee picked his submission, Ralph's pride was tempered only by the knowledge—perhaps tactfully revealed only sometime later—that there were only two entries in the contest. In any case, the committee asked Paul and Mary Pegors, who had some musical training, to meet with Ralph and go over the lyrics with him to make sure they were singable. After some minor changes, the song was officially adopted with the fairly straight-forward title, "School Hymn." Known for posterity to anyone who ever spent at least a semester at MCS, are the words below:

Nestled 'neath the great Himalayas
Far above the plain,
Stands the school we love and cherish
More than earthly gain.

CHORUS:
  Built upon a firm foundation,
  In God's hands a tool;
  Shaping lives of dedication,
  Murree Christian School.

There within her halls of learning
Wisdom's torch burns bright;
Where indeed her students grasp
The Good and True and Right.

Teachers, students work united
Towards this common goal:
Christ to serve with consecrated
Body, mind and soul.

Lord, with thanks and praise we honor
Murree Christian School;
May her life and fame and service
For Thee ever rule.

—Ralph E. Brown

*   *   *

In the early 1960s everyone went to Holy Trinity Church in Murree for the Sunday morning service, even during the spring and fall. That big stone church could get really cold! Because there was not enough room in the bus most of the older kids walked the three miles each way.

Mr. Butterfield often served as organist and he took these duties seriously. Because of his somber demeanor he was the butt of many student laughs, and once in a while the object of a practical joke. Sunday mornings presented a unique opportunity: while he was concentrating on the first stanza of a song at the multilevel keyboard someone might be able to sneak up behind the organ and remove the heavy lead weights from the bellows, which were powered by an electric motor. This altered the air pressure and had an acute effect on the operation of the organ—some notes wouldn't sound at all, others would wheeze, and the volume would decrease. One can only imagine Mr. Butterfield's consternation when this happened. He would feverishly look for clues to the malfunction, but his troubleshooting abilities were limited since he had to do his best to keep playing for the congregation below. Before the song ended the prankster would replace the weights, and miraculously, everything worked perfectly once again.

*   *   *

In 1964 Murree Christian School held its first high school graduation ceremony. The three students honored on this historic occasion were: David Davis, Paul "Skip" Lundgren, Jr., and Robert Tebbe.

That year George McMillan and Inger Gardner joined the staff. While George would stay at MCS for only five years his lasting legacy was putting together a school band. George replaced the exuberant, classically-educated, and thoroughly English Mr. Butterfield as the school music teacher. Short and already balding, Mr. McMillan looked like the lab technician he indeed had trained to be. He had assumed there would be no place on the mission field for his first love, music. After Mr. Butterfield's high-minded proper British authority, George had to struggle for discipline. But he quickly made up in enthusiasm—and shouting—what he lacked in stature, and gave MCS students the gift of hands-on experience with music as well as a cultured appreciation of it.

When George saw how many kids were present with trumpets, trombones, clarinets, flutes, as well as staff members and missionaries in the summer community in Murree who played instruments, he felt there must be some way to get all these instruments organized and "make music together." One student, Tim Rock, was there with a French horn, of all things. So George needed to add a bass horn. Somehow, he found one for sale in Sialkot and Billy Johnson, who would prove to have considerable musical talent, took to it right away. The Hamm family owned a baritone horn and David was playing countermelodies in no time, leaving the trumpet to his younger brother, Glenn. Mr. McMillan had no trouble convincing Bill Tebbe, who was taking voice lessons with him at the time, to learn the snare drum—once George was able to locate one. JoAnne McCurry found her place keeping time with the big base drum, and with the help of a few staff members Mr. McMillan had within a year put together a full, twenty-five-piece brass band.

The transient lives of missionary kids was a great frustration. George would just get a cohesive ensemble together and all the good musicians would leave. Musical talent seemed to run in families—such as the Hamms, Christys, Cutheralls, Browns, Philbricks, and Ralstons—and when one or two of these families left for furlough it decimated the band. But new talent kept arriving, too. One on one they were a pleasure to work with—such potential! But bringing them all together and trying to keep twenty-five seventh- through twelfth-graders focused was an exhausting task. Mr. McMillan often yelled till he was hoarse. Between the cacophony of instruments tuning up and Mr. McMillan's earnest harangues, what an dreadful racket echoed through the chapel chamber! But for George it was worth all the strain and struggle when the band played Mussorgski's "Pictures at an Exhibition" or "The Calif of Baghdad" at the Spring concert. Evelyn Calderwood soon became renowned for her clarinet solos. Equally memorable moments came from eleventh-grader Bill Tebbe, towering over his snare drums, which blended casually with the rest of the band till at the top of a musical flourish the whole ensemble suddenly stopped in an expectant pause. Then Bill—already a legendary six-feet-four—would tap a triangle, sending a delicate ring across the silence. And as a singer: even the first and second graders were enthralled by Bill's haunting baritone solos.

Speaking of haunting, Mr. McMillan was also famous for his recitations of "The Cremation of Sam McGee." On special occasions, like the first night back in boarding, the entire high school—all twenty of them—would gather for an after-dinner assembly in the big dining room at Sandes. With a huge fire popping in the fireplace, and George's musically-trained enunciation used to impressive effect, all loneliness and fear would be temporarily forgotten as the story unfolded:

> *There are strange things done in the midnight sun*
> *By the men who moil for gold;*
> *The Arctic trails have their secret tales*
> *That would make your blood run cold;*
> *The Northern Lights have seen queer sights,*
> *But the queerest they ever did see*
> *Was the night on the marge of Lake Lebarge*
> *I cremated Sam McGee.*

Bundled in blankets and flannel-lined bed slippers, huddled in that drafty wooden hall of Sandes Home that was always cold, the climactic verse of Robert W. Service's popular poem was appreciated for more than its humor and surprise: After a long journey with the corpse of his partner, the narrator finally finds a derelict ship and he proceeds to keep his promise, the last request of his dying friend. He stokes a good fire in the ship's old boiler and stuffs the body in it. Later, thinking he is finally done with the whole dread project, he opens the boiler door to check.

> *And there sat Sam, looking cool and calm, in the heart of*

the furnace roar;
And he wore a smile you could see a mile, and he said:
"Please close that door.
It's fine in here, but I greatly fear you'll let in the cold and
storm—
Since I left Plumtree down in Tennessee, it's the first time
I've been warm."

That Mr. McMillan's oldest son was named Sam didn't hurt the poem's enjoyment any.

*   *   *

The young institution now had an official school song and a proper school band. But the school basketball team had no uniforms. One summer around this time, some of the mothers decided it was time to do something about it. The school colors had just been chosen—it was Rae Steeves who suggested gray and green, not only for their obvious representation of our mountain environment, but because they were colors of a fabric readily available in Pakistan. With the official colors established, a group of concerned mothers (that is, the ones who had sons on the basketball team) immediately bought green satin, had all the boys measured, and contracted with a *dhursi* half way down the hill in the Lower Bazaar of Murree to make the shorts. Then they purchased undershirts and each mother sewed her boy's team number onto one in the same green silk.

What a proud group of parents, the day the newly-uniformed team ran onto the court and began their game. How handsome they looked!

The "court" in those days was two-thirds of the main floor in the old church. Toward the front end was the chapel area and during official games the pews were turned around and used for bleachers. Naturally, George McMillan's band was set up on the stage (formerly, the chancel) to play at half-times. Also naturally, the school being as small as it was, several of the boys that played basketball also played in the band. So, they came off the court, sweat and all, huffed on their horns, dribbled their drumsticks, laid down their instruments and ran back out again.

* * *

Rosemary Stewart had been teaching the TEAM kids at Abottabad for three years, while she studied Urdu. But when the TEAM school closed in 1957 to merge with the new school in Murree, MCS needed a boarding matron, not another teacher. Rosie agreed to this and her Urdu lessons proved invaluable in working with the Pakistani helpers. "Auntie Rosie" stayed at MCS for the next thirty years, teaching piano, Latin, American history, Bible, and kindergarten when needed. She also served as house mother for Middle Girls and, later, Junior High Girls. Additionally, she was in charge of the kitchen staff for many years.

"Auntie Inger" Gardner served as housemother of the Little Boys department (first through third grades) for fifteen years. Inger's family had come to the States from Norway the year before she was born and lived in a Scandinavian community near Chicago. Inger didn't speak any English until she was five years old and started school. When she was seven her mother got tuberculosis and finally began to learn some English in the sanitarium; Inger helped her. Her mother died when she was eleven.

After Inger's husband, Elmer, died of complications following a second heart attack, Agnes Davis (mother of Dave and Charlie) from TEAM encouraged her to go overseas as a housemother and three years later she arrived in Pakistan with her youngest son, Paul, then entering eleventh grade.

Eunice Hill—sweet and pretty and only twenty-three years old—had arrived at MCS the year before to take care of the first- through third-grade girls in boarding. Irv and Liz Nygren also came to MCS in 1963—Irv to teach English and later serve as vice principal, Liz to manage the school office. The Nygrens, Roubs, Calderwoods, and Murrays—these four "first families" became the cornerstones of the teaching staff; Rosemary Stewart, Paul Davidson (from New Zealand), Eunice Hill, and Inger Gardner all worked on the boarding side. Over the next three decades, these "twelve apostles" would contribute a total of almost 300 years to Murree Christian School.

The dedication and commitment of these long-term staff, and others who came later, contributed immensely to the stability and continuity of the school, so that children moving through the different stages of growing up could have an emotionally safe and reliable, home-like environment. By contrast, in the first decade of the school's operation there were more than 125 staff members, including many missionary language students who helped out temporarily or part-time as boarding parents.

Ian and Isabel Murray (from Scotland) and Eunice Hill are still at MCS and "Auntie Eunice"—enthusiastic, and faithful as ever—is now caring for the children of some of the boys and girls she taught in second grade thirty years ago.

Ralph Brown, Don and Evelyn Calderwood, Agnes Davis, George McMillan, Tim Philbrick, Gene Purdy, Rachel (Steeves) Fairchild, and Rosemary Stewart contributed material for this chapter.

8

The First Date

Tim Philbrick, '65

From the earliest years at MCS both boys and girls were aware of the opposite sex, and, even in grade school, from time to time one's heart would flutter when thinking of or looking at a particular person. Your friends would be entrusted with the secret that you "liked" someone, you would be teased unmercifully ("Joe and Suzie, sitting in a tree . . ."), and perhaps the object of your attention might even learn of his or her special status and there might be some occasional blushing. Once in a great while these immature romances spawned "marriages," conducted with all due hokum and fanfare and celebrated with one of KZ's cookies substituting for the wedding cake. Generally these relationships, if you can call them that, were brief, and apart from heartthrobs, nothing happened—in fact, in grade school no one ever wanted to be too close to anyone not of one's own sex.

That all changed when MCS's first classes "came of age." Now we had boys and girls who had moved from the "liking" to "loving" mode, so to speak. To be sure, there was still the occasional reluctance to openly admit one's attraction, but once the barrier had been broken and the initial embarrassment endured, couples felt the need—or obligation—to communicate

91

and demonstrate their amour. Since there were no telephones, notes were common—sometimes delivered personally with the wink of an eye while changing classes, more often surreptitiously through a trusted mutual friend. Some couples generated absolute flurries of notes, and for the most part this was tolerated, unless it became a distraction in class or study hall; in such situations a chit's confiscation (or threat to read it aloud) produced the necessary restraint. Much more worrisome to the staff was the tendency for some couples to be together at every opportunity. Some were more involved than others, and when staff thought they were "seeing too much of each other" they were so informed, with consequential restrictions. Naturally, this was never popular with those concerned—they grumbled privately, resorted to more prolific note writing, and waited for the earliest chance to quietly ease into their former tendencies.

Meals, the walks to and from school (we all lived in the Sandes environs in those days), and the time before and after evening study hall were the more common weekday "together times." Of course, for a variety of reasons, not every couple could take advantage of all of these—often the parties were separated by two or three grades and therefore ate at different tables, or after school sporting activities precluded an afternoon walk home. On the weekends there were of course the meals (particularly Sunday noon, when everyone sat where they wished, often accompanied by younger siblings), the much longer walks to and from church in Murree, and, if lucky, church and singspiration. But the best—and most relished— times were Friday night recreational activities and Saturday night movies.

On Friday nights we frequently walked back to school for things like Halloween parties, games and roller-skating. Romantically-inclined twosomes would subtly try to elude the staff escorts' eagle eyes by jockeying for position in the procession, then speeding up (if ahead) or slowing down (if behind) in order to sneak in a little forbidden hand-holding. Without a doubt, some zealous chaperones must have been exasperated in their attempts to keep an eye on anything suspicious. On Saturday nights after supper the tables were moved to the back and sides of the wooden floored drawing room in Sandes. Benches were brought in from the dining room, and a projector was set up near the dining room door, with a large screen at the opposite end of the room. When everything was ready, the kids took their places, little "chuts" on the floor in front, then the others, working back in order of age and size. The final row or two, mysteriously, seemed reserved for couples, who were always slicked up and dressed for the occasion. If one was sitting with his or her belle or beau, easily the best seats in the house were on the last bench, as far to the left as possible, away from the light and any curious staff member. While everyone else was engrossed in the USIS feature of the evening, amorous duos—with as much inconspicuousness as they could muster—held hands, or with the aid of the table behind them, put their arms around each other's waists. From time to time some staff member would suddenly produce a flashlight and shine a beam along the rows of legs, which immediately produced an equal number of innocent hands. When the flashlight went off, one by one the hands found their warm partners and again disappeared.

And so it went for several boarding terms, MCS's love life being relegated to whatever opportunities presented themselves in the daily and weekly routine. Then, in the fall of 1963, four members of the Class of '65 changed things. As it happened, Kathy Hamm and I had just started "going together," and in the course of an evening conversation which included matters of the heart, my friend, classmate and confidant, Don Lotze, suggested that we "go on a date." My response was something like "Whaddya mean?," whereupon Lotze laid out the concept: I'd take Kathy, and to be a good sport he'd take Nonie Lundgren and we'd go to Fircos (about the only Western restaurant open at that time of the year) for a Friday night dinner. I expressed my doubts about whether "they" would ever let us do it, how we would get to and from Murree with two girls at night, and raised every problem I could think of, but Lotze was confident, and not to be deterred. "Don't worry, man," he said, "I'll talk to Pegors (Paul Pegors—the older boys' boarding master)." Within a couple days he had done so, and had everything arranged. A couple weeks later, on Friday, October 11, 1963, we four nervous but brave souls rode in the school car (a Volkswagen minibus, probably driven by Mr. Roub or Pegors) to an almost empty Fircos, where we ate chicken curry and drank tea. About an hour and a half later, the car came back and returned us to Sandes, thereby ending the first official "date" in MCS history.

No one else duplicated our scheme that fall, but in the next two years (and undoubtedly, subsequently) several parties successfully negotiated and carried out dates on a similar pattern, the most ambitious of which (in the spring of '65) involved four couples. With Mr. Nygren as driver and chaperone, we enjoyed an evening meal at a classy Chinese restaurant in Pindi, followed by a brief stop at a scenic park overlooking the lights of Pindi and Islamabad. (Mr. Nygren may not have fond memories of that trip—he had to visit the "invisible mender" to repair a trouser leg, torn in a fall at the park.)

The night after we returned from winter vacation in March of 1964 we were called together in the dorm before devotions and informed of a new set of dating rules. Henceforth dates would be limited by grade: seniors could have six a term, juniors five, sophomores four, and freshmen only two. Pity the poor freshman or sophomore who liked an eighth grader, because eighth graders were out of the question. Assuming a couple went together for an entire boarding term, they were effectively limited to the number of dates allowed the younger member—and at that time, for example, it happened that two of the three seniors (all boys) were going with freshmen.

But the real bombshell was the definition of a date—from now on it was not limited to off-campus dinners and the like, but also included Friday night activities and Saturday night movies. Furthermore, if the staff thought a couple was spending too much time together at meals, during free time, or going to and from school, they would arbitrarily assess them one date each. To put the icing on the cake, dates would be applied for, in writing, a certain number of days in advance.

After the shock and disbelief wore off, teenage ingenuity set in. If a couple was severely limited in numbers of dates, they naturally had to get the biggest bang for the buck, so official dates were used for those occasions which promised the best return—that is, the best opportunity for privacy and time with one's sweetheart. This gave rise to a number of group outings to Murree, for which the student negotiators usually tried to include as much time as possible to facilitate private after dinner walks on the generally secluded Cecil Hotel road. On Saturday nights "non-dating" couples simply changed their seating arrangement—the girl sat directly in front of the boy and dangled her hand behind or even leaned back into his arms. On the numerous other "together times" (for which no one would ever waste a date credit) couples played each situation by ear—if a strict or rule-conscious staff member was present they watched their step, but if an event were supervised by someone unaware or unconcerned with the rules they'd take advantage of every opportunity.

9

The First Graduate

Dave Davis, '64

I went to Murree pre-hostel, pre-grade school building, and pre-interschool conventions. I even went there before Noah, and he went there before Murree had hills and water. Murree now has hills but still no water. The present-day basketball court was an open field in which we all played "three feet in the mud puddle"—and really meant it. I was at MCS before Charlie's! We could get tea in Pakistan even back then, though Charlie's fine establishment had not yet been established. We bought cakes from the "pastry walla" who walked all the way from Murree with a tin trunk containing a bakery shop-full of goodies balanced on his head. He came to the MCS gate and for two annas we could make it through recess.

I had the distinct privilege of being the very first graduating senior from MCS. That was only because my name is first in the alphabet. But I was in the top three in my graduating class. That looks good on a resume. Skip Lundgren, Bob Tebbe, and me. What a trio. Skip was good in sport, Bob was good in grades, and I was good in eating. I still remember Mr. Roub walking down the center aisle in the "chapel," carefully pacing himself to the tune of pomp and happenstance, side-stepping the basketball pole, and continuing on up the aisle to the platform. He had an unusual gait and the widest ties this side of Istanbul. My dad, Carl Davis, was chairman of the board then, too, so he got to give me the very first diploma. It is wonderful to be famous!

I was on the original basketball team, the MCS Panthers. My mom bought a "singlet" in the lower bazaar and sewed grey felt numbers on the "uniform." These numbers had to be taken off every time the vest needed washing, which was after every game. In those days we mostly played against pick-up teams of our dads and other missionaries who were in Murree for the summer. I remember one game against the Conservative Baptists. Oh, did they have a team! Frank Dobra had a hook shot you couldn't stop. Ralph Brown had a half-court two-handed shot that was maddening. Ray Buker, Jack Christiansen, and Paul Pegors rounded out the best team on the hill that year. We used to play the Pakistani language teachers and army teams but these games always turned into tests of control because they were masters at fouling. Irv Lotze was always the best ref. Doc Christy fortunately was kept busy in Taxila most of the time and we were glad, because he could drive around the best of us and score. He got his training at Woodstock.

Years later I went back onto the court at MCS as part of an elite team known as the Hillside Panters. We too had singlets from the lower bazaar. These had a picture of a face with tongue hanging out on the front and fractions on the back. We all had the furniture disease, where the chest has fallen into the drawers. We usually got whipped by the young jocks. They loved it and we learned lessons in humility which every missionary needs.

* * *

Boarding was a combination of learning to be tough and also some of the most fun I have ever had. My brother used to cry when Mom and Dad left us. I tried to comfort him and stick up for him when Bobby Harmon would pick on him. I cried, too, on the inside, but tried to be a tough guy on the outside. I will never forget the time my parents dropped me off for my first term in boarding. I was ten years old and trying very hard to be brave for them, so they wouldn't be worried about me. I remember standing by the huge tree in the center of the lower parking area below Sandes Home and watching the back of our green Chevy Carryall as it disappeared down the road; the tail lights blurred into a red splash just before it turned the corner out of sight. My eyes stung and I blinked them clear, walked up the steps to Sandes, up the old wooden stairs on the right, and down the veranda to Room 1. There, I comforted myself by reading through a pile of old comic books.

Another time, my parents drove my little brother, Charlie, and me back to Sandes for the spring term. There was snow everywhere. Charlie and I promptly donned our boots, coats, and hats and took off into the hinterlands. My parents unpacked the car, took our trunks into the rooms, and after a couple of hours decided they had to leave. We finally returned to sanity and went back to the parking lot only to discover Mom and Dad had left. We felt bad. Insensitive brats. Our next letter from home informed us that our behavior had been less than satisfactory and it better not happen again. Years later Mom told me that she cried half the way home that day.

Boarding was fun because you got to be with your friends again, you got to see all the stuff they got for Christmas, goodies their moms had sent in with them, and the latest bicycle junk. Every Saturday we had to change our bottom sheet, throw it into the *dhobi* pile, and put the top one on the bottom. We had to shine our shoes and write home or we couldn't go out and play. Play was important, so we got to our tasks with a vengeance. I learned good habits at MCS. They stand me in good stead even today.

*   *   *

Two new teachers came to MCS when I was in high school, namely Irv Nygren who taught me Chaucer, Keats, Browning and other useless stuff, and Ian Murray, kilt and all. He sashayed into MCS and tried to teach us chemistry and physics. The book was new to him, the accent new to us. He gave us problems as long as your leg. These usually took about two pencils and sixteen pieces of paper to figure out. In one experiment we just about got the end of his nose with a cork coming out of a test tube boiling over a spirit lamp. We missed his nose but he got us with the erasers. He gave us some "gali" in good Scottish Gaelic and we dutifully went back to experimenting.

Mr. Lawrence was the clerk when I was there—one of the few, and most enduring, of the Pakistani staff at MCS. He was also my friend. One particular day stands out. He and I went to Fircos in Murree. We drank tea and talked until the seventh pot was empty. He was one big tea drinker. He never did learn how to say "ahuh" and "uh-uh." These Americanisms were too much for his babu English tongue.

Khan Zaman was the school cook from the very beginning. Over the years his reputation grew to legendary and paradoxical proportions. Even his name was fitting: In Urdu, "khan-sama" is the word for cook; but pronounced, or written, as two words it literally means "King of Stuff." While kids (throughout the Western world, at least) will automatically complain about cafeteria food, some of K.Z.'s concoctions severely tested the limits of the human palate. On the other hand, his source market was pretty limited; we often had to endure seasonal vegetables every day, resulting in a lifelong aversion to cucumbers or cauliflower for some of us. I still can't look a kidney bean in the face. For better and for worse, there was always plenty to eat, though. No one ever went hungry at MCS, unless you missed supper as punishment for something.

K.Z.'s quandary is illustrated by his donuts. His doughnuts were delicious—the first day; but by the third day they were hard enough to kill someone. Skip and I decided to conduct a Mr. Murray scientific experiment. We put said doughnut on the driveway at the school gate and began kicking it towards Sandes. We got all the way to the big curve half way to Jhika, just before "King's Cliff." An overly enthusiastic boot sent our physics experiment over the "kud" where it shattered against a rock below. We will never know if it would have made it up the shortcut.

* * *

Bike trips down the hill to Pindi were a favorite activity. One eventful day, Kathy Hamm missed a turn near Company Bagh and flipped herself into a big rock. While this was most certainly preferable to going over a cliff, it rearranged a significant portion of her face. A couple weeks later Skip Lundgren took pictures and she was every color of the rainbow. She was still cute, even after that. Actually, Kathy's accident was probably the closest any student came to getting killed while at

MCS. She spent several days in the hospital, and her recovery was accompanied by a very tense prayer marathon at the school and throughout the missionary community in Pakistan.

On another trip to Pindi it began to rain near Chara Pani. Now, in those days we used to keep our bikes polished and gleaming, rims too. Those polished rims almost killed me. We were trying to make a record to the "halfway bridge" at the eighteen-mile marker, so we were zooming. When the rain began we zoomed even more. The only problem is that Chara Pani has that very steep hairpin corner. The others were zooming on ahead of me. I pulled the brake bars as hard as I could and kept right on zooming. Heavy weights tend to sink faster than light weights (I learned that in Physics, from Sir Ian). The corner came and I was headed for the edge. As those of you who know that spot will recall, it has a rock wall on the side of the road and then drops off about twenty feet. I knew I was going over. All my sins flashed in front of my mind and I remember saying, "Lord, here I come." I was trying to lean into the corner and that saved my life. I hit the mud on the side of the road, the bike swerved sideways, swung the back wheel around, I righted myself and zoomed on. I was shaking all the rest of the way to the bridge. We didn't break the record, but we did get it down to thirty-four minutes.

My brother Charlie had a similar brush with destiny. It was the day before the train party was to leave for the Christmas recess, 1962. Ground breaking for the new boarding hostel was to take place during the school's end-of-year ceremonies. It was a bright, spring-like day. After the ground was broken, awards given, and speeches ended, the climactic event was to be the felling of a huge pine tree that was in the middle of the future dorm building. Unfortunately, the pine tree did not want to fall, despite ropes, men pulling, and incessant hacking at the base of the tree. The ceremony ended, somewhat unceremoniously, with obligatory rituals of foot shuffling and awkward explanations, and finally people drifted away. At about noon, three or four hours after the moment planned for the tree to fall, Charlie and a couple of his sixth-grade cohorts got bored and decided to investigate the workings at the base of the impertinent tree. Three or four men were still hacking away at the base and it seemed incredible that the entire tree could possibly remain standing. No sooner did Charlie and his buddies make the round of the tree when they heard an ominous creaking and cracking. They all scattered amid shouts and the increasing noise of the falling tree. In all the excitement, however, Charlie forgot to look and see which way the tree was going to fall and just took the clearest path away from the base of the tree. When he heard its branches crashing into the tree dead in front of him, something clicked in his brain, and he did a ninety-degree turn to the right. A half second later the tree hit the ground with a tremendous shock, right where he had been.

Both Charlie and I believe in guardian angels, and that God had his hand on us for some purpose.

* * *

In those far distant days of ancient middle eastern history we got two dates per semester. Having staff escorts for dates in Murree meant finding the most lenient staff; Mr. Nygren was always a favorite choice. Being the first teenagers to go through the school complicated an already difficult time in life. There were no traditions and everyone—parents, teachers, and students—all tried to set the agenda, which shifted constantly. It was a wild time: sometimes exhilarating, often unnerving.

Discipline at MCS varied depending on who your boarding parent was. Some were good, and frankly some were terrible. I remember being angry at "injustice." Young people will take what they deserve. They will complain, but they will know it is justified, but when you are punished unjustly—that is very hard to take. From punishment I deserved I learned justice and respect for my elders. From unfair punishment I learned that I could get angry and bitter or I could let God work on my character. I'm not sure I let him work enough.

For some reason, it seems that a lot of wounded adults ended up at MCS as staff in those early years, and great emotional damage was done to some kids, lasting long after they left Pakistan.

I got my first and only caning (I was lucky) at age twelve, and I learned that a cane can lift a welt at least a quarter of an inch high for some distance. But canings did not crush the spirit nearly so much as the weight of incessant authoritarianism and petty rules. Tossing around a hard-boiled egg leftover from breakfast could result in a tirade about stewardship and gratitude. Even earnest questions could provoke a smack or being grounded for the day.

After several semesters of particularly rigid control and canings the Pegorses came. They were a breath of fresh air. The junior high and senior high boys lived in the top duplex on the hill behind Sandes. Paul Pegors was in charge. Mary Pegors was a friend. She cut our hair, she listened to our stories and complaints, she was a real *mom*. The Pegors were fair.

Other staff, such as Ian Murray, Don Calderwood, and Keith Mitchell, were people of such integrity that they, along with several missionaries I had contact with in my early childhood, have had a large part in my continuing Christian journey. There was a realness, a holiness, and an openness in sharing their spiritual lives that has provided me with a sure footing in this messy world.

At MCS I learned to love people from other cultures. I learned even Scots can be understood. I learned that there is no substitute for godly teachers that care. I learned Pakistan affected me more than I realized until I was gone and didn't feel at home in the States. I learned that nestled 'neath the great Himalayas, far above the plain, stands a school I love and cherish . . . that helped me become what I am today. For all this I am grateful. If any of those ancient staff ever read this blather, THANK YOU for giving to the Lord and for giving to me.

10

Train Party

Paul Asbury Seaman, '76

My parents worked in a Punjabi village-turning-town called Raiwind, thirty miles south of Lahore. My mother was a nurse; my father taught agriculture at the Christian mission school and ran an experimental farm that was an outpost of the Green Revolution then sweeping the Third World. Our red brick ranch-style house was about a mile from the main railway line—just the right distance to faintly hear the breathy chugging of freight locomotives and the *clickity-whisk* of passenger trains making their way across the landscape. The deep sigh of their whistles tracked the passage of time, day and night, a wistful counterpoint to the muted pounding of wheat mills and the squeaky see-saw sound of Persian wells pumping water into neatly-squared irrigation ditches. These slow rhythms filled the green, near-treeless plains of mustard fields and rice paddies, filled the days and nights of the winter vacation months spent at home..

As a major freight junction, the Raiwind train station was a popular bombing target during both wars with India. For passenger trains it was just another whistle stop; and express trains, if they stopped there at all, did so for only a few seconds. Once, when my three sisters and I came back from boarding,

103

we hadn't gotten all our luggage off when the train started pulling out. Dad was frantically throwing footlockers off the train all the way down the platform till finally leaping off himself. After that, when it was time to return to school, we usually took the family's Land-Rover the hour's drive into Lahore to connect with the train party in a more dignified way.

On trips to Lahore we sometimes got stuck at the level crossing just outside the city, where the train tracks crossed the Grand Trunk Road. The "G.T." Road ran roughly parallel with the main rail line north and south the length of the country, from Karachi on the Arabian Sea to Peshawar in the North-West Frontier Province. Once, stuck behind a gate that had been closed prematurely, we watched the train that we were trying to catch pass by. But most of the time these delays were merely a sweltering nuisance. The "level crossings" were never actually level, of course, usually consisting of a sharp "S" curve and an incline that brought the road up to the raised track bed at a proper perpendicular angle. A heavy backup at these places seemed more often like a carnival than a traffic jam. Vendors came around to all the waiting buses and cars, taking advantage of their detainment. You could examine pretty bangles and pocket knives, and all kinds of sweets, maybe even buy something. But at night—especially if you were on a less-travelled secondary road—you prayed not to encounter a closed level crossing. Sometimes the gatekeeper locked the gate and went to bed, and Dad had to go and find him. Even though the trains usually ran an hour or more late, the gates were faithfully locked according to the printed schedule.

The castle tower facade of the Lahore Train Station, rising behind the black-and-silver shrubbery of a thousand parked bicycles, faces a downtown roundabout. Horn-blaring buses, screeching taxis, horse-drawn *tongas* form a crazy carousel, whipping around while little motor rickshaws with their deviously tiny two-passenger seats dart in and out. An entire family, seemingly with half their worldly belongings, is packed into the cloth-flimsy cab of one of these three-wheeled scooters; five white-turbanned farmers cling to each other in another, balancing an assortment of seed bags and a goat.

When our Land-Rover pulls up to the station entrance on a bright March morning we are swarmed by beggars and insistent coolies. Inside, the air is thick with the warm smell of deep-fried *pakordas* (vegetable balls) and *samosas* (triangular meat-filled pastries), sweaty bodies, dirty clothes, and exotic perfumes. Color and motion fill the station, filtered through smoke and shafts of sunlight. The creams and grays of village dress jostle with Western suits on Pakistani businessmen; brown military jerseys highlight khaki against a cluster of green and white private school jumpers fastened to shiny smart girls; black full-length *burkas* cover traditional Muslim women observing *purdah*; and the dull reddish flame of soiled coolie uniforms flickers in swirling red lines along the platform.

A couple of coolies carry our trunks and suitcases and *bister-bunds* piled high on their heads, well-cushioned under great scarlet turbans. My father has prudently copied down the porter number from the brass badges on their arm bands. I race ahead to find Tim Old, a classmate. As soon as we spot each other we go wild, leaping at each other, hugging and pounding and kicking with mock hostility. But even the urgent tales and well-practiced banter of ten-year-olds eventually winds down, giving way to the restless limbo of waiting for a train that is all-too-reliably late.

Finally the Khyber Mail arrives, pulled proudly by a great, puffing steam engine. The huge black barrel of its boiler swells into the station, hissing and clicking importantly as it passes us on the platform. Carriages bang and clatter against each other as the train squeals to a stop.

We push into the doughy mass—all urgent and inevitable—till we find relief in the sanctuary of a reserved compartment. It is a familiar routine, after eight train parties, going to boarding or coming home. On the platform, vendors cry out in their hoarse, nasal drone—*Chai, garum, chai! Ice cream wallah; eyezzzz ka-reem wallah!* Tea, hot tea . . . ice cream; sweet meats, sweet-and-salty—as adhesive beggars pester for *baksheesh.* The greatest show on earth: right here, fresh fruit! Step right up. See strange and wonderful things, nowhere else; right here. You there! Buy something? Buy, buy, buy! Bye-bye. The train pulls out while the vendors are still haggling, insisting, hurriedly exchanging rumpled paper packets of hot *jalabees* or peanuts for rupees or paisa. Tea cups are handed back, empty or not.

This time I do not get up when Dad reaches out to say goodbye and he leans awkwardly under the overhead bunk to give me a hug. I smile reassuringly and turn my gaze back to

Mom who is already waving from the platform. I don't want to seem clingy. What would the guys think of Dad's emotional farewells? Once again, Dad jumps off at the last minute, landing awkwardly at a stumbling trot so as not to lose his balance. At the end of the platform he stops and waves his hat, the one he bought to wear to funerals, but it's really too hot for Pakistan. I watch till he fades into the city haze then pull my head in. Leaning back into the seat, I wonder for the first time how long my father stood there after the train had gone.

The train picks up speed, *thkk-thkk . . . thkk-thkk . . .* SHRIEE-EEK! And we become separated from the world, gliding away on our own levitated platform. This year, my parents had taken us to Karachi for a week's vacation at the beach just before it was time to go back to boarding. We took camel rides, collected shells, and followed turtle tracks. We saw giant sea turtles minding their eggs, and watched brand new baby turtles push out of their sandy cradles and scurry down to the ocean. I couldn't wait to tell the guys all about it. But when the station master rings the big brass bell announcing our train's departure it reminds me of the dinner gong at school. It would be cold in Murree. Maybe there would still be snow on the ground, and the *chowkidar* would have to shovel a path to where the bell hung from the big tree in front of the hostel, so one of the cooks could come out and ring it. I wonder how many times a day the bell was rung: wake-up call, breakfast, start of school, lunch, the five-minute-wash-up warning that called the kids in from play, and then the dinner bell . . . . Even if there is no fresh snow, the huge drifts or piles that always slid off the roof of the school would provide ample material for building a fort.

The thought of snowball fights melts into the dusty heat of the train. In early March, the plains are already summer-hot. By habit, I watch the landscape slip by: wall after wall of dirty white-washed tenements with small, barred windows and courtyards facing the tracks, where children and women come up to the railroad embankment to defecate, turning their exposed bottoms away from the city as if *we* were not there. At the main level crossings traffic is backed up two miles: cars, tongas, buses, and wildly painted trucks, end to end with bullock carts stacked with hay to impossible heights. Outside of Lahore we cross the Ravi River on a stone arch bridge that looks like a Roman aqueduct. Looking back I can see the massive red clay towers of the gate to Lahore Fort. Then the endless salt plains . . . wheat fields . . . and a horizon as wide and flat as the ocean.

A couple of hours pass, and just before Gujrat we cross the Chenab River, almost half a mile wide. Day or night, there is no mistaking the loud clatter of the long metal bridge: crossed support beams whip by like a passing train, as if all the windows and doors of the train had suddenly been flung open. Tim and I jostle with other boys for the thrill of sitting on the steps of a gaping doorway and looking down to the river below. Beyond the shoulders of older boys and the fast-flicking racket of bridge girders, the rusty stone pilings of an old bridge glide past above pale mud flats. The dry-season river, shrunken into sluggish brown fingers, winds through a splotchy green flood plain laced with winter wheat; then solid ground again, up close, and the quiet rush of air.

Lunch consists of stale sandwiches and fruit, and Kool-Aid out of big blue dispensers that tastes of plastic even through the sweetening.

When the afternoon reaches the restless side we cross the Jhelum River. Shortly after that the train stops, to wait for another train to pass we suppose. We idle in the dry countryside for an hour and then another. It turns out the train has hit a water buffalo. Tim Old and I wander along the track, seeing how far we can go before one of the parent or staff chaperons calls us back.

"Let's put some coins on the track!" I suggest. Whenever a few of us found ourselves near a railroad line, a favorite pastime was to place one-paisa or ten-paisa pieces on the track and wait for a train to press them into foil-thin ovals of tin or copper. Some of the boys said that putting coins on the track might cause a train to derail, but we did it anyway—with a guilty thrill.

"We'll be gone when the train runs over them, stupid," Tim says.

"On the other track—stupid," I reply, pointing to the second line a few feet away. But Tim thinks this is a boring idea—probably because he didn't suggest it first.

Not really old enough to get permission, we risk defying the rules and walk up to the front. The great locomotive towers over us, trembling with power and glistening with steam that drips off the lower edges like sweat. The engineer looks down like a knight from his horse. He wears a tattered brown military jacket over pajama-like Pakistani pants. His sinewy face and long white beard carry more authority than any uniform might have. Today we are lucky and he lets us climb up into the cab, which is suffocatingly hot from the boilers. The novelty wears off pretty quick.

And the dead buffalo is starting to stink. We head back to our own carriage. Eventually we are off again.

The thick yellow light of late afternoon tints the rolling grasslands and little rocky canyons with an antique glow. These badlands remind me of the Old West, and each time we pass through them I imagine playing in their moon-like crevasses, taking all day to explore their secret gullies snaked with little creeks.

Because of the delay, darkness falls while our destination is still three or four hours away. The order comes down from the adults that all the elementary children should unroll their *bister-bunds* and take a nap—or at least lay down on them. Some of us chafe at this slight to our maturity, but the small band of kids from the Sind are only too happy to turn in. They have been on the train for twenty-four hours already, through desert heat and dust, some of them all the way from Karachi. Among each other, their superiority to those of us who have been on the train less than eight hours, is a given. It is an elite camaraderie born of mutual hardship, but one that lasts only as long as the circumstances that give it relevance. Tomorrow morning, when the train party is forgotten, other interests will effortlessly reshuffle relationships and loyalties.

Bister-bunds are the Pakistani version of sleeping bags. A mattress, sheets, and blankets all fit into a canvas covering with a tuck of pockets at each end for pillows, pajamas, and toiletries. They are plenty cozy and, slept in or not, they are an inseparable part of the train party ritual. I lie on the lower bunk next to the window, feeling the familiar rocking of the train, back and forth; the lickety-clack of the tracks almost merges with the whir of the overhead fan. The quiet, steady pitch of the carriage breaks suddenly with the roar of a passing train, barrelling through the night in the other direction: WHHOOOSSHHH! The windows rattle loudly as shadows whip across the ceiling—*rumble-rumble-rumble-rumble*—then the roar fades abruptly, leaving an imagined echo in the vacuum.

Snuggling securely into my *bister,* I listen to the soothing sound of the tracks, *thkk-thkk . . . thkk-thkk . . . thkk-thkk . . .*

After that everything is a blur of disembarking the train, jostling through another station, someone shouting, and being herded onto the school bus. And then another kind of sound and rhythm lulls me back to sleep as the bus rises into the mountains, pulling us through the darkness, up the winding road, shuddering around hairpin turns, climbing ever upward, till we are home. I drift through the dreamy chaos of trunks and suitcases in the narrow dormitory halls, find my room assignment for the new term, select the bunk I want—or settling for the one that is left—and roll out my *bister.* The boarding mother says that because it is so late we don't have to make up our beds proper, just for tonight. After a quick good-night kiss from "Auntie" Inger, I huddle into the blankets, which smell of mothballs from their recent storage. All I can think about is how cold it is! And I wish I had taken the time to fill my hot water bottle.

When the lights are switched off, silence falls with the darkness. Each bunk is set adrift, a world unto itself. Before the shivering stops and sleep closes over me a terrifying loneliness pours into the void. I feel abandoned. In the nights to come we will whisper excitedly about important things or nothing in particular, to put off this moment as long as possible; but now everyone, dead tired, seems to have switched off the instant their heads hit the pillow.

Wake up, wake up! I cry silently. *Let me show you what I got for Christmas; tell tell me what great adventures you had during the winter break.* In the days to come I will revel in the freedom of the woods around the hostel, the wide open hillside with its constant surprises—packs of monkeys, mysterious holes, secret clay "mines" that supply the construction of our "dinky towns." I will treasure the invigorating privacy of escaping into imaginary adventures without interruption. But now I long for the carnival atmosphere of the train party, where we were all too busy racing around and laughing and arguing to think about what we were leaving behind and what might lay ahead.

What will this term be like? Will old friends hold true? Will I make new friends? The rhythm of the train lingers—like the way the weight of roller skates remains awhile after they've been taken off. *Clickity-clack . . .* the train rolls down the tracks; my body sways imperceptibly as I listen to the train and feel it rock, back and forth inside of me, like the pendulum of a clock. I watch the tracks unfold before me as the train slips over the gravel stream, tie after tie, rails telescoping in endless extension, like ladders in seamless connection.

The last thing I remember is the jackals howling in the woods, strangely human—like old ladies cackling, we always described it—laughing at some joke I am not in on.

This chapter is an excerpt from "Train Party" in Paul Seaman's forthcoming memoir, Paper Airplanes in the Himalayas: Reconstructing a Missionary Childhood.

In March 1956, this old British garrison church became a school for m sionaries' children in Pakistan. Part of the new elementary building can be seen in the background; the boarding hostel is behind it. *(photo: 1973)*

(All photos courtesy of Ian and Isabel Murray, MCS archives, George and Glennis McMillan, John Lotze, Chuck Roub, and Margaret Spoelman.)

CENTRAL ASIAN REPUBLICS

Hunza

GILGIT

K2

Nanga Parbat

KASHMIR

KABUL ◉ *Khyber Pass*

Murree

Srinagar

Peshawar ● ◉ ISLAMABAD

N.W. FRONTIER PROVINCE

Rawalpindi

AFGHANISTAN

River

Lahore ● ● Amristar

Mussoor (Woodstoc

IRAN

Dehra Du

● Quetta

PAKISTAN

Multan

PUNJAB

DEHLI ◉

BALUCHUSTAN

Sukkur ●

Indus

Mohenjodaro ∴

SINDH

Karachi ● ● Hyberabad

I

ARABIAN

● Ahmadabad

OMAN

SEA

● Bombay

| 0 | 100 | 200 | 300 | 400 | 500 |

Kilometeres

| 0 | 100 | 200 | 300 | 400 | 500 |

Miles

AFRICA
↙

1996 LOUIS SPIRITO CARTOGRAPHIC DESIGN

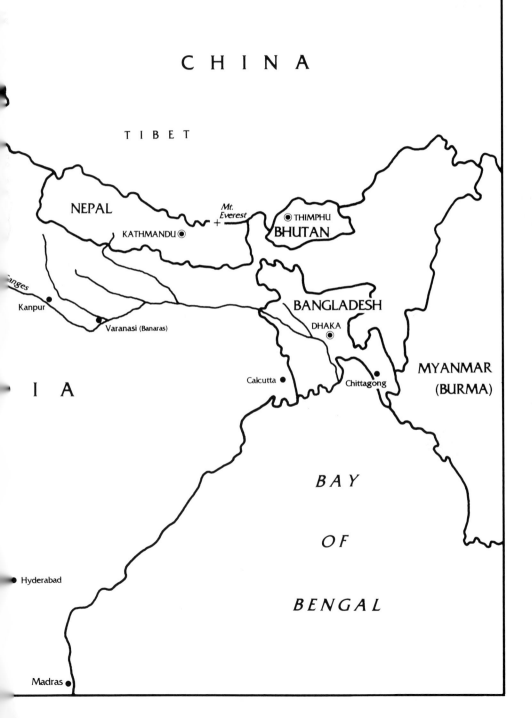

SOUTH ASIA

CHINA

TIBET

NEPAL

Mt.
Everest
+

⊙ THIMPHU

BHUTAN

KATHMANDU ⊙

Ganges

Kanpur •

Varanasi (Banaras) •

BANGLADESH

DHAKA
⊙

I A

Calcutta •

Chittagong •

MYANMAR
(BURMA)

Hyderabad •

BAY

OF

BENGAL

Madras •

Opposite page: The interior of the school in 1967, before the stage was built. The front of the former sanctuary serves as an assembly hall, the rear as a gym. Classrooms were built into the sides and the wings. The high school library (*top*) is on the third floor on the left, with the science room and lab on the other side *(below)*.

Don Calderwood confers with Chuck Roub in the principal's office, 1969.

Behind the school at recess: the picnic table traditionally reserved for teachers' coffee breaks and the equally-memorable sandbox, 1969.

Evelyn Calderwood teaching math, 1969

Sandes Home, 1993. How many of us appreciated the irony that such an elegant place, dowdy with Victorian nostalgia and designed to soothe convalescing soldiers, should be given over to the frenetic terrors of rambunctious teenage boys?

Opposite page, top: Sandes Home (at lower left) as seen from the north end of Murree, above Jhika Gali.

Opposite, bottom: A typical view.

Above: Students David Hamm and Tim Rock discover why the old school bus was so hard to start. (1965)

Below: The "new" bus, which seemed like a spacious luxury model, was built on the chassis of the school truck. (1973)

The main hostel, located on the school property, was completed in 1965 and houses the elementary students and high school girls.

Behind the hostel, the forested hillside descends out of the picture to the right. In a large courtyard above the stone retaining wall, students eat lunch—and exchange threatening gestures with over-eager monkeys.

Opposite page, top: Hostel dining room. Lunch is served across kitchen counter—on pre-formed metal trays. *Middle:* Head chef Khan Zaman in the modern kitchen of the new hostel, 1966. *Below:* Senior high girls' dorm lounge.

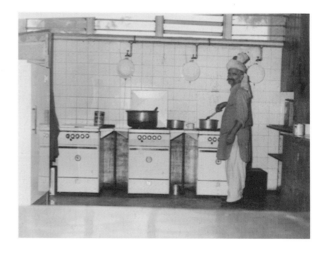

Above: The basketball/tennis court between the main school building and the elementary classroom block, shown below. (The referee is a beardless Ian Murray, with Bill Johnson shooting and Tim Feldmann looking on, 1969.)

Below: Above the elementary classrooms are living quarters for single teachers, more recently used as the senior high girls' dorm. The main hostel is just out of the picture to the right. (1973)

Above: Elementary school choir, c. 1968,

Below: Ninth graders Marty Feldmann and Nancy Addleton perform at annual music recital, 1974.

Ad hoc staff choir, 1973/1974.

11

Young Lions and Ladybug Farms

Jonathan Mitchell, '79

The Little Boys had to endure one-hour naps every Saturday and Sunday afternoon. I now suspect that this was less for our benefit than for that of Auntie Inger, our houseparent. We never slept. It is asking too much of six- and seven-year-olds to lie still on their beds without making any noise. But there were ways to keep busy without attracting too much attention. Often we would tend to our ladybug farms. In the spring there would be a boom in the ladybug population in Murree and we would have competitions to see who could catch the most of the cute little red spotted bugs. Those caught we would dutifully place in cozy containers built for the purpose. These would be lined with handy bits of fluff and grass or whatever else seemed appropriate. These were ladybug farms. My farm was in a little green metal box which could be locked. Never mind that I didn't have a lock, no one else had a hasp on their farm and this gave mine added value. Later I would use this box for all my electrical parts, and I suppose it would have been a good place to keep love letters, had I received many of them. But we needn't dwell on that. Tending ladybug farms during rest period consisted of exercising the ladybugs. We did this by first pulling strings from our bed spreads, tying them

111

together, and stringing them from bed to bed. By the end of the hour we would have an arrangement resembling a spider's web, with numerous intersections of string suspended several feet above the floor. Onto these strings we would place our ladybugs which would promptly run along the string as fast as they could go. We would stage races with as many as twenty ladybugs at a time, though we were careful not to cheer for our entrants too loudly for fear of attracting Auntie Inger. I now suspect she would have enjoyed the spectacle as much as we did, and I regret that we didn't include her in the fun. Maybe we were afraid she would guess where we got the string. The best fun of all resulted when we sent long lines of ladybugs along a number of strings which intersected in the middle of the room. There would be a huge traffic jam, better than anything in Los Angeles, with ladybugs crawling all over each other suspended several feet over the floor. We would keep sending more bugs on their way from all directions till there was a fist-size collection swarming where the strings intersected. At this point the whole clump would usually fall off, scattering ladybugs all over the place while we gasped in awe at the splendor of it all. In their fright the bugs would release a bitter yellow juice which stank up the room something fierce. We would then scramble to open the louvers to get a gasp of fresh air. We were surprisingly refreshed after these "naps," which was doubtless used as an argument for continuing the tradition.

After the school acquired some triple-bunk beds, their novelty was fully exploited, nap time or not. As pirate ships, submarines, or helicopters, they made great props for rowdy adventures—with the predictable crop of broken arms (not mine).

It is strange how I use the anonymous "we" in reminiscing about these early years. To tell the truth, I remember the ladybugs, Auntie Inger, and "us." "We" were one, and seemed to experience things collectively. Our individuality emerged years later. This was one of the unique things about Murree—many of us were there for most of our school years, and, while a variety of memorable people came and went, there was a core group of us who experienced all the rites of passage together. Tim "Waldo" Wilder, Sunil "Slugger" Lall, Dwight "Tweets" Burton, David "Wiggan" Heaton, Tim "Schlonsy" Johnson— these friends and others took on their individual identities and earned their nicknames when we entered junior high. In grade school "we" did things, and the individuals involved in specific memories are almost interchangeable. "We" would line up after afternoon tea for "feastings." Feastings consisted of various edibles brought into boarding or which arrived in the mail from home. (Auntie Inger would wisely ration these, or they would have disappeared in a few days of gluttonous revelry.) "We" would play Prisoners Base, Poison or Three Feet during morning recess. "We" would listen to the jackals howl at night. "We" would throw pine cones at the wild monkeys. It was only the extraordinary occasions which lifted one above the collective anonymity.

One such occasion is permanently etched in my memory. Miss Perry, our legendary first-grade teacher, had the greatest of art classes. We would finger paint or build clay models or fool around with crayons. These are risky things for a first-grade teacher to initiate and I remember well the temptation to decorate Janet Selby with a good dollop of green paint. But Miss Perry ran a very tight ship and none of us would have dared step out of line. In fact, she would count the crayons, every little piece of them, after each session and conduct a hunt for any which had gone missing. On this occasion the count was one short, and the hunt began. When nothing turned up, she instructed us to put our heads on the desks and take naps. There we were taking naps again. But there was no ladybugging under the watchful eye of Miss Perry. It wasn't long before Andrew Lohr leapt from his desk, madly blowing his nose and jumping up and down furiously. This was most extraordinary, and I would have given anything to get up and see what was the matter, but Miss Perry was strict and anyone expressing interest in the matter risked being placed out the window as punishment. Yes, she would actually place us out the window for a few minutes; fortunately we were on the ground floor! (Miss Perry's room was the old Music Room in the alcove to the left of the stage; a large church window dominated the far wall and from the outside a short flight of stone steps mysteriously came up almost to the window ledge.)

Surely Andrew knew better than to behave like this. He was a "Squirrel" after all. The class was divided into the "Squirrels," "Rabbits," and "Kittens." The "Squirrels" were smart, the "Rabbits" were middle of the road, and the "Kittens" were stragglers. The "Squirrels" got to spell words like *glistening* and *beautiful,* while the Kittens were struggling with things like *PET, CAR*, and *GATE*. I can still recall her little ditties like "When two vowels go walking the first one does the talking." Therefore "goat" is pronounced "gote" rather than "gate" since the "o" appears before the "a." I remember chuckling to myself when I overheard Miss Perry mention to my mom that we had no idea we were divided into ability groups. We had it figured out before the end of the first week. So here was a "squirrel" hopping around the room when he should have known better. We might have understood a "kitten" carrying on like this, but Andrew was the class brain. Actually, he had a very good reason for the ruckus. It turned out that the missing crayon was stuck up his nose and they had to take him to the Civil Hospital in Murree to have it removed.

Andrew Lohr was not the only one elevated to fame in Miss Perry's class. Another of "us" was similarly blessed, but I won't mention his name. He had the misfortune of wetting his pants. We had set times for using the bathrooms, and he had somehow misjudged his ability to hang on. Yet this alone wouldn't have distinguished him. Rather, the picture which remains in my mind is of him walking up to lunch in a pair of shorts which would have been several sizes too big for Mohammed Ali. The poor little guy would have found room to spare in just one leg of these shorts, and I am sure we could have used them as a tent on one of our campouts. They were cinched up in the most imaginative style with shoelaces, and they came together at his waist in a way which made him resemble a wasp. From his waist they ballooned out and dragged along on the ground. He attracted the strangest looks on his way up past Roub's house, and I am sure the memory is still fresh in his mind. Miss Perry had fished these shorts out of the lost and found, and even now I would like to know whose they were.

Meal time at the hostel was unique, and it took newcomers several days to figure the system out. We would stand behind our chairs and begin with a song: "For health and strength and daily bread we praise thy name, oh Lord," or, "The lion's young may hungry be, And they may lack their food; But they that wait upon the Lord, Shall not lack any good" were typical. Some of us couldn't figure out the words of "The Lion's Young" and I remember well my brother's innocent version of it, which he sang at the top of his lungs:

The lion's young may hungry feed
And they may like their food
But they that wait upon the Lord
Shall not like any good.

This song was taught to us by "Uncle Jim Hunter", who wa
Scottish—he of the sternly protruding lower lip, rosy cheeks
and, when some impertinence was perceived (which was often),
a stare that could grab you around the neck. To our young
American ears, he always sang the last line, ". . . shall note leck
enny GUDE." So my brother did *rah*ther well under the circumstances.

After the song we would noisily drag out our chairs, sit
down and wait for the bearers to bring the food. The dishes
would begin at the head of the table and would be passed coun-
terclockwise. If we were hungry we knew not to sit on the left
side of the table since the food reached this side last. There was
always enough food, we simply were impatient. We learned to
say things like "Pass the potatoes, and no on the ways." "No on
the ways" prevented anyone from helping themselves as they
passed it your way. If you didn't add that phrase the dish
would be empty when it got to you and you would have to wait
a few minutes with your hand in the air waiting for the bearer
to bring refills. When you asked for the food you had to be prepared for the standard question, "How do you want it?" The response was one of "Air Mail," "Sea Mail," or "Submarine." Sea
mail had to slide along the table, whereas submarine was
passed under the table. Air mail (the regular way) was boring
and not often requested.

Before you could drink any water, you first had to dispose
of the milk in your mug. This usually had a sour taste and we
were not very fond of it. Rumor had it that the cooks washed
their hands in it. I remember bribing Phillip Avery with sweet
eggs (tiny hard candies) to drink mine. We also observed enforced times of silence when things got too noisy. Auntie Eunice
would ring a bell, announce the duration of the penalty, and
the only sound in the dining room would be that of silverware
clattering on plates. After the meal we would have to wait till
the last person was finished at our table before we could leave.
You could deliberately drag out finishing your dessert just to
watch your comrades fidget, but if you did this too often no one
would sit at your table.

Friday night was the most exciting night of the week. We would squirm all day in Miss Perry's class in anticipation. After supper we were allowed to go down to the basketball court and run and run and run. We would sometimes organize running games like Prisoner's Base, but usually we little kids just ran around with no particular purpose other than to express our exhilaration. When it began to get dark Auntie Inger would usually organize a game of Flashlight Beckon. I never understood the game, but I had a grand time hiding behind bushes and walls giving three short flashes of my flashlight toward anyone I could see. I was always careful that my mom packed a flashlight with a button designed for flashing. A regular switch wouldn't do, and had she not complied I would surely have been wounded for life. At some point in the game Paul Seaman or Bruce Bagwell would announce that I had been caught, and I would follow them around for the remainder of the game. It was great. And at eight o'clock we would have tea and cookies in the dining room before heading up to our department for storytime and devotions and whatever skullduggery and mahem we could get into with Auntie Inger for the rest of the evening. Our favorite "bedtime" activity was DRAG-OUT, with Auntie Inger as the hapless victim.

How this began I will never know, but for anyone who has had Auntie Inger as a houseparent it must be one of the most prominent memories of Murree. The game simply involved dragging Auntie Inger—a nicely plump, widow lady in her fifties—down the hall. We didn't fake it either. We would all congregate in the playroom, jumping on the couch and climbing the cupboards in our excitement. Auntie Inger finally entered the room and for a moment all was quiet. When she announced she was ready we charged at her with all our pent up energy. Some went for her legs while others climbed on her shoulders in a vain attempt to bring her to the floor. She was extraordinarily strong (the Norwegian stock, I suppose). Try as we might, she was usually still standing after the first assault. But we had a special weapon in reserve. On the second or third attempt, one of our lookouts would shout a warning and those of us near the couch scampered out of the way to make room for Gene Stoddard's charge. He came rushing in like a football player and pushed the whole pile of tangled arms and legs to the floor. With a loud whoop we each grabbed our piece of Auntie Inger and triumphantly dragged her down the hall to the Little Girls department. She would be laughing so hard when we finally let her go it took her several seconds to catch her breath. Then, with our victory complete, we would crowd around her on our way to bed. Friday nights were definitely the best.

Saturday mornings weren't bad either. Breakfast was later on Saturdays so we could sleep in, but we were so excited we would wake earlier than usual. We got to change our bottom sheets on Saturdays and this made for great fun. It was a chance to tear our beds apart, pile the tangled blankets on the floor and leap into the mess from the top bunks with shouts of "Geronimo" or "Timberrrrr." I don't seem to recall putting it all together again, but I tend to forget the duller moments. And making the beds wasn't the end of the chores. We had to pre-pare for Auntie Inger's "white glove inspections." She would come around with a white glove on her hand and wipe anything we were to have cleaned. The idea was that dirt would show up on the glove, but it was turning a bit gray with use and it wasn't hard to pass the test. Although we found this final ritual quite exciting (which was probably her motive anyway), pre-paring for inspection was not. I would slyly announce my in-tention to beat the rugs and head out in front of the hostel. There I could take my time swatting the rugs with a broom handle and watch the Middle Boys getting their hair cut on the oval inside the driveway, while my roommates were busy clean-ing. This tactic had an added advantage: I would listen care-fully to the wisecracks of the older boys and later impress my brethren with them.

If the barber still had time after buzzing the Middle Boys it was our turn. News that Mr. Hunter was coming would spread down our hall and we would all rush to hide. Haircuts weren't terrible, but no sense having one if you didn't have to. Mr. Hunter would bellow out a command to get in line and the more intrepid of us would venture forth and stand at attention. Mr. Hunter would then run his hand through our half-inch long hair and arbitrarily select those destined for the clippers. After the danger had passed the rest of us would slink out of our lairs to taunt those in the haircut line. It was great fun.

One of the events which became a legend at MCS occurred while I was having my hair cut. David Hamm came running up to the hostel to announce that an apple truck had fallen down the *kud* near Elephant Rock. This was exciting stuff and I was most upset at being imprisoned in the barber's chair at the time. The Middle Boys were off like a shot and came back with tantalizing stories of what it looked like. We little chaps were not allowed off the school grounds without Auntie Inger so we appointed a delegation to negotiate with her. If she would take us to see this wonder we would forgo the traditional afternoon walk. She had an uncanny ability to know what was important to her little boys. Even before the white glove inspection she proudly marched her troop the half mile or so to what is now known as "Apple Turnover." There were the bruised apples and mangled truck, down the *kud*. We watched for half an hour, wishing we had been there to see it crash, before heading home to finish our chores. We somehow knew that Auntie Inger had done something special for us, and we scurried around like little beavers to leave the Little Boys' department spotless. We were proud of Auntie Inger.

As I recall, Auntie Inger took us on a walk that afternoon anyway, after our "nap." While this was undoubtedly generous of her, with our energy we probably would have just gotten into mischief at the hostel. These walks were no ordinary affairs. There is a little stream behind the hostel surrounded by fields of daisies, buttercups, wild strawberries, and lollipop pines. We called them lollipop pines because the local villagers would lop off the lower branches leaving the upper tufts looking like a lollipop on a stem. The stream was full of tadpoles and various water bugs which were most suitable for harassing the girls, but the water itself was the main attraction.

The stream bed wasn't more than about three feet wide and the water meandered back and forth as it flowed from pool to pool. It was rather too peaceful for our tastes so we devised a way to pep things up a bit. We would split into groups of two or three and assign a pool to each group. For about an hour we would build dams on our assigned pool, rearranging rocks to form a foundation and carting all manner of material to plug the leaks. Pine cones, branches, clumps of grass, and hunks of dirt were all artfully combined to raise the level of the pool a foot or two. There was one pond where we could raise the level almost four feet if we were careful with the foundations of the dam, but you had to be very careful when standing below it. When our dam was complete we would scamper up and down the stream inspecting and assisting with the other dams, our excitement mounting all the while.

Finally, when we were satisfied that the dams couldn't be improved upon we would gather at the first dam. The anticipation was so great we could hardly contain ourselves. The makers of the dam would locate a weak spot and coax it loose with great ceremony. This required a good measure of finesse. The idea was to introduce a leak which would grow and finally destroy the dam. To forcefully break the dam would have been too crude, though inexpert dam builders sometimes had to resort to this.

With the collapse of the first dam a pulse of water would surge down the stream and crash into the next dammed pool. Ideally, this dam would break under the onslaught, but usually we had to help things along. At this stage there was no attempt at finesse. If we waited too long, the slug of water would pass over the second dam and we would lose our chance to amplify it. Amplification was the primary goal so we usually resorted to frenzied dam bashing when the pulse of water hit. We would then race along beside the rapidly growing flood screaming our best rendition of blood curdling war cries, destroying dam after dam on our way.

It was a powerful experience, and the adrenalin rush was usually enough to last us till the next week. We were awed by our ability to transform the peaceful little stream into a roaring torrent, and when it was all over we would head back to the hostel wishing we could watch a real dam like Mangla or Tarbela break.

When we weren't traipsing through the woods we might hike around the back of the mountain past Birthday Rock to "the Lookout" and throw paper airplanes. We became experts in the design and manufacture of various types and threw them all with the vain hope that one might land in Indian Kashmir, whose snow-capped mountains we could see off in the distance. When our paper supply was exhausted we continued around the mountain on a back route to Jhika Gali. At this tiny burg of smoky tea shops, fruit stalls, and little general stores we would spend our weekly allowance, which we had been fingering since morning. Some of us bought sweet eggs or *jalebis* while others invested in *patakas* (fire crackers). The kind we were allowed to buy were harmless noisemakers shaped like a Hershey's Kiss; wrapped in thin, pastel-colored paper twisted at the top, they "popped" when thrown on the road or against another hard surface. What to buy was always an agonizing decision since no matter what you purchased, the other group seemed to be having more fun.

If we took the road around the hill and returned to school via Apple Turnover and Pee Corner, we had walked about three miles.

*   *   *

Having a special friend for your first boarding term at Murree was important. The friend would fill you in on all you needed to know to survive. When you are six and away from home for the first time things can be rather daunting. Details such as how to get away without brushing your teeth or washing your hands, how to sneak feastings into your room for a midnight snack, or how to win the kissing fights with Auntie Inger were crucial for a successful first term. But a good friend could also be a source of other kinds of wisdom. I remember Jamie Blanchard at the end of his first week of the fall term asking me to go to the nurse with him. His throat hurt. I asked him more about it and realized he didn't need the nurse. He needed Auntie Inger. I had experienced the same thing myself—he was homesick and had a lump in his throat. Auntie Inger was the place to go for a quick dose of the cuddles. She was the sweetest person, and a wink from her twinkly eyes was powerful medicine. One of these winks not only chased away any thoughts of mischief but left us with a strong feeling of being deeply loved. She was like a grandmother rather than a mother to us—mothers have to discipline more often.

12

A Girl's Life

Brigid (Anderson) Murphy, '68

My early memories of boarding are tinged with homesickness—the goodbyes to parents on the station platform as
we joined the train party; the loneliness of the first night at the
realization of a whole, seemingly endless, term stretching ahead.
I remember one particular "Singspiration" in the dining room
at Sandes. Sitting next to my sister, Tisha (the brave one)—we
must have been about ten and eight—one of the hymns filled
me with a wave of homesickness and I started to cry, quietly at
first, then louder and louder. Tisha gave up trying to comfort
me and joined in. I only remember being aware that our chorus
of crying seemed to have drowned out the singing!

The homesickness never lasted long, and as the years went
by, it became less and less—replaced by the anticipation and
excitement of those early romances. There was always a great
interest in who was going out with whom. I remember the thrill
mixed with almost paralyzing fear of my first date to the school
banquet with Jim Tebbe. There was also the fashion at one
point of couples getting matching shirts and dresses made. Eric
Pulliam and I had a set; I wonder what happened to them

when we broke up. We were only allowed so many dates a term, always a chaperon, and no kissing.

The woods are my most idyllic memory. We used to play for hours in them—they seemed to stretch on for eternity, an unexplored land begging to be discovered. There was never anything frightening about them—in the innocence of childhood, they seemed like heaven to me: the wonderful smell of the pines and the sound of the wind whispering through them; the sudden, unexpected glimpses of snow-covered mountains; the ground softened by dry needles, ivy and moss covering the tree trunks. I loved those woods and I still dream of them to this day.

Sharon Erb, '75

I established some notoriety in my early years (around fourth grade) for being "naughty" after "lights out." We would get out of bed, look out for The Houseparent, and run down to the other end of the hall where the Little Boys lived. Once there, we would throw a note in, say something silly, or just turn around and run back—or hide out in the bathroom, if we heard The Houseparent coming. I was not the only "naughty" one, but my bed was the top bed of a triple-bunk, so I would never quite make it back into bed before the ominous image of The Houseparent loomed in the doorway. I was always "caught in the act" (sigh). Our punishment (horrors!) was that we would have to forego "toast and *chapattis*" at breakfast the next morning.

At the breakfast table, hot toast was the big thing—as it was usually cold and soggy. When fresh toast was coming, we would place "dibs" on who got the first piece, second piece, and so on. I remember rolling up *chapattis* with cream and sugar (yummm!). And "white glove" inspections (good grief!).

I was generally intimidated by teachers and houseparents, but there were some notable exceptions:

Miss Eunice Hill: my first- or second-grade teacher—she was so pretty, so sweet, so gentle and soothing. Her presence made me feel safe and cared for and gave me someone to admire. I needed that.

Miss Lea Virtanen: The Senior Girls housemother in the

early 1970s, she was a true advocate of students. Once she said, "I am here for you—not for the administration." This stands out in my mind. She was not concerned with "controlling" us, but rather attending to our needs. She could relate to young women, and made time for singing, sharing, and just being available.

In my sophomore year, some friends and I created a "prayer chapel" in a small room in the basement of the hostel— a sanctuary, a place to hide out and experience comfort.

I never cried during all those years—except once when I learned that David Hover's father had been killed in a car accident. I broke down and sobbed and sobbed. At the time, I thought, "How noble that I only cry for others," but I understand now that this tragic loss allowed me to shed tears for all the losses and disappointments never mourned.

Esther Corcoran, '79

I was only at MCS for one term but during that time I developed friendships and teachings that have influenced me for a lifetime and it was an experience that I would not trade for anything.

My favorite staff member was the Senior Girls dorm mother, Debby Rupe. Many were the times that we'd gather in her room for an evening of fun, and she always had a hug when we were depressed or a roar of laughter when we were acting foolish. I'm sure there were times that she longed to kick us out, especially when we sampled things in her kitchen that didn't always turn out right. I can see her yet when she confronted me about smoking and told me that I had to write to my parents and tell them, then informed me that she had to ground me for two weeks. I knew that I'd hurt her by abusing the trust she'd placed in me. It certainly taught me a lesson—not to get caught. Ha!

The teacher that frustrated me the most was Mr. Murray. He always called me "Ruth" because he claimed that he couldn't remember my name. He was a strict teacher but always had something funny, or nice, to say out of class.

I think I was blessed to have the two nicest roommates in my class! Shelly Walsh (whose parents worked in Bangladesh) and Miriam Dalton (from Abbottabad). Of course, we had our spats, especially Miriam and I over Phil, Shelly's brother; but we always seemed to come through and become friends again. When I think back, I still have to laugh at Cindy Irwin—she was the class comedian! She climbed into the cubbyhole above our closets one night and waited until we were all settled into bed before jumping out at us—we just about died of a heart attack. You can be sure that, after that happened, we always checked above our closets before going to bed.

During my stay there, I "sailed" with two Davids. One, in the eleventh grade, was British and the other, a twelfth grader, was Canadian. The late night walks on Friday and Saturday nights to Jhika and the Saturday night movies certainly helped to make things more romantic! One of the most frustrating things, though, about the walks was that it put the guys close to Sandes so a lot of time I ended up walking back with the girls. Of course, the camp-outs helped to fuel romantic feelings—especially the campfires.

Monkey Hill camp-out comes back to mind as clearly as if it were yesterday! We got into a water fight and by the end of it, there was not one dry person around! Yes, boarding school did have its fun times.

But, of course there must a downside to everything. The *cold* classrooms in November, the watery eggs for breakfast, and the *tiny* bathtubs. All of these were also part of life at MCS. The morning bell always seemed to ring so early; then started the rush in order to make it to breakfast in time. Why? I'm not so sure—the toast was usually cold and soggy, the porridge was sticky, etc. Ha. The favorite break of the day, though, was afternoon tea time. I never did figure out why that was, though.

Laundry duty was my most hated duty—everyone complaining that socks were lost, name tags were missing, and clothes were sometimes still damp. But everything added together to make for a very interesting life.

The hardest thing I went through while at MCS was homesickness. When one gets tired or lonely for home all the good times get forgotten. Though I'd made friends and had an excellent dorm parent, nothing can replace home and parents. That is probably the biggest drawback that I would have, even now, of sending a child away to boarding school—the child misses out on a close relationship with his or her family, especially the very young ones. Sometimes when relieving the dorm parents of the first through third graders for a evening, I would hear the little ones crying. Upon checking, their answer was always "I miss my mom and dad."

Sabine Munzinger, '87

Snow-covered mountains, moonlit walks, a sweet warm *chai* at Joe's, leaking busses, creaking bunk beds, prowling snow leopards, howling jackals . . . These are the images that spring immediately to mind when I think about Murree Christian School. Other pictures, sounds, and smells come back, too. But these are the impressions a tourist could have brought back from a visit to Murree; they are excuses for the lack of courage to reveal my true thoughts. If I let my heart do the talking it would say this:

I had the privilege of being one of the few students who actually made it through twelve years of MCS—*plus* kindergarten—without a single interruption. I define the latter as my "Tower of Babel" experience, sitting in a class of kids that all looked like me but when they opened their mouths the strangest language came out. Elementary was more enjoyable because I realized that what they had been speaking was English, and I was so fascinated by the new language I was learning that by the end of the first school term I had trouble communicating with my parents in German.

Being one of those fortunate children that seemed immune to homesickness, I looked forward to coming into boarding to hear Auntie Eunice singing in the halls, to be around my best friends as much as I liked, to play "Three Feet in the Mud Puddle" with them and shake our heads at those naughty, naughty boys.

My heart pauses to ask me why life is so full of paradoxes. In spite of the beautiful childhood memories, elementary turned out to be the worst time I had at MCS. When stronger kids notice the weaker ones among them, they turn life into a horror story for these—even at MCS. I have to tell my heart that I don't know why, and I hastily ask it to continue.

Seventh grade at MCS is the magic number, letting former noisy sixth-grade rowdies think that they have finally grown up. The staff handled the situation well, giving us respon-

sibility and putting trust in us and I thank them for treating us
so wisely.

I laugh at the picture I see before me of a panic-struck junior high student quivering at the thought of having to ask the
question of life or death, "Will you go to the Formal with me?"

Junior high meant "real" movies (no more kid stuff), raiding the boys' dormitory without the presence of a staff member,
endless discussions about whose turn it was to sort the laundry, carved hearts with initials in desks, whispers from best
friends to best friend for hours after lights-out. But junior high
was also a time of discovering that we are all human and learning to cope with the reality of it. Coping with friends turning
their backs on you, with cruel gossip, with rules you did not understand and coping with homesickness you were scared to admit.

When I think of senior high my heart smiles. Having sur-
vived the most critical point of puberty, we were given the
chance to make use of what we had learned. Not only could we
give voice to our thoughts, but we had the opportunity to try
out ideas, be creative by organizing activities. Our teachers
made school interesting and enjoyable for us, causing us to be
eager to increase our knowledge, motivating us to question and
discuss what they had taught us.

We did so at the same time not failing to question the rules
and boundaries, testing the authorities by trying out how many
sets of drawers belonging to the opposite sex we could empty
without having to polish furniture in return; how many monkeys we could feed with the school food without getting caught;
how often we could escape from the library to the *chai* shop
without a pass and not land in the principal's office. Even now
my heart stops and reminds me that even high school was not
just sunshine but had its share of storms.

In senior high, cultural differences became evident. MCS,
being under a great deal of American influence, had its own set
of traditions that expected students to join all activities. For example: unwritten laws about dating and conforming to the
American way of dressing, speaking, and thinking. Consequently, a non-American lifestyle was "out."

I forgot all that though. I can forget it because every chapter of life has its highs and lows. MCS is important to me because it gave me two things: faith and friends.

MCS made Jesus very real to me, it helped my faith to

grow and that is the faith that still lives in me and is the most important factor in my life.

The deep friendships that started in Murree have remained to this very day: friendships that enabled us to work and pray through problems together at MCS, especially when parents could not be there to help, friendships that make it possible for us to meet again after six years of separation and give us the chance to pick up where we left off as if we had never been away. And that is what made MCS come alive: the friends. People I laughed with, cried with, grew up with, fought with, struggled with—people I loved. I understand why the memories I started off with are so precious to me. They remind me of the friends I enjoyed them with: gazing at snow-covered mountains from the student lounge, a sweet warm *chai* at Joe's with friends after a moonlit walk, listening to the haunting howl of jackals while secrets wandered from bunk to bunk, laughing at the intruding raindrops in the school bus . . .

Marie (Dalton) Lehmann, '74

Until I was in fourth grade, everyone stayed at Sandes and walked to school with all the little kids paired up in lines, two by two. And almost every day I tripped over a round rock that stuck out of the ground by the side of the road. I tripped or ran into things because I was too busy talking to notice obstacles. One day Becky Cutherell tripped and our first-grade teacher picked her up on her shoulders and carried her to school. I guess I was too tall even then for such special treatment, or maybe our teacher realized she'd have to help me every day if she started! One day I walked into a telephone pole and bruised my hip and shoulder! Another day, coming home from school, Miss Cunningham stopped the class to warn us about the fresh holes in the street on the way to Jhika Gali. But I went on talking to my partner and sure enough, suddenly one leg disappeared! I scrambled out so fast and was too embarrassed to ask for sympathy.

One day in school someone got caught cheating on a spelling test. The teacher grabbed the cheat sheet and ripped it up in front of us all. On the way out to P.E. on the field, I was madly licking and rubbing off the spelling words on my hand! I was afraid of what the teacher would do to my hand if she saw it. But as I went out I talked with a friend piously about the evils of cheating. I don't think I cheated after that fright.

One day in Miss Cunningham's class we were to give oral book reports. I stood up to give my report, thinking fast because I hadn't read a book. In the gym some adults were setting up for the Hobby Show and outside the classroom window I could see a cake for display. I started talking about a squirrel that jumped in the window, onto a cake, and so on, and ended lamely with, "If you want to know the rest, you'll have to read the book." I took my seat and then Miss Cunningham asked for the biographical information on the book. I hemmed and hawed and realized I was found out.

Once, in boarding, we got some yummy peppermint-tasting toothpaste for a change. The next time it hailed we pushed our tin tubs out to collect hail and make peppermint ice cream. We were squeezing out the toothpaste when our houseparent came yelling. Ginny and I ran off and the others got in trouble.

I am thankful for my elementary years in boarding, a time of mostly pleasant memories, and because it taught me at an early age that I could always pray about my troubles.

During summers in Murree I enjoyed the best of both worlds: nights and weekends with the family and school days with my friends. The school bus was the place for catching up on the latest gossip before classes started. I remember Patty Irwin, Ginny Stoddard, and I had a crush on the same guy, Mark T. We took the wooden spool out of a toilet paper roll and carved on the wall of a bathroom stall, "PL+GM+MN+MT." We thought we were so sly because we used our middle initials. These letters were five inches tall, so it was no small act of vandalism! But after I spent a weekend with Mark's family I was convinced I didn't want to marry him. On the bus I convinced Patty and Ginny, too, and as soon as we arrived at school, we ran to the bathroom and crossed out the evidence as proof of our seriousness. That grand engraving to fickle love only got erased when the whole stall was eventually tiled.

The lack of privacy was probably the hardest thing for me at MCS. Those little toilet stalls came to represent privacy in my life. We used to change clothes under our night gowns or under our covers in bed! And yet, in another sense, we had too much privacy—dictated by the Islamic culture we lived in. And these restrictions were much more confining for the girls than for the guys.

The weekend walks in junior and senior high offered a welcome relief—a chance to get off campus for a while. The open road under the stars, the chance to be alone with your thoughts for awhile, the prospect of tea and omelets at Charlie's in Jhika Gali (which the guys could enjoy anytime they wanted), all made the evening walks a special time, even if you weren't romantically inclined.

My favorite high school teacher was Miss Glennis Brown. (We called her Glennis the Menace, but meant it affectionately, most of the time.) She took an interest in my art work and got me really interested in reading. I remember her reading *I Never Promised You a Rose Garden* to our class. One day she was talking with us on some other subject and Mr. Roub stopped in for a "spot check." Miss Brown, cool as ever, quickly switched back to discussing the novel we were reading and we all helped out, answering questions, joining in the act! When Mr. Roub left, she sighed and thanked us. That was fun.

Mr Murray was so exasperated with me because I couldn't understand the word problems that involved playing cards. I said they were against the rules, so why should I understand them. He finally drew the cards angrily on the board to explain once and for all. Just then Mr. Roub came up the lab stairs with a visitor! Mr. Murray was so embarrassed and flustered he was speechless. After they left, he excused himself and ran after them to explain. I thought it was poetic justice for all the times Mr. Murray had made me blush by teasing me.

*   *   *

Stress was a word rarely used at MCS, but it took its toll anyway, compounded by guilt and embarrassment. I nearly reached the breaking point once. After a bonk on my head during volleyball practice, I did my usual 100 bicycle exercises that night; then, as I sat down in chapel the next morning I clunked heads with someone again! I went up to my dorm room to rest for a while. I lay on my bed and started thinking about all the demands of the upcoming interschool Cultural and Sports Convention (the first MCS participated in), Algebra II, and living in such close community: girls, girls, girls.

Poor Kathy Wilder got a shock when she came up from chapel. I freaked out and begged her to stay out of the room. Lea Virtanen came in with a pill and left it on the edge of the bed. That helped me calm down. I was taken to Taxila for x-rays with a suspected whiplash, but all I needed was rest and less stress. After a few days at Bach Hospital, I returned to MCS to find out everyone had been praying for me. There were rumors that I had gone crazy. Kemmie Philbrick had made me a lovely poem book. The support from everyone is something I will always treasure.

I can't remember why I didn't go on a certain campout, but I ended up with a boyfriend as a result. It was Sunday morning and I entered the back of the gym, saw the row of girls I would normally sit with and, with sudden boldness, refused! I went and sat by Kemmie Philbrick. After the service Paul Seaman came up and, assuming that we were "going together," asked if we wanted to join him and his sister Ruth for lunch at Sandes. What a break from the routine and life with the girls that I was sick of! So off we went and after talking all afternoon we ended up sitting down by the tennis court at school. We decided to go steady, or be "boat and sailor," as MCS lingo put it. When the campout bunch returned, some got wind of where we were and came around back of the hostel to throw pine cones and tease. It was fun to be really "somebody."

13

A Saturday Evening Walk

Kem Philbrick, '74

Suspended in a daydream about the end-of-term train party that will carry me home, I lie on my back in a patch of grass just below Sandes, soaking up the warmth of a lazy afternoon sun. My reverie is shattered by a burst of clanging as the first supper bell rings, a sure sign that boarding is still very much in session. I get up slowly and the warmth of this early November afternoon gives way to a sudden chill as the sun begins a more rapid descent and shadows abruptly lengthen.

Up the front steps, I disappear into the bowels of Sandes to find a bathroom, scoop a bowlful of water from the bucket to the basin, and wash my hands before joining the migration to the dining room. My brush with homesickness is elbowed aside by the mounting anticipation which greets the arrival of evening. Supper is no drawn-out affair tonight and even the apple crisp dessert is accorded short shrift. Floor boards creak beneath hurrying feet as the high school boys retreat to their rooms. Some change a shirt, some brush their teeth, others wash their faces and try splashing a little cologne. As for me, I stock my pockets with dry handkerchiefs, ready to do battle against my first head-cold of the autumn. Behind me, bathed in his mellifluous whistling, Tim DeHart checks his long, five-cell

131

flashlight to be sure all the batteries are fresh, primed for light-hearted mischief later in the evening. The floor boards are quiet once again as the last of us hasten into the nightfall which becomes even more dense as we leave the Sandes drive-way and duck into the woods.

Our feet stutter on the rocky, make-shift steps of the short-cut, a hasty staccato broken by an occasional silent spot on the soft pine needles. Down, down, and down a little more until we round the bend from which the road is visible through the trees as a pale grey ribbon. On Saturday evenings it is a short mile to Gharial when the hostel, films, refreshments, and, if all goes well, a walk lie in store. Every bend and rise in the road feels like the handshake of an old friend, predictable and unchang-ing. The uneven blacktop, the dusty shoulders, the sagging guardrails, the whispering pines—all exude a familiar warmth, joining in the prospect of an evening designed to nudge long-ings for home aside, at least for a time. I drop behind the others and peer into the deepening darkness, trying to force the fa-miliar out of the shadows. Of course, my home is down on the plains with my parents, but then what exactly is boarding? Is there a path to lead me to an answer? I walk along, glad at least that I know *this* road.

Rounding the last big bend, I hear welcome voices hanging in the crisp night air from the teashop across from school. A lit-tle closer and the voices mingle with the redolence that only a Himalayan teashop can offer: the smoke of hissing pine cones in the fireplace, the mouth-watering fragrance of curry along-side freshly-baked *chapattis,* and the creamy steam of *chai* cresting to a boil. The hostel lights break through the trees and before long the scrape of shoe leather on blacktop gives way to the clatter of the driveway's gravel. A few quick strides, and I step into the energized chatter of the hostel dining hall. My eyes skim the room, seeking a familiar figure who, I hope, will grant me some reprieve from my pensive mood.

Up front, one staff member spreads the stubborn three legs of the film screen, while another patient soul checks and re-checks the aging projector in the rear. The evening's fare is passed along the grapevine until most everyone knows what lies ahead: a documentary on wheat farmers in Nebraska, an-other on an expedition to the Antarctic, and (maybe) a short cartoon on good hygiene featuring "Careless Charlie." Some boarding mates regroup with siblings, others find security in a knot of friends. A few glance nervously about as they watch the clock tick towards starting time without the appearance of a current flame. Those who have already traversed the shoals of fledgling romance sit contentedly side by side, occasionally holding hands (even with the lights still on) as a flag flown proudly from the mast.

Here and there is evidence the "canteen" was open: BP toffees crackle as they are unwrapped and Sweet Eggs boxes rattle as they yield their multicolored treasures. Adrian Coupe, all of seven years old, and sitting in the second row, turns around long enough to reveal a mustache of powdered sugar. His hand is clutching a half-eaten, sugar-dusted brownie, retrieved from some cherished hoard received in a package from home. I too know the comfort of savoring some treat which could only have come from home, but tonight I seek an alternative answer and, spotting that familiar, sought-after face, I feel a smile well up from deep within. Our eyes meet, shyly exchange greetings, and then scan the rows of chairs for two adjacent. I rather like redheads.

After a brief announcement, a contagious tide of "Shhh!" sweeps the room and the overhead lights surrender to the lone bulb of the projector. Around the room, necks crane to afford a clearer glimpse of life in that faraway place some call "back home in the States." A few necks do not crane at all, belonging to those content with their present milieu. Among these, a few hope tonight will launch a new romance as they sit on the kitchen counter at the rear of the room, scanning the horizon and plotting their intended course for what remains of the evening. Others have more proximate concerns: will she let her hand drift over (aided by a forced cough, a feigned itch, a false air of preoccupation with the film), and if so, is tonight the night to cross that Rubicon and actually hold her hand? Two weeks ago tonight we did, albeit briefly. I catch myself wishing for an encore. Furtively glancing down, I lift my palm from my leg and let it hover between us in anxious proposal. My mouth is threatening a cotton mutiny by the time she notices and rotates her hand in acceptance.

Ah, the confluence of untold stories huddled in that room, dancing in silent deference to the whir and steady *tick-tick-tick* of the projector. Up front, freshly scrubbed and clad in flannel pajamas and worn robes, more than one of those brave little urchins would gladly exchange the sight of a wheat field at harvest for the security of his father's lap, but it is not to be. I know because I was once one of them. Maybe I still am. Further back, an uncertain girl, caught in those awkward middle years and poised on the threshold of womanhood, might sacrifice even the convulsive humor of a brief cartoon for an evening with her mother. Instead, she is learning to pour her thoughts into words and entrust her questions to manila envelopes with twenty-paisa stamps: questions about boys, and how does God understand what it feels like to be a girl in Pakistan, and why do you have to be so far away? And in the back, obscured by the bravado now well-honed by those of us who have made these Saturday night pilgrimages since our youth, the uncertainties of adolescence jockey with disciplined defenses. Usually the defenses carry the day, but I have seen the occasional momentary infirmity, betrayed by an unexpected silence, a weak laugh, a quiet retreat, or a wistful eye.

Whatever private longings and exertions may converge in this hour when reality is challenged by importing far-off worlds, they are apt to be drowned in the raucous welcome accorded the refreshments as the projector moans to a standstill, then revives briefly to rewind the evening's respite. We sit with our sweaty hands clasped a moment longer, unwilling to let the moment retreat. (And I wonder how long I will be able to hold her hand before my nose threatens to drip again.) Her shoulder touches mine as the little kids surge by. I watch their eyes and suck my breath in sharply as a sliver of memory slides between my ribs. I lean against her, glad for the reassurance that tonight at least, I will not have to fight the ache of putting another week to bed entirely alone. Too easily I remember crawling into cold sheets after an evening's entertainment and wondering why the glow faded so fast. It gives me pause: did we welcome the refreshments because we were hungry or because they enabled us to pass over from unanswered longings to the more comfortable domain of immediate distractions?

The thump of a foot against the swinging doors of the kitchen heralds the bearer's entrance, grasping two dented, steaming aluminum pitchers in each hand. With a little luck, the contents will approximate hot chocolate. Khan Zaman's cookies follow shortly: broad and flat, yellow with browned rims, sprinkled with granular sugar and crowned with half a walnut. Not at all like my mother's, but I pick up two just the same. They never last long, and after the young ones are shepherded off to bed, Roy Montgomery successfully cajoles the bearer into producing an additional tray of "seconds," the existence of which he playfully denied only moments before.

The cookie trays are empty, and the girls disappear upstairs, then descend the back stairs clad in jackets and scarves. Before long, the high schoolers make their way outside onto the gravel driveway. I watch as she pauses to finish a stairway conversation with Carolyn Pietsch before turning and offering me an almost involuntary wink of reassurance. "I am coming," says the wee twinkle in her eyes.

The junior high contingent, largely clustered in groups while still in the light of the hostel, moves down the road and, reaching the school gate, turns right to skirt the upper field. The senior high lingers a few more minutes, waiting to learn which staff will accompany us tonight. Once they appear, we become a ragtag procession stretching down the hill. Three shrouded figures in the teashop look up from their huddled vigil near the fire as the first of the crew reaches the main road and takes a left towards Jhika. A time-honored institution of the boarding experience, "the walk," is underway.

And so, by twos, threes and more, the senior-high wanders into the night. In a world where more typical familial boundaries have long since been breached, it is a time for the surrogate family to embrace conversation which reassures us that we are not alone. Here is a breath of tenderness, there a peal of laughter; behind a flare of irritation, up ahead a wisp of loneliness. Nearby a patient ear plays midwife to a solemn thought, while further out words tumble precipitously forth. Many voices and a few hands reach out in search of understanding, taking up rhythm with the muffled cadence of our scattered feet upon the mountain macadam. Reciprocity hangs in the air and she takes my hand as we too join the chorus of voices.

Weekend walks under the protective shroud of night also open other routes of youthful commerce. I remember a few short months ago, when, unwilling to risk public discovery, I had turned to tow-headed Nate Irwin whose sister's discretion was beyond reproach.With nervous instructions, I entrusted my dignity to Nate, in the form of a soul-baring note which he then delivered to Patty for the intended recipient. That common piece of notebook paper, into which were folded the hopes and prayers of my week, passed discreetly from palm to palm until, in the course of an evening, it arrived at its final destination. Later, safely ensconced in a bathroom stall to ward off prying eyes, the red-headed one read the note. Honoring its creases, she folded it back up, savored the sentiments expressed, closed her eyes, and began to compose a reply. After all, there was promise of another walk the following night, and an opportunity for return post. Such were our early lorries of romance.

Just as I am on the verge of reminding her of those early awkward days (so that we could share one of those we-were-so-young-then smiles), we are interrupted by the approach of a lone Pakistani. Some pass him in silence, others offer a quiet, "Salaam." We are strangers in his land, yet I feel a particular kinship. He nods to Mr. Murray, everyone's favorite chemistry teacher, who with his wife is bringing up the rear. Suddenly, the approach of a 1957 Chevrolet is announced by a familiar wheeze and muffled ker-plunks born of a rough road, exhausted shocks, and eight men in a six-passenger car. Mindful of the cultural consternation with which a car of Pakistanis might regard the late-evening spectacle of young men and women walking with arms entwined, our chaperon bellows, in a voice that would cascade down the years of our memories, "DISENGAGE!" I drop her hand as Ian Murray's fearful Scottish brogue ricochets on from one couple to the next until, by the time the flickering headlights cast their momentary spotlight on us, their only target is a scattered band of school children. The receding rattle then signals it is once again licit to rejoin hands. Who can tell what our Pakistani neighbors think of this curious phenomenon of venturing into the night with no apparent destination in mind?

No discernible destination, perhaps, yet before heading back to school the evening's stroll would culminate in a much-anticipated stop in Jhika. Both narrow footpaths and sinuous roads chiseled out of the mountainside converge at this slender gali. Fresh from the darkness, laughter finds renewed vent as we emerge into the dim light of Jhika's teashops. Those in the lead head for a glorified hovel marked by the carved wooden shingle that reads simply, in English and Urdu, "Charlie's." (Boarding regulars had recently made this sign for their favorite teashop owner to hang outside his door.) I take my turn holding the sagging door open as we swell the crowd even more.

Just inside the door, flowered cups and saucers—some once broken but now wired anew—lie upturned on a board, patiently waiting for the bearded proprietor's deliberate reach. Eggs and spices, raised aloft in skeletal wire baskets, hang from the screened windows that look out on the nearly deserted street. Further in, just beyond the fireplace, a dirty rag waits on an uncertain table. Alongside, an iron chair, polished by years of use, leans against the blackened plaster of the wall. A bare sixty-watt bulb dangles from a fly-specked electrical cord, issuing weary light still strong enough to fade President Ayub Khan and the sultry cinema stars whose portraits adorn the walls. The filthy floor—buffeted by a sudden mountain gust—shivers beneath the fireplace's brave bursts, or do the boards give and bounce reassuringly against the heavy tread of Charlie's smoky shadow? The wobbly benches welcome us and we cram ourselves in, six to a side. I bask in a warmth that feels like family.

Having gathered our requests, Charlie reaches into those scant wire baskets and, with the distinctive crack of an egg, the ingredients yield to the chup-chup-chup of his wooden mixing spoon. Then into a frying pan popping with a wedge of *ghee* and in minutes we are enjoying omelets and piping hot *rotis,* a simple feast without rival. The girls relish the escape from the hostel's circumscription. And the guys welcome the novelty of having the girls alongside in the usually segregated teashops. I watch her fingers tear a piece of *roti,* capture a shred of omelet, and tuck it into a smiling cheek. For a moment, I wish the hands of my watch would stand still. Now comes the tea . . . and more tea. It is a time of shelter—not only from the bracing wind outside but from the occasional nasty gust of loneliness which catches you unawares in boarding. Somehow the aromatic sizzle of the frying pan, the steady steam off the tea, the gentle laughter rebounding off the walls, the quiet smile which plays upon Charlie's face, and, ultimately, the glint of a four-anna piece resting on a rupee, purchases a reprieve from the unspoken ache for home. For some, the refuge inherent in this curious community renders the unspoken almost unknown. For others, the unspoken is a forceful undercurrent not so easily resisted. Regardless, there is a redemptive strain for all of us in these hours of walking in the moonlight, talking in the shadows, eating and drinking in the embrace of Jhika.

Too soon the saucers are tipped and drained for the last

time, and, sated in more ways than one, we pry ourselves loose from the warmth of Jhika's teashops and set our faces reluctantly toward Gharial once more. A few head straight up the long, steep driveway to Sandes, but most of us retrace our steps, taking a more gradual route to close the evening. Past the short-cut, now the short-short-cut (hear the trickle of water?), the curve where the apple truck went over the edge . . . every ten paces of that road owns a memory for those who have known it from their earliest baptism into boarding. Two-by-two in first grade, twice a day, rain or shine, and then on down through the dozen years that follow. Small wonder the road seems now to anticipate our every footfall, she and I, in a more grown-up pairing.

The mile-long amble ends in the brief climb to the hostel followed by lingering good-byes. We walk around to the back of the hostel and stand for a moment in the shadows to look silently over the stone wall into the darkness below. Absurdly, I think of the monkeys who are often so plentiful there in the daylight. Do they gather as families for the night, I wonder? Smiling at myself, I squeeze her hand and turn to take in her gentle smile of farewell, framed in red. She squeezes in response and almost in unison we murmur, "See you in church tomorrow." Then Marie is gone. Up the back stairs, pausing for just a moment to turn, smile, and hint at a wave. I am happy. I am sad. I watch while she follows the last of the girls upstairs.

Heading back towards Sandes, I spy a few dim figures and the flicker of a flashlight ahead. But tonight I'd rather walk alone.

14

The Old Maid's Club

Regulation, Isolation, Socialization

Ruth Feldmann, '74

My earliest memories of MCS are from kindergarten. Every day I carried a little basket—bought in the bazaar in Murree, I'm sure. My basket held one cookie, probably, or something similar. One day I was wearing my favorite purple dress with the purple sash, and walking home from the bus with my Dad when I slipped and fell in an enormous, fresh buffalo-pie! Yicch. This resulted in the ever ready tetanus shot.

I also remember breaking my arm playing dress-up with Allison Thompson. At the hospital in Pindi I saw a telephone and an elevator for the first time. Skip Lundgren and I were allowed to ride in the front of the bus together because he had a cast on his leg and I had one on my arm. I felt pretty special, since I was in kindergarten and he was in high school.

Entering boarding at age eleven was pretty traumatic. It was summer boarding of grade six. Everyone said that summer boarding was the most fun, but I always thought that the people who said that were never in summer boarding. We ate our lunches off of metal trays that grew steaming hot in the sun while the lucky kids had lunches from home. Grass is always greener on the other side! We did do some fun things, though, with extra trips to Pindi, picnics, and so on, and some of the rules were relaxed a bit.

I'll never forget the "Going-Back-Into-Boarding" feeling. It seemed like it was always raining in Murree the day boarding opened. Many times the electricity would be off. Kids would be screaming up and down the halls, boarding parents were everywhere, coolies were hauling up trunks and bisters, homesick kids were saying goodbye, train party kids were trying to tell better stories of their adventures. The first meal was always a let-down, and going to bed with a roomful of others was mass confusion.

Every morning we had to face those "wonderful" breakfast cereals, *suji* and *dahlia,* except Sundays when we were offered puffed wheat. I could hardly wait to be in the "Big Girls" department when eating breakfast was a choice and not a regulation. KZ was the cook when I was at MCS and "KZ" was also the name for the tummy trouble we always had. Other meals featured "monkey grits," "bombs," and something that was called liver, but looked like something unmentionable.

Every morning with breakfast, little black and yellow vitamin pills were passed around the table. They had a shape and texture like M&Ms, but you wouldn't want to bite into them! The nurse was famous for her "little yellow pills," some sort of antihistamine good for making a person sleepy or drying up a cold. We were convinced she handed them out for almost any ailment.

We were always having water shortages at MCS. In the winter we'd get buckets of snow and melt them over the kerosene heaters (what fumes!) to wash our hair. In the summer we had to go with our buckets to the nearest stream and get water to wash in. We prayed for rain so often. We were allowed one bath a week and could only use two inches of water! I didn't feel clean very often. My hair always felt itchy, stringy, greasy, dirty.

And the toilets stank. I don't know why no one put lids on the toilets. We weren't allowed to flush them. Unlucky monitors came around twice a day and performed that task. Sometimes there was so much paper (among other things) in the toilets that they would back up. *Yichh.* The toilet paper we had was those slippery little folded over squares of what felt like waxed paper. Whenever you pulled one out of the box, several more fell out and littered the floor. The poor "potty monitor" had a really bad job ahead of her.

Speaking of regulations, we girls were under the strict "regs" regarding dress lengths. In the days when miniskirts were very fashionable in the States, we girls wore dresses to our knees. Straight skirts had to touch the floor when we were kneeling and full skirts could be a couple inches off the floor when kneeling. How we hated those rules! I wore skirts more than dresses because they could be rolled up to the desired length when teachers or housemothers weren't around.

We all had at least one "daddy shirt," a white shirt that was too big for us. I got one from my dad, although I'm not sure I told him I had it! These shirts were great because they were long enough to do the necessary as far as being modest, and they were also what the "in" group was wearing. It was so important to be like the "in" group.

During the winter I was in grade nine we kids from the Abbottabad/Bach Hospital/Mansehra area made a special trip up to MCS in February to decorate the new student lounge. This was the first time the high school kids had their own little space and we wanted it to be nice. We put in a dropped ceiling of tie-dyed cloth, painted the walls orange and black, laid carpet, and added curtains and furniture. It was freezing cold in there and hard to get warm, but we had fun. I was disappointed though, when we were in school the next term, that the lounge quickly became a place where the "in" kids hung out, and so no one else felt comfortable in it. It hurt to have put so much effort into it and not feel good being there.

In grade ten we tried to have as many birthday parties as possible. The guys would get rolls and chai from the shop across the road and we'd "feast" instead of having geometry. It was such a good break that one term I had a couple birthdays until Mr. Calderwood caught on.

Peer pressure was very strong at MCS and made kids do things that they didn't have any desire for, like playing certain games or liking/not liking certain foods. It wasn't "cool" to like French and to admit that you did was really humiliating. The favorite game was Rook. I didn't like it, wasn't good at it, never really understood it, and yet played it to be "in." Since leaving MCS I don't think I've played it once.

Then there was the pressure to have a date to various events. Those unlucky girls who weren't selected really felt the sting of defeat. Trying to live with all these unspoken rules and rigid expectations was one of the hardest things for me at MCS. About four of us formed a club called the "Old Maid's Club." We had rules, traditions, and regular meetings. Once, two of the guys petitioned to join and we held a meeting to discuss the matter. They were rejected and told to form a club for old bachelors.

*   *   *

My favorite housemother was Auntie Inger, although she was never in charge of any department I was in. Auntie Inger was great. She did everything from kissing fights to roller skating. She was a good sport and had thousands of stories to tell. She fell off a bed during a kissing fight once and broke her nose. It was a noble wound.

I was most in awe of Mr. Murray, whose bark was usually worse than his bite. Once he poured rubbing alcohol (spirits) down the back of my dress for not paying attention in his class. Another time (same infraction) he threw chalk at me and made me stay after class to pick up the pieces. He was a good teacher. I wish I had paid more attention! His inspections were famous (six-inch straightedge, four-inch pencil, eraser, notebook with all the pages intact), as were the five paisa fines if we didn't have one of the necessities. Mrs. Murray made good fudge using our fines, which we got to enjoy at the end of the term.

Study halls were a good time to catch up on a nap, write notes to a friend, or look around at who might be holding hands with whom! Possibly some of us actually studied.

We had fun on camping trips. Mirianjani, a beautiful high mountain area, was a favorite spot. One weekend, we arrived at the trail entrance late and it was very dark on the hike up to the government rest house. Cindy Webster fell over the *kud* at one point and lost her glasses. The next morning some of the guys went back to look for them and realized that she had stopped rolling down the mountain just a little way from an edge that would have certainly taken her to her death if she had kept sliding. They found her glasses too. God was really taking care of us.

Something was planned every year for spiritual emphasis. Someone's father would come and hold meetings. We would learn new songs, have special sessions, get out of classes. Many of us made commitments to the Lord at these times. Sometimes special singing groups from England or the States would find their way through our neck of the woods. These also gave us a chance to learn new songs and envy their shorter dress lengths. It was good to have some input from the outside world.

15

Frivolous and Philosophical

High School Days Revisited (1970s)

THE MUD AT KUND

Rob Bailey, '78

Campouts were always the high point of each semester. There was never any other event to rival them for sheer height of expectation and amusement. Usually by that point in the term, most students were badly in need of a change in scenery, and often we found ourselves anticipating them purely for the opportunity to abandon homework for a few days. Out of their deep respect for our diligence, or perhaps due to a recognition of the futility of assigning homework over a campout weekend, most teachers would send us on our way without any assignments due the following Monday. We were then free to abandon ourselves to complete lethargy, a task which we undertook with vigor.

I suppose that each era of Murree history had its favorite locations. During our era, Kund rose to prominence as the choicest site. Kund was the very tip of the peninsula of land at the confluence of the Indus and Kabul rivers. It was heavily forested, and filled with all types of prickers and brambles to ob-

144

struct easy progress. We had to remain on guard against un-detected thorns in the selection of places to sit or sleep. There were innumerable insects, mice (a reality of the place which the girls were not overly delighted about) and, above all, it was hot. On the Indus side, the shores were rocky beyond description, and we would get sore feet from the sharp edges.

The river was regulated by the spillways at Tarbela Dam some miles upstream, and the level of the river would rise and fall by several feet throughout the day. On the Kabul side there was nothing but a putrid septic mud. There were few of us who showed any interest in the Kabul side for long. Instead, we spent our time wandering among the rocks and stones of the Indus shore. Some of these were huge boulders, almost the size of a house, and when the river was high they provided a sta-tionary object in the midst of a moving and turbulent land-scape. It was a fabulously isolated location—for obvious rea-sons, and only accessible by a barge drawn across the river by cable. The girls enjoyed the freedom to wear swimsuits in broad daylight without drawing a crowd of men to stare at them.

This open display of female anatomy added to the weekend an unparalleled element of tension, and produced dramatic and often comical behavior in the guys. However we might have masked our attitudes, we were at an age where girls, and the pursuit of girls, was one of the primary consuming interests of our world. For this reason, campouts at Kund were looked for-ward to by most all of the guys as a perfect opportunity to enjoy the scenery, and chase women in a circumstance where they couldn't escape far. The other pronounced advantage which Kund held was the glorious mud which collected around the larger boulders in huge and lovely pools. As it turned out, at Kund, I always found women to be an elusive quarry, and the pursuit of them was rife with anxiety and frustration. The mud was invariably a soothing and wonderful escape from these oth-er pressures. It was to this solace, for lack of any better, that the guys would retire by mid afternoon, to cool themselves, and to bond with their fellows.

This was unusual mud, to say the least. The eddies and currents would deposit sediment to depths of four or five feet around the larger rocks, and with some effort, we could work it into a pudding-like texture. If one stood in the middle, and worked both feet alternately up and down, the mud would engulf us up to our necks. The Indus river silt is very fine—not filled with sand and grit—and by early afternoon, with the river at low ebb, there was a veritable paradise of mud pools. It was every man for himself.

Most of the girls loathed the mud as much as they did the mice, and they expressed their distaste in every possible way. The most common of these was simply, "E-E-e-e-w-w, you guys are so gross!" And it always had that inimitable whining delivery that almost made you feel as if you were covered with a putrid slime. Another type of female response was curdling condescension—usually some statement about the maturity level of the wallower. This latter form of response was much harder to bear, since it was a direct attack upon the ego, unlike the former, which was merely an ignorant statement of opinion. As a result, we would find that the girls, in their wanderings about the river bed, sometimes gathered in small groups to express their incomprehension, but mostly they kept a fair distance. It was as if we could hear them saying to one another, off in the distance, "Oh, the guys are doing *that* again."

A few girls eventually dared to enter the mud, but not without encouragement. I believe the first one to do so was Jutta Windszus, who happened to be standing by observing our repose with frequent diatribes on the juvenile nature of our behavior. Of course, under these circumstances, it didn't take long for our scheming little minds to plot a wicked revenge upon her. We immediately emerged from the mud *en mass*, and rushed her. We took great ceremony in swinging her by her arms and legs, and finally hurled her into the middle of a large and well-worked mud pool with an exquisite splat. She took it in stride, and after expressing her great gratitude to us, she took off to clean herself in the river. The objective then became to hunt down and hurl each girl in turn into the mud. This project occupied our interest for much of the rest of the weekend. The task was made more difficult by the fact that some of the girls would deliberately sequester themselves in the rest house, especially once word got out of what we were up to. I do not recall whether we ever got them all that weekend. Somehow I doubt it.

Being covered with mud from head to toe was no small achievement. Nor was it a small task to clean up afterward, especially considering that the river water would clean mud off the outside of swimming trunks, but it took special effort to get it off the inside. On our senior skip weekend, which was also at Kund, we tried a novel approach. All of the guys, together with Paul Mason, the senior class Bible teacher who was there as our chaperon, decided that a skinny dip was appropriate, in broad daylight, no less. We had just finished a foray into the mud pools, and felt that it would be an easier task to clean difficult areas if we had our trunks off. All of the female members of our entourage were napping at the rest house, about half a mile distant, so we calculated it to be relatively safe. Skinny-dipping is something that everyone should do at least once, just to say that they have done it. Mostly it should be done at night, for obvious reasons, but exercise caution if there is a bright moon. Those who are more experienced in this activity will attest to the fact that butt cheeks are highly visible in moonlight, even when submerged. A broad daylight skinny dip, on the other hand, is a brash and dangerous exercise in any situation, and not for the faint-hearted, for there is truly nowhere to hide.

This occasion happened to be my first skinny-dip and I was highly concerned that we might be discovered by someone. My worry faded into surprise at the unique feeling of buoyancy and liberation I began to experience. While I was trying to get used to this sensation, the others discreetly hid my shorts, and then they staged something which I still wake up in a cold sweat remembering. They raised the alarm that the girls were coming toward us, and all began frantically putting their clothes back on. I was in a panic—realizing that my shorts were gone; I didn't want to get out of the water to search for them, but I could hardly remain where I was. The others enjoyed my terror for a minute or so, before they let me know I had been put on.

* * *

Pakistan was an earthy place—often times raw, and harsh. We lived with many things which our American counterparts would certainly regard as crude, and even disgusting. I saw that squeamishness many times on the faces of the kids from the International School of Islamabad. They looked with disbelief, and incredulity at the living conditions which we had to "endure." On the contrary, I far preferred this life on the "visceral edge" than the comfortable existence of the diplomatic community. While at times it created hardships of one type or another (the lack of water for showers, for example), it also added a certain exhilaration, and enhanced the sense of appreciation which I developed for back country adventures and for "roughing it" in general.

My first semester of eighth grade (after my family returned from an extended furlough) was a trauma of transitions —both for me and for the school. Many of the problems of previous semesters still cast their shadow of influence, in the attitudes of students and staff alike. Those problems were from a time in which MCS had seen some unusually difficult situations, and yet they had been dealt with, and put behind. As time went by, I came to enjoy boarding, once I felt I belonged. By my last years, I thrived, and revelled in it. Boarding was never perfect, even in the good times, but neither is the world at large. Despite the difficulties, and the scars which I still carry, I look back on it with a sense that it prepared me very well for later life. I am thankful.

ADOLESCENT ANGST

David Hover, '75

Adolescence is terribly involved with your own ego, so it's not easy to sort out what is David and what is communally MCS. And the emotional undercurrents involved with growing up seem to attach themselves arbitrarily to certain events.

For example, when I first arrived at Sandes Home, I hitched a ride to school on a truck with a group of others. This was strictly forbidden and I felt terrible; so after much heart-searching, I confessed to my boarding parent who clearly didn't want to know. It was my first experience with the diplomatic approach to truth and a step into the adult world of tints of grey. A few years later, when I was hauled up in front of Mr. Roub on suspicion of smoking, I asked him whether he wanted the truth or an acceptable version of the incident. As soon as the words were out of my mouth, I realized with horror that my philosophic honesty was social suicide and so it proved to be.

When I think of it, in fact, this proved a tough social nut to crack throughout the time in MCS high school. Boarding parents and teachers were there to make sure rules were kept. Kids at that age are becoming adults, and rules are useful things to sharpen your teeth on. The usual tacit working relationship between the two is losing (that is, being caught red-handed or being snitched on) and winning. This breaks down when things become a question of open honesty between the two sides. Either you lie, or the person in authority has the uncomfortable choice between punishing you for what you did, or not punishing you to keep your confidence. The two have a tough time coexisting.

* * *

I have no recollection of sexual or social frustration. Surveillance was not that rigid and most discoveries appropriate to my age were possible with a little imagination. Remember the glued-together pages of advertisements in *Time* of girls with wet T-shirts, carefully unglued with as little noise as possible during library periods? That wonderful library: refuge of lovers during various Friday and Saturday night activities, scene of my first kiss in the dark among books, and the touch of a tongue which tasted funny.

In the same vein, Simon and Garfunkel's "Cecilia" was banned—with a general rush to memorize the lyrics (still remembered) before the tapes of *Bridge Over Troubled Waters* were doctored or confiscated.

Days of the Carpenters and Led Zeppelin . . . wild flowers gathered in the woods on the hill between Sandes and MCS for your girlfriend, and toothpaste to cover the smell of a smoke along the walk. The kids from Islamabad who came from another cosmopolitan world but, from my point of view, without creating the slightest desire to be like them.

Grey days are associated with wiping Mr. Murray's chemical bottles clean when he was not throwing bits of chalk at you. Or arriving at school with fingers stiff from the cold and having to pound on the keys of pre-war typewriters in first period (but thank you for teaching me the skill!).

Eleventh grade taught me that I do not have the slightest talent for business, with a run of failures in raising money for the senior banquet: There were badly made ice creams bought from the restaurant opposite the church in Murree; a waffle "restaurant" at the carnival, where we were rapidly submerged by numbers while the volunteer mothers tapped their heels with impatience in the kitchens; and leathery angel food cakes offered at Sports Day . . . Catering was rapidly crossed off the list of my ambitions.

Religiously, my memories are happy ones. I was allowed to work my own way and express my opinions without the slightest pressure. I remember a period of genuine interest in apologetics, and probably spoke pretentiously about it. Literature of all sorts was available, and I discovered Kafka and Camus while I was there from the MCS library. More importantly, perhaps, people were gracious enough to let me, openly not a Christian, co-lead a prayer group with Scott Kennedy. The sum total has been a legacy of religious sensitivity and tolerance which I find uncommon and am deeply grateful for.

*   *   *

My father, a medical doctor working in the Sind, was killed in a head-on collision with a truck while I was in boarding. Those who remember my family from MCS days may wonder how the death of my father affected me (I was eleven at the time). There's not very much to say, really. I wasn't particularly traumatized.

Like many missionary kids, I didn't know my father very well. Apart from a couple of weekends in the summer, the only time I saw him was on the long holidays and even then he was occupied more than full time in the hospital. Quite honestly, I never missed him very much. It was different for my sisters.

I don't know how far his death affected my Christian belief. Adolescent rebellion and intellectual questioning would probably have done the trick anyway. Perhaps early responsibility robbed me of some of my adolescence but then again I managed to fit in long hair, smoking, and the infamous "streak" with Mark Pegors, so I didn't do too badly.

*   *   *

There are regrets. I've been back to Pakistan twice. My Urdu gets tolerant smiles in a country where everyone speaks a handful of languages, and my ignorance of Indo-Pakistani poetry, literature, and history is almost total. I understand that the curriculum is heavy and that adolescents have other things to do, but the sense of MCS's existence seems to be one where such subjects should be compulsory. It's easy, of course, for me to say that in retrospect. While I was there, the staff tried Urdu lessons and I remember kicking against them. But now, going back, there is a shame at how ignorantly Western I managed to be.

ROUB SAHIB

Jonathan Mitchell, '79

Our passage into "Middle Boys" in fourth grade marked the beginning of our fascination with girls which we tried desperately to disguise with a feigned disdain. I went so far as to co-found with Brent Ralston the Anti-Girl Association, or AGA for short. Tim Wilder fashioned a suitable green flag complete with a dagger symbol, and to this the entire troop of us pledged our fealty with a chant remarkably similar to the American pledge of allegiance. This did little to dampen our curiosity, and we would dream up ways to innocently interact with the girls. My favorite method was to head to the woods behind the hostel with David Heaton and Jamie Blanchard to collect skinks. We would return with a jar full of these cute little lizards, wander down to the girls dorm and threaten to sever the skink's tails unless the girls ransomed them. This was a perfect guise: we had a chance to show off, it got the girls angry, and it raised money with which we could pay off our ice cream debts. One term, we got nearly thirty rupees from Maylene Dalton and Elizabeth Blanchard.

But Murree was a small place with a long memory. Years later I was somewhat reluctant to have a "serious" girlfriend. The former president of the AGA was bound to attract some extra razzing when he finally bit the dust. Sunil "Slugger" Lall fell into this trap as well when he declared himself president of the "Sub Club." At Murree we had an elaborate and complex lingo for dating. It was called Sailing. Those who were not so serious were "in harbor" or "near shore," while those more involved were "out on the high seas." The guys were the sailors and the girls were the "boats." The sailors could sail a variety of boats such as tugboats, battleships, or clippers depending on how cute the girl was. In this system everyone at Murree fell into one of three groups. There were the Sailors already described, the Air Force composed of retired sailors, and the Submarine Club made up of those sworn never to sail and whose job was to sink ships. Slugger was the proud president of this club, but was the only member by the time we graduated.

I suspect that everyday life at MCS was more mundane than the impressions I choose to recall, but my memory is selective; it filters out the more miserable side of things, leaving the fonder memories shining brightly. There's always some specific recollection attached to more general routines—like our daily walks to school. The shortcut from Sandes Home through the woods emerged at "King's Cliff" on the road below. In the mornings, we raced down this familiar path, over the rows of neatly-placed stones that formed occasional steps; but at night we groped our way up, doing our best not to trip over these protrusions. On one particular dark night I used my newly-purchased calculator with "8888888888" on the display to make my way up.

I have read about POWs in Vietnam spending their years in captivity building a house nail by nail. In such a situation I would simply relive my years at Murree. I am sure I could last for years on what I have stored up. At the same time, I have complete sympathy for those whose experience tilted their feelings about MCS another direction. I can't say what was "typical," but I know that I was fortunate. For some, leaving Murree was a liberating experience, a chance to leave old molds and set off in new directions.

*   *   *

One might think that in a boarding school situation the significance of one's parents would be somewhat diminished. In fact, the opposite was true. I attribute the bulk of my positive Murree experience to the knowledge that my parents would drop their work immediately and come if I needed them. They told me as much, and I knew they meant it. I now realize that my parents were somewhat unique in this respect. In fact, for some students, it would have taken a serious disaster to drag their parents away from their work. After all, the Lord's work came first and the Lord would take care of the kids, or so the theory went. This type of attitude tarnished the Murree experience for many students. I am convinced that relationships within a child's family and their position in the hierarchy of their parents' priorities had more to do with determining their

Murree experience than any other single factor. The school itself was essentially neutral, you could make what you wanted of your time there.

Parents need to make it clear to their children, who are already confused and insecure—at least at some level—from being "sent away" to boarding, that you will drop everything if they need you, that you will support them to the end even when they are in trouble. While this is not a complete formula for success (I know of no such formulas), it is an indispensable ingredient, and it is what was lacking for many of those who found Murree difficult.

When I look back on my time at Murree, my fondness is not so much for the place but for the people who made it what it was. Maybe my experience was unusual, but I was always much accepted by my friends, and our antics were less adolescent foolishness than revelling in a sense of belonging. Granted, I have lost touch with many MCSers, but I have stayed in contact with a good number as well. They form an extended family and give me a sense of belonging that I now realize is increasingly rare in the modern world.

I was richly blessed (to use an abused phrase) to have been at Murree. Rather than being the rootless MK misfit we were warned about, I am part of something more permanent and meaningful than anything my peers here in the States have ever experienced. I deeply appreciate my time at Murree and I treasure the group to which it afforded me entry. I would not trade it for anything.

*   *   *

We had a very dedicated staff at Murree—not just the Roubs and the Murrays, but many others. I was fortunate to have a succession of fantastic houseparents. Not only did they do their best to nurture us, they made their little homes ours as well. Consider Auntie Inger, in whose one-room kitchen, living room and bedroom we were always welcome; Karl and Shirley Smith who brought all of us model cars from the States and invited us to share in their gunny sack of peanuts; Mark and Joy Jones who took us camping; Wayne and Joy Hildebrand who helped plan our raids; or John and Margaret Sommerville who let us prepare our midnight feasts not only in their kitchen but with their ingredients. These people sacrificed their own privacy to give us a home.

And none more than Jim and Alison Hunter, for whom some of us had little appreciation at the time: As new boarding parents of the Middle Boys and Middle Girls departments they lived with their baby in one of those tiny one-room efficiency apartments designed for the hostel staff—the single ones, that is.

Nor were the teachers any less giving. Most of them taught six or seven classes a day and took turns leading Friday chapel, Sunday School, or Sunday evening singspiration. They were also involved in student council and participated in weekend campouts. After school they would often coach the sports teams. Such a schedule leaves time for little else but school responsibilities. How these people were able to maintain such a pace year in and year out I may never know. And yet maybe I do know. The staff at Murree were a godly group. These people were committed to serving their Lord, and they gave us students everything they had. We did not always get along with all of them, and they often made mistakes. They had to deal with their own failures, insecurities, and weaknesses, but we could not question their dedication or motivation. And we could not know till much later what a significant impact they had on our lives.

* * *

Chuck Roub was principal at MCS for my entire time there. I have many images of Roub Sahib. His driving was wild, he had a way of shifting his weight from leg to leg as he spoke during Friday chapel, and he had a powerful voice. He also had an uncanny ability to uphold the conservative rules of the school without shoving them down our throats. I include the following snippet by way of illustration.

While eyeing the girls and basking in the sun one lunch period, Marty Ketcham and I noticed that the school gates could be lifted off their hinges. Normally one hinge points up and the other down, preventing the theft of the gate, but someone had made a mistake with these. It was, of course, necessary to let Roub Sahib know of this serious weakness in school security, but he was a busy man and merely telling him wouldn't convey the importance of our observation. So we decided to steal them ourselves.

We spent the evening in Charlie's tea shop warming our hands by his cooking fire while we ate his famous omelets and sipped tea. Thus fortified against the cold we headed for school sometime after 10 pm. As usual, Roub Sahib was still in his office, and for a normal raid this would have been a problem, but we were stealth personified as we carted the gates down into the woods. Before we left for our cozy room at Sandes we slid shut the outside bolt on the *chowkidar*'s quarters where he was contentedly snoozing. Of course, this was also in the interest of school security.

The next morning we arrived at breakfast to hear that there had been a robbery at the school. A taxi had been stolen from the tea shop and the thieves had made off with the school gates. The *chowkidar* had made a brave stand but was finally overpowered and locked in his room. This was quite a piece of news. We knew something about the *chowkidar* and the gates, but the taxi business was a bit ominous. Maybe the police would get involved. But we would have to wait to hear of the outcome—Ketcham and I had arranged to ride down to Pindi with the junior high swimming party.

Unfortunately, the robbery rumor had come with another small wrinkle. Roub Sahib was canceling the junior high trip until the perpetrators of this outrage confessed. What a hassle. We would lose precious time taking public transport to Pindi and would have to pay the fare. Finally, though least in importance, the poor little junior high squirts would lose out. We therefore decided to head to school, knock on Roub Sahib's door, and announce our guilt.

He wasn't angry. He sat there behind his desk and apologized for forcing our confession. He knew we were just having fun, and, no, it wasn't a big deal, but there were standards to uphold. And no, he hadn't heard about a taxi being stolen (what a relief!). He then read us a poem which had something to do with someone's bucketfull of patience, energy and goodwill being depleted by friends removing a teaspoon's worth at a time. We had just taken a drop, not much, but his bucket was nearly empty.

We had never given much thought to how our antics affected the staff. We knew Roub Sahib's job wasn't entirely pleasant, and it was certainly possible that his bucket was nearly empty. Maybe the fundies on the board were hassling him again, or possibly some parents were threatening to pull their students from the school because he refused to ban our Beatles tapes.

But, his bucket notwithstanding, Roub Sahib was true to form. He asked us which afternoon we were least likely to be at school and announced that our punishment was to be banned from school for two hours on that afternoon. He then agreed to further delay the junior high bus at Sandes so we could catch a ride down to Pindi.

Following that event, I would have done anything for Roub Sahib. He certainly had a way with people and could turn a sour moment into a treasured memory. And that may be why he was so good at his job.

16

The Hand at the Helm

Charles Roub (1960-1985)

I grew up in Blue Earth, Minnesota, where at age twelve I determined to give my heart to the Lord. It was through the influence of my older sister that I was saved. I joined the Army Air Corps in 1943, when I was nineteen. And it was in Trinidad (then the British West Indies), where I served for two years as a radio operator in the Signal Corps, that I got a firsthand glimpse of missions and clearly felt God's call. Several missionaries of different denominations opened their hearts to me, allowing me to work alongside them. In one of the local churches I taught a Sunday morning Bible study that quickly grew from five or six people to about forty. This period brought great encouragement to me as a Christian and a growing conviction in my heart that, if God would allow me to serve him overseas somewhere, I could never remain in the U.S.

After I was discharged, I went to Bethel College and Seminary in St. Paul, and also began serving a small Baptist church as a student pastor. I studied hard at Bethel and spent many hours in the library. I checked out many reference books, and then one day I checked out the librarian. Eloise and I were married in 1949. We applied to the Conservative Baptist Foreign Mission Society (CBFMS), and arrived in Pakistan at

157

Easter time, 1955. I spent those first years diligently learning Sindhi and trying to comprehend the Muslim mind and faith. I had gotten my bachelor's degree in education and had a real desire to teach kids, but also desired to be faithful to God's call. Nevertheless, I was just unhappy in "Muslim evangelism," and when the new school for missionaries' children needed an English teacher, I made known my readiness to come. The board acted on that offer, and to our amazement voted to ask me to come as principal.

That summer (1958) we returned home to the States for an eighteen-month furlough in order for me to complete a master's degree in Education Administration. I finished my thesis on the ship returning to Pakistan and we arrived at Murree Christian School in February 1960 with our two small children, Ron and Becky. (I was thirty-six years old at that time, an average of five or six years older than my colleagues.) I took over as principal from Don Calderwood when the Calderwoods left for furlough in June 1961. MCS was five years old.

On the first day of the new school year my first official act was to hook my jeep on to the front of the bus, which wouldn't start in the rain by rolling it down the hill, and towing the thing until it finally did start. Up to that day, Don Calderwood had always managed the bus so easily, it seemed to me (Help, help—Don, come back!).

Two of the high points of my time at MCS were the first graduation in 1964 and the completion of the new hostel on the school grounds in 1965. The occupation of the hostel was delayed by war between India and Pakistan that year and I was on furlough (home assignment) in the U.S. when it opened. Enrollment over the years ranged from a peak of 185 just before the war in '71 to a little over a hundred. When Pakistan lost Bangladesh [East Pakistan] in 1971 we lost a lot of students.

Participation in inter-school sports meets—flag football, field hockey, basketball, soccer—and student council conventions with other Western international schools was good for MCS students. But it was a real pain getting visas and re-entry visas for athletes going to India, and on one occasion a staff member's briefcase containing all the kids' passports was stolen! (The passports were never found. Presumably they brought someone a good price, to be altered and used by others, and some of them probably furnished free passage to terrorists.)

MCS joined the South Asia Inter-School Association (SAISA) in 1973, but for some years prior to that we had been holding athletic contests with the American school in Pindi, which later moved to Islamabad.

The kids at MCS seemed to get confused between April Fool's Day and Halloween, playing pranks and conducting mischief both times. Among the senior high boys, practical jokes were not limited to any special occasion, and these surprise "raids"—often involving firecrackers, and usually at the expense of the senior high girls—soon became an MCS tradition, despite official sanctions against them. Sometimes these middle-of-the-night escapades became very annoying to administration and staff—especially when the Pakistani army thought we were shooting each other, or that two groups of soldiers had gotten into a fire fight. Sometimes they were just plain funny, but often it took me longer than most to see the humor of it! Sometimes I never could.

Our relations with the army were usually quite friendly, especially so with the officers. In the early days we were allowed to drive our jeep into the compound, go to the barracks and hold Bible classes for the Christian soldiers, who often brought their Muslim buddies. That changed as anti-American sentiments and anti-foreign attitudes increased. Christian army officers were a blessing to us. A Christian station commander (the highest official in Murree) got us the permit to build the hostel; otherwise, it may never have been built!

Local bureaucrats could be a problem sometimes. Relationships ranged from the president of the Murree municipality one summer asking the Christian missionary community to entertain at the centennial celebration of the establishment of Murree (or some such occasion) to the man in the same office sometimes denying permission for the school bus to go to Murree in the afternoon. The chief officer of the Cantonment Board gave verbal permission to build at Sandes, and for a time we seemed to be just one step away from losing the entire newly renovated building because we didn't have a permit. That was in God's hands, too. But when we were days away from the dedication of the new Sandes building, and finally confronted the station commander about the permit, and still didn't have the permit to build in the first place, it seemed pretty dicey.

*   *   *

Recruiting staff was always a fun thing and, at the same time, very trying and challenging. The school was so organized financially that if a person would sign on to come for three years, the school could finance the term independently. In those days most of our staff were mission-supported teachers and boarding staff sent out by the various missions to do that ministry. When I left in November 1985, there were twenty missions affiliated with the school. Like the staff and student body, they were based in many countries: England, Scotland, Wales, the United States, Canada, Finland, Norway, Sweden, Germany, New Zealand—to name a few. Virtually all recruiting was done by letter, but there was another very effective way. Missionaries on "home assignment" (it was called furlough until the 1980s) found and recruited staff on their regular deputation rounds. I found my successor to the office of principal while on a short home assignment.

I remember the great work the Holy Spirit did in all our lives. The common ground amongst staff was always Christ—and our relationship to each other through him. We used to have some pretty rough staff meetings, but we could always talk things out and when we left a meeting, no matter how "hot" it may have gotten, we left as friends. The few staff members who could not buy that philosophy left very quickly—either because they'd "had enough" or because the board eventually asked them to leave. The latter happened *very seldom,* praise be.

What kind of issues were controversial or caused tension in staff meetings? Definitely not doctrine. All of our staff knew Jesus Christ as Savior and all of us were agreed that he and his atoning death on the cross for us was the central issue. If we had unity on anything, it was our faith. And we were pretty solidly united that our purpose was to work and plan for the welfare of the students, not the staff! We didn't care if our brothers or sisters baptized by immersion or by sprinkling, infants or adults, as long as they loved Jesus. We didn't care if our fellow staff members liked to dance or see a movie or drink alcoholic beverages, so long as they loved Jesus. We were not, in that sense, legalists.

The kinds of things that caused controversy among the staff were: 1) the amount of homework some teachers gave; 2) the conduct of study halls, in the library or in the evenings; 3) the kind of music the kids were listening to; 4) student dress, specifically for the girls—for example, covering tops, short dresses—all this mainly caused by the need for sensitivity to the Muslim culture in which we lived; 5) curriculum—the introduction of British courses of study, necessary for GCE students but a burden to American students; 6) lines of responsibility between teaching and boarding; and 7) the number of school days required in a school year. Other staff might remember other issues as the major ones.

I have been asked, "How is it that a conservative evangelical culture—almost, in fact, a fundamentalist one—came to dominate at MCS?" I never know whether to boast or plead guilty! The description does seem to be used in a pejorative sense; I think the word "dogmatic" was also used. But there is another word missing from this context—a word I like even less than some of the others, but one that probably describes our greatest shortcoming in the early years of MCS: legalism. I think legalism describes one of the negative aspects of fundamentalism. While legalism was not our aim at MCS, I'm sure the rules and guidelines often created that aura or feeling. I speak now of the kind of legalism St. Paul hits on in his letter to the Galatians—a list of dos and don'ts that, if obeyed, makes one a Christian, or a better Christian. While I don't think we ever taught this per se at MCS, having always been very clear that salvation is of grace not of works, I do think that at times our students may have read this from the rules and the ways in which they were enforced. I have a deep regret for errors in communication, of which I must have been a part, that conveyed this impression. I do not regret my conservative, almost fundamentalist position at all, because I think it was far closer to the heart of God than what the world has today, even the Christian world.

But back to the question of how this position came to dominate at MCS. I can see at least four factors:

1. It is simply a matter of majority rule. In 1956, the vast majority of parents involved with starting the school wanted it that way! Or at least, their elected representatives to the formation of the school, those who spoke for the parents, wanted it that way.

2. It would be fair to characterize the Conservative Baptists and TEAM as conservative evangelical missions, and that

label fits the overwhelming majority of their members. It would *not* be fair to say that all the blame (or credit) for the dominant attitudes exhibited at MCS lies at the door of these two missions. In the other missions, especially as time went on and other faith missions joined the school, there was still a strong, if not overwhelming, majority of the missionaries who were characterized by the same conservative evangelical positions. And some of them held a far more strict code of conduct than I, a Conservative Baptist, held in terms of what Christians should do or couldn't do. Would you believe the number of letters I received from parents who felt our rules at MCS were too liberal? No particular missions held sway, although of course in board meetings their voice was more clearly heard if they had four representatives on the board instead of only one. That simply means, as you can understand from representative government, that they were speaking for four times as many people.

3.   The conservative culture came to dominate at MCS also because we were operating in a conservative society. One of our conservative rules had to do with the dress code for girls. That was a sore point, especially for the girls, and for their sympathetic friends. We could not see in those days, and we cannot see today, how we could possibly allow our girls to be about in the bazaar in short, short skirts, or without the protecting *dopatta* over their shoulders, to bear out modesty. It would have been offensive to our Pakistani neighbors (and sometimes was) and dangerous for the girls themselves because of the message it would have sent! Similarly, it was easy to go along with a no-movie rule when all of us missionaries were regularly treated to such comments from our Pakistani friends as "Look at the kind of stuff you Americans send to us in the English language movies you export to Pakistan; we are being invited by America to live like the people in these movies." As Christian missionaries, the parents of most of our school kids were there to demonstrate a Christian lifestyle, not one that allowed more "looseness"—as Pakistanis saw looseness—than did Islam itself. We weren't extremists. We never required or suggested that the girls wear *burkas.*

4.   Religious conservatism came to dominate at MCS also because I was the principal for twenty-five years. I was, and am, a conservative. I have never felt, since I was twenty or so, that all movies are sinful or wrong. I have always felt, however, that there was enough potential danger in and out of Holly-

wood that the Christian ought to be wary. As you know, the content of popular movies is currently a major controversy in America; it is not just a missionary, or a conservative Christian, issue. Granted, most of the junk in movies today did not appear in movies in the '50s, but we saw stuff there that we did not like and we knew that in the '60s and '70s it would be increasing.

Today I read that estimates go as high as thirty to fifty percent of kids from evangelical Christian homes are sexually active in high school years, and even in junior high. Conservative Christians believe that sexual intercourse before marriage is wrong—and that our kids should be protected from that which is sin. You don't have to be conservative to figure out that what kids are fed through their eyes, what they listen to in their music, and what they engage in on the dance floor certainly influences them to go all the way sexually (as just one illustration). While few "evangelical" Christians are as conservative today as they were in the 1950s, there is even greater need in our time to ground our children in basic Christian values.

Admittedly, it's hard to get the balance right. My early Christian life was shaped by a Christian subculture in the Midwest that was very legalistic and probably too strict, but it suited my nature. I was guilty of having too many "don'ts" in my philosophy and I tended to place consistent Christian living parallel to salvation by faith, rather than following it.

This confusion was understandably misconstrued at MCS; part of the misconstruing was our fault, and sounded like legalism. In some cases it was. But it kept a lot of us from outright sin because we had lines we would not cross and boundaries we would not transgress. Today, the boundary lines are not clearly drawn. Kids are asked to make decisions for themselves they cannot wisely make, and then they live with all kinds of consequences. I will stand with "too much" guidance before I will with "too much" freedom of choice.

There were only two major discipline problems that I remember dealing with: experimenting with drugs, and offenses that left a bad taste in the mouths of our Pakistani hosts. There was the running-away problem, but that only happened a couple of times. Infractions were handled in consultation with the vice principal and the boarding staff involved, which still didn't mean we always got it right. I remember only once that I made an arbitrary, unconsulted decision concerning a student who got drunk at an inter-school convention. Even now, I see it as a major error on my part. I didn't always agree with the treatment we meted out, but I always tried to be faithful in administering whatever punishment we did decide on, and with students and parents alike, always owned any decision as my own.

I do want to speak a moment in favor of suspension from school for "major" offenses. In almost every incident I can remember, the suspension worked for the good of the family. The parents appreciated having the kids home for the extra week or month, almost like a holiday. They did things together; parents found themselves listening to their children. Consequently, the parents were able to bring back helpful criticism of the way we on the staff had managed the situation, or the things leading up to it. The kids found out their parents cared. Sometimes they found out their parents sympathized with them; they learned new truths about authority; and both parents and kids learned how to communicate better.

*   *   *

I have many fond memories of MCS, and they are much more prominent in my mind—and, I think, the reality—than my errors or the hardships we all faced. I will just mention some of them in closing. Any given class marching down the church aisle in their baccalaureate service, and down the aisle in the school for their graduation (I've always felt sorry for those MCS students who couldn't be there to share that moments with us). The long winters, especially in the early years when we were the only family in Murree, when we could do the winter's work at a relaxed pace and have time for each other as a family. The completion of our hostel at school, the first major building program, which included the staff housing at Sandes. Some of the "Spiritual Emphasis" weeks or weekends, when we saw God working in our lives and in the lives of our students (and sometimes, staff!). Summers in Murree, when all the parents were there, bringing with them their own ministries; the Murree Convention, and Sundays at Holy Trinity Church where missionaries (and other Western community members) worshipped together, heard great messages, and talked about their work all over the country—and at the school. And, of course, I always cherished news that our alumni were continuing on to serve and live for the Lord.

The Lord's call for alumni to return to Pakistan as missionaries seems particularly strong; some of our graduates have gone as missionaries to other countries as well. In 1992 and 1993 there were at least twenty-five former MCS students serving in Pakistan as missionaries or in "tentmaking" professions (witnessing to their faith while employed in a secular occupation). The debate rages on as to the pros and cons, the good and evils, of boarding schools. I tend to see the positive side of boarding. In many cases, life-long friendships were formed during grade school. Several of the romances begun at Murree Christian School ended in marriage. And the many reunions are one exhibit of the lasting relationships formed at boarding school.

More than 110 former students—about ten percent of the total MCS alumni—have been involved in at least short-term overseas mission work in thirty countries.

17

Glennis Brown's School Days

Glennis Brown Fields (1970-1974)

My first recollections of MCS can be summed up in three words: *cold, damp,* and *cramped.* Without central heating, even the mild winters were sharp, demanding layers of clothing to keep warm. The classrooms, in the old stone church, had tall but very narrow windows and the thick walls kept the sun from penetrating into the room unless it was able to shine directly into the window opening. Even electric lights never seemed to brighten these small rooms with their high ceilings. Kerosene heaters took the chill off a small area around them, but they were never sufficient to warm the whole room. During the summer and warmer months we had classes outside where it was much more pleasant. During the monsoons, the damp penetrated even the thick stone walls and one never seemed to completely dry out.

When I first saw those black monsoon clouds rolling down the mountainside, I was sure a horrible fire was about to engulf us. Nothing was as it seemed. A thousand unspoken formalities, one by one harmless and incidental, sometimes even humorous, were straw on the camel's back. I remember the simple pleasure of eating lunch at the staff picnic table and seeking out the sun to enjoy our afternoon tea. And I remember getting

166

scolded, good naturedly, for stepping into someone else's "sun rights."

There were people everywhere, big and little, loud and subdued, harsh and gentle. Students of all ages inhabited all the corners of the compound; one had little if any privacy or quiet solitude. With the lack of space both inside and outside, the cold and damp seemed to take on a presence of its own, like an unwanted companion.

My first night at MCS was spent with the Huffakers, who were in charge of boarding. I was pleasantly awakened in the morning with a cheerful, "Good morning, Auntie," from little David who was then about four years old. Being single, this familial appellation never ceased to cheer me.

The morning after my arrival the acting principal, Irv Nygren, sent word that he would like to see me down at the school office. Rather than getting a guided tour, which I rather expected, he said, "I know you would like to get right into the classroom. When do you want to start? Tomorrow morning?"

I stumbled over the words that I heard myself say, "No, I would like a few days to roam around, get acquainted, and get my jetlag readjusted." The matter was quickly and abruptly settled when I became very ill—no doubt the combination of weariness and dysentery, a malady better known at MCS as a "bad belly." I wanted to die. I knew no one; I felt helpless, alone, and anything but a missionary teacher. I lived in the staff housing just below Sandes, under the Murrays. Isabel Murray brought me cups of tea and snacks, God bless her; but for her cheery face and cups of tea I think I would have gone into a state of complete despair. Somehow I did recover, not to teach, but just in time to head south for three months of language study during the winter break.

While my health improved dramatically in the warmer climate, I continued to feel very isolated trying to adjust to a new situation and a new country, especially as a single woman in an Islamic culture. I met very few people from my own mission—the Roubs were home on furlough the year I arrived—and everyone seemed so well settled into their routines.

I came to Pakistan as an English teacher, well-trained and experienced, but even in my job it seemed that I was on my own. As the new kid on the block, I became the unsuspecting object for jobs that the old-timers did not want or had done and realized the pitfalls. I was young, eager to work and eager to please, and that is how I became student council advisor. I became the buffer for the students between Irv Nygren and Dale Huffaker who did not see eye to eye philosophically. So I took some good bumps from both sides and was often hard put to explain to the students why we were not making much progress with their ideas or projects and still maintain their level of respect for these men who were in charge!

My other extra-curricular assignment was director of the annual school play. I had limited experience with drama, but in the States we had had great success with the play *Harvey*. Naturally, I chose something familiar. This was the story of a brother and sister who lived together. The sister was very high-strung and nervous; the brother was kind, gentle and low-keyed, but had developed the hallucination of a huge white rabbit that he called Harvey and with which he had conversations. The sister tried to get her brother into an institution. Her presentation of herself led the authorities to believe that she was the one who needed admitting. So they whisk her away, strip off her clothes—"off stage," of course—and give her the cold sheet treatment. In the meantime, Elmer Dowd, her brother, and the niece come looking for her. One of the attendants makes a pass at the niece, or tries to. The final crunch comes when the rabbit must be condemned to Hell in order for Elmer to be free of it.

The kids thought it was great. Irv had a copy of the play and had given his approval. We started rehearsals—my having no idea that with this play I was about to run afoul of the traditions at MCS. Parents and other missionaries arrived on the hill for the summer and things began to boil over. The first sign of trouble must have been in the form of questions from some of the parents whose children where in the play. When Irv came to me and asked me what I thought I was doing, I had no idea what he was talking about.

When he finally got specific, I said that I didn't think I was doing anything except putting on the school play. There were objections, he said: first the sexual innuendoes when the attendant tries to touch the niece, which never actually happens; then there was the trouble of the sister being admitted and having her clothes removed—which also doesn't really happen! The final problem was the word "Hell." I told Irv that it was not used in swearing, but rather was naming the place. If this were deleted, the play would lose its punch line, or one of them.

Then the girl who played the niece wanted to drop out. Another single missionary teacher came to me and asked me if I realized what a furor I was causing on the hill (around Murree); everybody was talking about the play. I had no idea, but was beginning to get the message not only that the play was unacceptable, but also the director. What to do! Then Irv came through during a rehearsal and heard the word Hell; he about came unglued. I thought I might be sent back to the USA, persona non grata!

By this time I was getting the sounds of the buzzing on the hill. Yet throughout all this, not one adult came and discussed the matter with me. I decided that I had to do something before I was run out of Murree. I went to Irv and offered to stop the play and can the project. I also pointed out that there would not be time to do another: scripts had to be ordered from the States, and here we were already half way through the summer. Irv said he could think of more reasons to continue than to quit. So I asked for his support, and continued.

I grew more and more apprehensive as time for production drew near. I told the kids that I would sit in the audience, at the side door aisle, and they could come get me if they needed me backstage. The truth was that I was scared, and if things got bad I was going to make a fast exit. I tried to maintain a calm exterior, and we went into final rehearsals.

The night of the performance came and the house was packed. I had no idea what to expect. I sat in my escape seat, turned a little to the side so I could watch audience responses. The curtain rose and we were off. The atmosphere seemed pretty stiff to me, perhaps it was my own tension. Gradually, as the play proceeded, there were a few chuckles. Dr. Bavington, bless his heart, caught all the humorous irony on psychiatry. I think his enjoyment of the play broke the ice, at least for me. I began to breath a little easier. Then the cast began to get some open laughter. When the curtain fell there was solid and well-earned applause. I didn't run. Folks came to me afterward and said, I don't understand what everyone was so upset about!

I was allowed to direct one more play. I chose *The Family that Nobody Wanted,* about a calm family who adopted children from different nationalities. It lacked humor and zest. The kids felt that I had sold out. After it was performed I had only one person come to me and tell me that it was the kind of play that was wanted at MCS. When I was relieved of drama duty I didn't know if I was happy or sad. Some of both, I guess.

* * *

It has often been said that Pakistan, along with the other Islamic countries, is the hardest place in the world for a woman to be a missionary. As I read the various accounts of being a teacher at MCS—Ms. Fields' experience was not unusual—I wondered if, in fact, the staff had a more difficult time than those of us who knew the school, for all its limitations, as home. They were not accustomed to such a homogenous community— eating, worshipping, working, fellowshipping, and socializing with the same two dozen people—and sometimes the sense of claustrophobia could become quite acute.

Surrounded by a larger culture that required the segregation and seclusion of women, female staff at MCS experienced a double isolation. For all its religious highmindedness, MCS was like any small town, and not immune to gossip, petty alliances, and rigid social expectations. For example, single women who violated convention (usually unknowingly) and spoke to men after church, and not just to other missahibs, were sometimes labelled "husband-hunters."

Several staff members experienced severe depression during their time at MCS. And, of course, in that highly-charged religious environment, this "ailment" was usually accompanied and complicated by a lot of spiritual confusion. That senior staff members sometimes questioned the calling of newcomers already struggling with a variety of circumstantial difficulties, didn't help matters. Recent medical evidence identifying some of the chemical compounds present with Murree's infamous "tummy troubles" (hepatitis, amoebic dysentery) as the same ones linked to clinical depression should stimulate some new thoughts about that aspect of the experience.   —PAS

"When I first came out I think I felt a little apologetic about whether this was 'real' missionary work. It's hard to stand in front of your home church and say that as a missionary you're going to teach missionary children. But now I understand the importance of this work to the work in Pakistan. It is vital. So many missionaries wouldn't be here if it weren't for Murree."

—Karen Hicks, *SIMNow*, n.d. (c. 1990)

18

The Tree of Knowledge, the Fruit of Grace

Auntie Eunice had a lovely singing voice. She was pretty and always cheerful—the kind of woman a little boy wants to marry when he grows up. She may have been the closest thing to Pollyanna I ever met in real life, but for all her Christian earnestness, it was Auntie Eunice who taught us to sing "The Little Dutch Boy." I still remember the chorus:

> Oh Mister, Mister Johnny Rebeck, how could you
> be so mean?
> Now all the neighbors' cats and dogs will never
> more be seen
> They'll all be ground to sausage meat in Johnny
> Rebeck's machine!

We gleefully sang such ditties to pass the time on bus trips to 'Pindi, grateful for the change from the usual Sunday School choruses. Adding an exotic touch to her sweetness, it was rumored that she had a brother who was a movie star. Indeed, it turned out that one of her half-brothers is Arthur Hill, who starred in "Moment to Moment," "The Andromeda Strain," and other films. Auntie Eunice also taught us that wonderful hiking

172

song, "The Happy Wanderer" ("I love to go a-wandering along the mountains tracks. . ."), a graceful melody that hauntingly captured both the peace and the exuberance of the mountains we so loved. —PAS

Eunice Hill (1963-64, 1967-)

I came out to Pakistan in 1963 as a student from Westmont College in Santa Barbara, California. It was the Peace Corps era and very exciting to be in the first group from my college to go overseas. I was only twenty-three years old, and fifteen months in Pakistan at that time was a real adventure. The first thing I learned to do in my new room at Sandes was call over the back veranda—in Urdu—for hot water from the *bhishti.* It was good that I learned because after the first summer of teaching second grade I had little girls for boarding in that same area of Sandes. Every Friday we rolled back the rug and moved furniture to allow for six tin tubs, and the *bhishti* carried up hot water for twenty-three little girls' baths. It wasn't unusual for someone to complain that water was going through the floor boards onto the piano in the room below.

I had planned on teaching missionaries' kids since I was eighteen, when I'd asked a missionary from Brazil about needs—wondering whether to take up teaching or nursing. He mentioned specific needs at MK schools. It made sense to me, because I had spent three years at a Christian boarding school (Caronport High School) in Saskatchewan after my parents died. I'd been in classes with missionaries' kids who had been separated from their parents because of the lack of facilities in the host country.

I'd only been in Pakistan a matter of weeks when I was very ready to consider MCS long-term and hoping Brazil would find another teacher. I had such a sense of peace that this was where I was to be. I found out later that Grace Pittman, a Westmont alum working in Pakistan, got news of Westmont's short-term missionary program the same day a letter from Chuck Roub arrived telling of the need for a teacher at MCS for the summer of 1963. She stapled the letters together, sent them back to Chuck suggesting the program at Westmont might have an answer.

As I passed the bulletin board on the way to an English class in college I read Chuck's request for a teacher for MKs in Murree. I was so excited, I talked about it all through the English class. And now here I was! I started attending TEAM prayer meetings because my father had been legal advisor to the mission years before, so I had a natural interest there. I filled out my application papers for TEAM while on the short term project, went back for my senior year at Westmont, and after graduation drove straight to Candidate School in Illinois. I was back in Pakistan by the next April, 1966.

When I was twelve my dad died fairly suddenly of a heart attack. He was a barrister who had been in politics, but whose life was turned upside down when he realized forgiveness in Jesus. His last few years were filled with preaching, working with prisoners and ex-cons, starting churches, and helping to administer mission boards. My mom had had cancer the year before Dad died and it recurred within months after his death; she died a year later. Her calm response to the stress of that year, with two teenage girls, probably did more to persuade me of the reality of God than anything. She was convinced that if God took her he would care for us. He did.

I had come to Westmont after teaching in Winnipeg for two years, and although I had loved the six months as a boarding mother during that first stint at MCS, I had only considered teaching as my role on the mission field. After coming back with TEAM I began language study in Abbottabad and was dying to get back to Murree. I was due to start teaching in September 1967 after language training. I'd be taking over for Margaret Cunningham, the fifth and sixth grade teacher, when she went on furlough. This was a frightening thought, as I'd gotten to know Margaret and she'd be a hard act to follow!

In the spring the school had another of its staffing emergencies and I was thrilled to come up to twenty-seven little girls in boarding, even though I was just recovering from hepatitis. There had been many changes in boarding that year and it was Betty Ralston—one of the moms—who stopped me one day to ask if I'd ever consider staying in boarding. She saw it as a more crucial need for continuity than the classroom. I talked to Chuck Roub the next day and we both agreed to pray for a teacher, if I were to remain in boarding, or that a permanent housemother for the little girls would be provided, if not. The teacher came and I've been "Auntie" Eunice ever since.

I had first- through third-grade girls for the first thirteen years and then, as numbers dropped and Auntie Inger went to Bach Hospital to work, I had the younger boys as well. In 1977 numbers were back up and Patty Irwin came out to help for a year. I had ten lovely quiet little girls and seventeen very lively, delightful little boys. There was no question as to which I should turn over to Patty. I'm so glad she was a former "cherub" of mine or it would have been very hard to part with the girls. Within a year, though, I realized I had much more emotional energy and was able to see the switch as a real gift to me as I got older.

I've been with little boys for more than twenty years now, and they give a lot! Teaching kindergarten in the summer gives me a real change in schedule and a chance to meet new families as well as keep up with alumni visits. I am blessed!

* * *

There have been so many rewards in meeting up with "our kids" again as adults—over coffee in my room here at the school, or *chai* down the road, but also around the world: praying with a former student in a Finnish sauna; laughing over memories while going through an Australian zoo; visiting with kids in Britain, the United States, Canada, New Zealand, and Europe.

Often traveling together, Debby Rupe and I have been able to share in alumni weddings, college plays they've been in, winning college elections, and trips back to Pakistan with spouses and families and grandparents. We've had the privilege, too, of praying with them and sharing times of pain and tears of healing—for us as well. If I ever wrote a book of philosophy on being a boarding parent, a large chapter would be "Mistakes I've Made." We haven't done everything right! The encouraging thing now is I know there is forgiveness and God has made provision for those mistakes. I would have quit otherwise!

In the early years at MCS my own lack of understanding as to my acceptance in Jesus contributed a lot to my mistakes. I was very much into performing well and having everything "put together." Unfortunately, little children are not created to make us feel successful. It's taken me years to realize my need to ask God to show me the genuine worth of each child (not try to fake it) and then also ask him to help me create the kind of atmosphere where those lovely qualities can be developed. I've had to ask forgiveness of adults that I feel I hadn't accepted as children, especially some who had my problems: Because I'm not particularly tidy, somehow the children couldn't be too messy; I hadn't accepted that part of myself. Now I can say, "We have the same problem."

I also allowed some children to feel very rejected, without ever meaning to, when I allowed them to pull away after a punishment. I now realize that when a small child acts like she doesn't want a goodnight kiss after a punishment it's not sulking as much as needing the adult to move closer.

The missionary parents have enriched our lives so much by sharing their grown kids with us, even on precious visits back when time was limited. They've also been our best teachers and friends. I'm so glad that at MCS we have three months together in the summer, when the parents are in Murree for language school or vacation. In talking to staff from other boarding schools I realize how fortunate we've been to have such contact with the families. Visiting children in their homes on the plains during the winter break has also given a rich perspective. I took this for granted until I observed that some missionary schools are very isolated from the families they serve.

With the new, culturally-sensitive attitudes toward missions, some people are uncomfortable with so many Westerners gathering in a former colonial hill station. But having basically one place where missionaries go during the summer, a unique circumstance of Pakistan, has contributed immensely to the remarkable unity we have among so many diverse missions and denominations.

When Sarah DeHart Raiter (who had been one of my little cherubs) came back from Australia for the grandparents to see baby Joel for the first time, Don and Garnett DeHart let us know the time of the flight and Deb and I were right there behind them at the airport sharing in such a very precious meeting. Sarah's brother, Joel, was in my second-grade class when I taught the summer of 1964 as a short-termer. After graduating from MCS, he returned to work with Afghans and in 1991 was taken hostage by the Mujahadin. Sitting in devotions with another generation, around a kerosene heater, and praying for "Uncle Joel" in captivity was a privilege, but the real excitement came after his release when he returned to school to tell the kids of God's faithfulness. Now Joel DeHart has published a book, *The Upper Hand,* about that experience.

I have many "grandchildren" at MCS. In the summer of 1993 I had five second-generation MKs in my kindergarten class: Larry Cutherell's Tricia, Luke Cutherell's twin boys, Eric Pulliam's Corey, and Dale Stock's Esther. Luke's four boys have all been with me in kindergarten or boarding. I have Nate and Marty Irwin's son Tim in boarding at present. Tim is sitting at my side reading as I write this. A third grader, he's older than some of the rest and comes back to my room to read when the others are asleep.

I had Sarah DeHart as a six-year-old and later, when she was a senior, she became the monitor for my little boys. At that time I was praying with a young Australian English teacher who was very interested in her. He didn't let her know his feelings until a few years later, and when they were married in Murree Deb Rupe and I got to be bridesmaids. Mike and Sarah Raiter are now missionaries in Pakistan and their little boy Joel started boarding with me this fall. My first fall at MCS I held Esther Cutherell as a toddler during the groundbreaking for the hostel. I've now lived in that building for over twenty-five years. Esther went through MCS and came back to work at Abbottabad Christian School as a short-termer.

In 1988 Deb and I had a great trip with Esther to Malaysia for a conference on boarding schools. This was an area conference, sponsored by Dalat school in Penang, that grew out of the International Conferences on Missionary Kids (ICMK). We went with the request from our staff to find out two things: 1) How and where do you find good boarding staff? and 2) How do you keep boarding staff long term? All the schools were asking the same questions, but the others were desperate. Morrison Academy in Taiwan, which, with 550 students, was at that time the largest MK school in the world, had a total turnover of boarding staff that year. A board member had brought a new staff member to the conference.

The Roubs' long-term influence gave a stability to MCS that can't be underestimated. As principal, Chuck Roub kept a very busy but pretty satisfied staff. We had a sense of doing something bigger than just teaching or running a boarding hostel. We were serving a whole community and, above all, the Lord Jesus.

The ICMK conferences have been a terrific encouragement

to schools like ours. Stew Georgia [principal of MCS 1985-1993] and I were sent to the first one in Manila (1984). This conference in Manila was an explosion of learning for me. It brought form and substance to years of perceptions and instincts I had developed about our kids. Whereas I had spent years visiting kids struggling with their return to their "home" countries and felt guilty that somehow we were failing them, I came to realize that the problem of re-entry and of being a "TCK" (Third Culture Kid) was a much larger experience. No matter where they grew up or who their parents worked for, the children of expatriates shared a remarkably similar profile of traits and issues, skills and struggles. Studies had showed that transition back to the "home culture" carried with it normal problems— and that positive learning could take place in pain. It wasn't all just happening in our little school in the mountains of Pakistan.

In 1987, Deb Rupe, the Georgias, and I attended the second ICMK in Quito, Ecuador (where we met up with former students Joy Salmon and Joyce Bavington). Phil Billing, the Murrays, and John Brockman went to the Kenya ICMK (Nairobi, 1989). Deb and I also made it to Euro Comet (Holland, January 1992)—for a serious look at the specific problems of European MKs in our American-type boarding schools. We were reminded how important it is to make sure our European kids keep up with their language. And re-entry problems are a bit more severe in areas of Europe where it can be harder for young people to find supportive Christian fellowship. Unemployment seemed to be more acute for families returning to the U.K.

I've also come to appreciate how much MCS has benefited from the British involvement. I remember the tension at our first PTA meetings between what the British and the Americans wanted. The British had more formal ideas about school (wearing uniforms, a school crest, rules of discipline, and so forth), but their attitude toward religion was more informal. They could wear jeans to church; they liked jazzy music (I know Ian Murray did). The British saved us from legalistic fundamentalism. I look at other MK schools that are all American and they are so repressive. Americans are far more conformist than the British.

* * *

As far as doubts in my job, there certainly have been wobbly times, much self-doubt, but the most serious was after the first ten years. I remember thinking, *In Winnipeg* (where I started teaching) *they move teachers on to different schools after ten years: Should I consider going? Why am I here? Is it just because I'm happy? Am I vegetating?* In the middle of that summer I opened my journal in panic. I'd overscheduled and I couldn't see how I was going to meet commitments. I was teaching kindergarten in the morning, twelfth grade economics in the afternoon, and helping Isabel Duncan direct *Pygmallion* in the evening. And we had guests I'd promised to show around. When I saw the last entry in my journal—"Am I vegetating?"—it was as if the Lord said, "Relax. I can stretch you here and I'll let you know when to go."

Another hard time was in 1973 when all my support people seemed to be leaving at once: the two I had my days off with, the family I came out to Pakistan with, and my prayer partner. I remember really crying out to God that he would have to show me he was meeting my needs. Before leaving Westmont that first summer I was lying on my top bunk praying with such excitement and gratitude. I remember saying, "God, if you'll let me work with missionaries' kids, I'll gladly be single." Now, marriage—having one stable support person—looked very attractive. But God has been so faithful in meeting my needs that I've come to trust him in this area, too.

That fall he did it in an amazing way. Three new people to the boarding staff joined me for a day off. We had such fun we called it the "Thursday Off Club." Within days of that, the new administrator called me in to ask if I'd pray with her each day, and a new teacher arrived from Winnipeg. No one person was replaced, but God had met each need.

Two years later Debby Rupe arrived. I'm sure one reason I've been so happy here long-term has been her consistent friendship and encouragement. Deb is committed enough to the growth of others that I can share frustrations honestly and we can pray together without feeling disloyal. Deb is also very good about keeping the kids' confidences and they know it, so sometimes our prayers are general with only her knowing the specifics. One of the biggest gifts to MCS has been Deb Rupe's

Mom and Dad. They gave her such a loving and secure home
that she's had a very unusual consistent love to pass on, even
to some kids at a fairly hard stage of life. Deb always under-
stands that when kids are sometimes at their unloveliest is
when they need love the most.

*   *   *

*I will always remember Debby Rupe—a godly example,
wonderful house-mother and, best of all, a true friend. Deb truly
cared about each one of us and was sensitive to us as individuals. Ever ready with a cup of coffee, she took time to listen
to us, to our joy and our sadness. Her door was always open and
we'd sometimes hang out in her room late at night, arguing
with Deb about the no dancing rule, or skirt lengths, or how late
seniors could stay up. We tried our best to give her a hard time,
but usually she just threw back her head and laughed at us.*

*One thing Deb was known for was her alter ego—Bill
Skitch. She would slip out of the room and a minute later Bill
would appear. He looked remarkably like Deb, except for his
buck teeth and black moustache. He would always say, "Where's
that cute Debby Rupe? I love her more than life itself!" Then he
would go off in search of Deb, who would soon reappear as herself. When we told her Bill had been there she would be so disappointed. He was the love of her life, but she had never had the
chance to meet him!*

—*Amy Jo Inninger*

Debby Rupe (1975-)

I came to work with MKs in a round about way. For a number of years before coming to Pakistan I had been planning on
working as an evangelist in the province of Baluchistan. This
became impossible from the Pakistan government's point of
view and my mission then suggested I come to MCS since I was
a teacher. I felt this was the right thing to do, but I prayed that
the Lord would give me a burden for MKs. I didn't just want to
use MCS as a way of getting into the country. I always say this
was my best answered prayer. After being here about two
years, I felt very much that MCS was where I wanted to stay
and that MKs were the greatest people to live with.

I became a housemother because of Chuck Roub. I was in Iran teaching first grade at an MK school and waiting for my Pakistan visa. Chuck wrote and asked me if I wanted to be the first-grade teacher or a senior high girls housemother. Housemothering sounded wonderful and I wrote back and said, senior high girls, please! I think Chuck must have been relieved, as I found out later he already had a first grade teacher.

I met Eunice that first week at MCS and very quickly realized she had a very special burden for our kids and a very special ministry to them. Her love and enthusiasm, as well as her godly perspective on our kids and on living, influenced me very deeply, and she has continued to be a big part of what God has done in my life. It has been great to share together in so many kids' lives and in this very exciting business of seeing kids grow, mature, and go on from here; to see them find their relationship with Jesus as the core of their being, bringing glory to God; and even being able to be part of the next generation.

I worked with the senior high for seventeen years, from July 1975, on my arrival, till 1992. I then became the housemother for junior high girls.

Reflecting on the past must include places where I have failed kids and the Lord. Like Eunice, I too have had to make specific things right with kids—at the time, or later as adults. I remember one girl who I felt didn't want me around. I pulled back. Only after many years, on a trip to visit her, did I feel our relationship was restored. I'm thankful that that experience was early on as I learned a bit from it and asked God to give me the grace to not pull away from kids, no matter what the signals. God is a very faithful God to our kids. I'm often aware of how much we miss of the needs of our kids—and that he doesn't miss them. I think of one girl who was only in my department a short time. I never really felt I got to know her well. Ten years later she wrote me out of the blue. Since then we have visited a number of times, talked on the phone and written. I realize God is now in the process of healing some very deep scars from her home background and he has allowed Eunice and me and another MCS classmate to be part of that.

A highlight of my time at MCS was Joyce Bavington Minnich Raglow's wedding. Joyce was one of the girls Eunice had at six and I at sixteen. I was able to be her bridesmaid and share in much rejoicing after the great time of pain since her first husband Steve's death. It's amazing how the Lord allowed Eunice and I to be part of it all. We had had the very precious chance to know Steve and become his friend during his time here in Pakistan. We loved Steve and were thrilled to think that he and Joyce, who also was back working in Pakistan, were going to be married. And after Steve's sudden death on their honeymoon, we sorrowed with Joyce, when she arrived back in Pakistan to fulfill her contract with the International School of Islamabad. Some years later as we were watching an alumni basketball game, someone pointed out a young man playing who was part of a group out with Phil Johnson. They said, "That's Greg Raglow. He's interested in Joyce Minnich." (She was back in the U.S. by then.) Eunice had him up in her room for coffee and we "interviewed" him. Once again, Joyce had a very fine Christian man interested in her. Needless to say, we were pleased. Our paths crossed again in Britain. Eunice and I were on a trip visiting kids there and met up with Joyce and Greg. It was at a crisis point in their relationship and it was a wonderful opportunity to be able to share and pray together. The following May I was in their wedding. Who wouldn't want this job?!

MCS is changing—new people and different ideas. I struggle at times with the changes. I do thank the Lord for his care and protection of MCS and its goal to provide education for MKs within an atmosphere of commitment to the Lord Jesus and his glory on this earth. It has been such a great privilege to work at MCS all these years, to have had so many special people be part of my life and cause me to know the Lord Jesus better.

Above: MCS viewed from the upper field. (1994)

Below: Shivering in their "greenies" on Sports Day. High school girls were obligated to wear this much-maligned "athletic" outfit, designed with discretion for the local Muslim culture. Boys wore white T-shirts and green shorts. Some parents wanted MCS to adopt a school uniform—a proposal that never gained serious support.

The "Jesters" (1969), with "Uncle Paul" Davidson in the center; Mr. Lawrence, the school clerk, standing in front of the left goal post; Irv Nygren and Don Calderwood kneeling at far right. Even with two-thirds of the high school boys participating, MCS was unable to produce a complete line-up of first- and second-string players for its soccer team.

The playing fields across the road from the school were part of the Pakistan army's summer training camp, which included most of the hill behind MCS as well. We used the upper field (photographed in 1967) for soccer and field hockey. A huge Russian helicopter once made an emergency landing nearby and was hauled up to the lower field for repairs. When it took off several days later, it blew the tin roof off the nearby barracks (visible behind the pole vault pit, next page).

Sports Day, 1969: Track and field events. *Above:* Jerry Selby going over the top; Jim Hunter in foreground with back to camera. *Below, l. to r.:* Giles Armstrong, Eric Pulliam, unidentified, Tim Meadowcroft, David Hamm.

George McMillan's school band, 1968. Note old wooden church pews in foreground with placeboards for the little hymnals we used.

Spring Recital, July 1993, after completion of new stage. A new library and classrooms have been built over the stage, preserving the vaulted ceiling above most of the main hall.

The Class of '75—first grade with Miss Gardiner: Jonathan Addleton, standing, back row, far right; Elaine Roub, seated, middle row, third from right; Paul Seaman, kneeling, far left. Even with attrition (three of us failed second grade, one skipped a grade, other families left Pakistan), this group remained the largest—and among the rowdiest—in MCS history. (With 15 graduates, its record has been broken only by the class of '79, which has 16.)

The Class of '75—senior year. *L. to r:* Mark Pegors, Steve McCurry, Emily Wilder, Ellen Christy, Debbie Nygren, Susie Pietsch, Elaine Roub, Margaret Tebbe, Bill Cutler, Jonathan Addleton, Joel DeHart, Nancy Kennedy, John Huffaker; *standing:* Robert Lotze, Steve Rock.

Class of '75—Graduation Day, with class sponsors Isabel and Ian Murray. Note Mr. Murray's Scottish kilt.

MCS boarding and teaching staff, 1971. *Back row, l. to r.:* Dale Huffaker, Eunice Hill, Grace Huffaker, Don Calderwood, Rosemary Stewart, Kitte Clark, Glennis Brown, Gene Fisher, John Unrau, Mark Jones, Irv Nygren. *Middle row:* Chuck Roub, Eloise Roub, Evelyn Calderwood, Inger Gardner, Margaret Wheeler, Wilma Wilson, Linda Fisher, Lea Virtanen, Margaret Cunningham, Joy Jones, Liz Nygren, Margaret Wilson, Mary Selby. *Front row, seated:* Eva Hewitt, Khan Zaman, Mrs. Zaman.

A well-preserved Paul Pulliam in 1996, forty years after he started "the Murree school" as a young missionary with a sick wife and three pre-school-age children. MCS opened on schedule, with eight children the first day, less than three months after Pulliam received this assignment from the United Presbyterian mission in Pakistan. (It would be another year before the several cooperating missions gave final approval to the school's constitution.) Enrollment has averaged around 140 students, with a high of 180 in 1990.

Photos of Stewart Georgia (Principal, 1985-1993) and Phil Billing (1993-) were not available at press time.

Charles Roub, Principal
1960-1985

Eunice Hill *(left)* and Debby Rupe. As of 1996, they have been boarding parents at MCS for 33 years and 21 years, respectively.

Ian and Isabel Murray with Paul Seaman in Washington, D.C., at one of the nineteen MCS reunions prompted by the Murrays' 1994 "research tour." In four months they interviewed 147 alumni about how the school could better prepare students for re-entry and adjustment to their home countries. The Murrays have been at MCS since 1962, longer than any other staff members.

After an early snowfall: Across the road that passes in front of the school, viewed from the iron fence surrounding the old church property. (See John Mitchell's "Watching the Descent of the Nomads in the Cold Sunshine," a marvelously evocative musing which appears in the second volume of this work, *Paper Airplanes in the Himalayas.*)

19

From the Other Side

Becky Roub Treb, '71

It was an interesting experience, coming back to MCS as a staff member—and being only nineteen years old. I wanted to take some time off from college in the States so, at my dad's suggestion, I applied for the position of Middle Girls' house-mother, and was accepted for the almost two-year period from March 1972 to December 1973. The staff graciously offered that I could call them by their first names! I had difficulty, however, calling Mr. Murray, "Ian." It was hard thinking of him as a fellow worker. Even in the winter time when we staff kids were allowed to call the teachers "Auntie" and "Uncle," he had always been "Mr. Murray," and always will be in my mind. As a student, I had chalk thrown at me more than once for day-dreaming. I spent the entire time in his class in the front of the room, where the poorest students sat, and I never once earned his famous taffy. Now as a staff member, I no longer had to live in fear and, in fact, Mr. Murray was very kind, spoke to me quite respectfully, and even joked around with me.

When I first came, the boarding staff seemed to lack leadership. Our weekly meetings never seemed to accomplish much. We talked about issues, but I seldom left a meeting feeling satisfied that anything was resolved. In the summer Isabel Duncan came to take over as boarding superintendent and things changed drastically. I liked her very much; and things got done, believe me. However, I remember a few conflicts when issues came up for discussion at our staff meetings and things were finalized with or without everyone's agreement. Isabel was pretty assertive.

One issue that bothered me was that students were forbidden to buy anything on Sunday. Corn cobs on the grill were the luscious summer treat which we looked forward to every week. In the late spring, before boarding closed, we rode the bus in to Murree to attend the big church in town. Because no motor vehicles were allowed on the mall, we had quite a walk from the bus to the church—almost a mile. That didn't seem like much on the way to church, but coming home after a long and boring service, and feeling hungry, it was almost unbearable to pass by the corn *wallas,* see and smell the corn cooking, have your mouth water for it, but not be allowed to buy any. Some of the kids often broke down and bought some anyway.

I was really torn about what I should do in this situation. Having no convictions myself about buying on Sunday, if I mentioned it to other staff members I would feel like a tattletale. Several times I brought the issue up in staff meetings, but the rule stayed. Furthermore, it was clearly expected that I would enforce the policy—and report the kids who disobeyed it.

Dilemmas like this could have been due in part to my youth, and my inability to separate myself from identifying with the feelings of the kids. Dan Mitchell was the boarding parent for Middle Boys (fourth-, fifth-, and sixth-graders). His boys used to come to me and complain about how strict he was. They talked about things like long and drawn out devotions, where if they didn't sit still and pay attention, he would punish them severely, with spankings or time-outs for long periods.

One Saturday, I was sitting out on "the wall" in front of the hostel, just watching the activities going on around and about, and I happened to look up at the second floor windows and saw a couple of Dan's boys looking out at me. I waved, and in a few short minutes they were sitting beside me on the wall. They said that they were supposed to be inside all day, on their beds, as a punishment for acting up in devotions. I asked them why they were out there, then? They said that Dan wasn't around, and they were tired of being punished. I know that I should have immediately sent them back inside with scolding, but I didn't. I did tell them that if Dan showed up I would disclaim any knowledge that they were supposed to be inside.

Dan was also in charge of water rationing at the hostel during water shortages—which, of course, was almost all the time. We were told that we couldn't bathe more than twice a week. Being a young woman, I felt the need to bathe each night, so I would go into my bathroom, draw my two inches of water, and bathe. One day Dan came to me and said that he knew that I thought I was being sneaky: even if he didn't hear me drawing the water because I always closed the louvers before I did it, he knew I bathed every night. I did not close the louvers to hide my water running, and I told him so. He did not forbid me to do it any more, and I continued my nightly baths, not in rebellion, but in genuine need, and with much frugality in water use. But it made me feel small and humiliated that he would accuse me like that.

That year, there were quite a few new boarding staff, most of them unmarried. I had been assigned Thursdays as my day off, with Eunice Hill and a couple of other younger staff members. Eunice and the others liked to drive down to Rawalpindi and spend most of the day shopping for things like copper and other Pakistani handicrafts. I couldn't afford to spend much, and didn't want to spend the day traipsing around with people who shopped endlessly. So, in the summer I asked to have my day off with Inger Gardner and Rosie Stewart. That was fine, Inger and Rosie welcomed me and I found them delightful to be with. I liked to go to Pindi with them, do some minor shopping, and then spend the rest of the day by the pool at the Intercontinental Hotel.

Meanwhile, my old group had begun calling themselves the "Thursday Off Club." I took no notice at first, but as time went on, it began to seem like the Thursday Off Club had turned into a Thursday-off clique. They spent their days off together *and* their days on together. The staff customarily met in the lounge at night, after the children were asleep, and have "tea" before going to bed, and it soon became evident that there were two groups in that lounge, the "in" crowd, and the "out" crowd. Just like high school! You are ignored or put up with, and when you leave they don't know the difference, and don't hear you say good night. I know that no one was deliberately snubbing anyone else, but I was still really hurt by this situation.

I went to m. mother and told her how upset I was, but she was sure, too, that I wasn't trying hard enough to fit in. I said nothing further to anyone until one day when Inger and I took a night and two days off and went to the missionary hospital in Abbottabad for some get-away time. We got to talking about what was going on with the staff as a group—Inger was the one who mentioned it first. I was incredulous that she had noticed the same thing, and that I hadn't been just imagining it all. By then both of us had stopped going to the lounge for tea because neither of us felt comfortable and, I learned that night, because the other of us wasn't going to be there.

Looking back, I certainly harbor no hard feelings toward anyone, but it does make me wonder if that sort of thing was going on with the teaching staff, too.

20

Dan Finds a Bride

Daniel Mitchell (1973)

In the fall of 1971 I was working as a journalist in South East Asia—seven years by then, the last three in Vietnam and Cambodia. Before that Singapore, India, Afghanistan, Indonesia, including several months in Riau, and Malaysia. Working this beat was just like being at home: my parents had been missionaries and I grew up in Indonesia and India. But the call to head to the USA was getting stronger. The Vietnam war was winding down, and on September 3, 1971, the Lord Jesus Christ had taken center stage in my life. I knew my life would be changing, so I started to do some serious thinking.

Not knowing what in the world I would get into next, the thought came to my mind that a wife was needed for this "old man." The best place to look was right where I was—South East Asia. With mission stations in every country and scattered all over, I began my search in Indonesia, where I was born. In exchange for photos taken and tapes made into some propaganda for the missionaries, I asked for a mat to sleep on and some simple food—a good trade, I thought. This was accepted and off I went to different stations looking for stories

187

and for single missionary women.

The stories were there, but the women were not; at least, not the one I was looking for. Asian women had always been attractive to me, but I knew that my family would not approve and so the guidelines were: American or European, active on the field as a missionary or born and raised on the mission field under missionary parents. Looks were important, but not the objective. She had to be stable, not given to emotion or overbearing. Her age would have to be within ten years of mine or less, and of course she must be committed to the Lord and his work. This last item was paramount and would be the focal point of everything.

I met some grand missionaries, even some whom I had gone to school with as a kid. I knew that missionaries are a special breed, they have to have that special force in their personality that makes them different from other people, and that was what I was looking for.

India was almost a hit when I visited Woodstock School, which I had attended as a kid for five years. During the fall months when my parents went down to the plains for their work I stayed in boarding. Landour was heaven on earth for a kid going into his teenage years. This time I thought it might be, too. A blonde bomb hit me real hard, a young smart kid from the States teaching in the school. We had some good conversations, but when I found out that she had protested the war in Vietnam and had some "left wing" ideas, I lost interest. Our spiritual ideals did not match, but there was some electricity there and India continued to be my home for over six months. There were some other serious "look-ats," but nothing took.

After spending some time in Afghanistan, it was on to Pakistan to visit my older brother David and his family of three children, whom I had not seen for some time. Pakistan was just like India: dusty, smelly and dirty—but wonderful. When my brother and family picked me up from the bus station, the first thing we did was go and have a good Pakistani meal in Rawalpindi. This was November 1972 and I thought I would be headed to the USA after Christmas, by way of Norway to see family there. Then, while I was staying at Bach Hospital, the Murree school principal, Chuck Roub, came down, and when he heard that I took pictures, he asked me to do a special for the school, a picture story on what MCS students did during their winter break. I agreed to do it and during the sessions I got to know some of the kids. I remember the Irwins, the Rassmussens, the Blanchards, the DeHarts, and others. I remember Cindy Irwin being quite a tomboy and the DeHart boys being more Pakistani than American.

My brother David introduced me to all of the missionaries that came by, and from time to time I went to Pindi with one of them to do some photo finishing. I was used to hitching because I did it all the time in Vietnam; many of my "hitches" were choppers or tanks. That winter I made some good friends with some of the Pakistani people on the place and would have meals with them.

It was during this time that Chuck Roub asked if I would be willing to work at the school for a semester as a boarding parent. I was game and agreed to do it. I had acquired a hernia around then and decided to get it fixed before school started. Dr. Blanchard did the job, with another missionary and some cute Pakistani nurses.

It was really great getting to know my nephews and niece—Jon, Jeff, and Joy. We had some fun times together, even snowball fights, after I recovered from surgery. On one occasion, I hit Jon with a hard throw well aimed, just as he was throwing. The thing he did not like about it was that I thwarted his attacking me. Well, life became too much for the family with me around. Being winter and cold, this warm-blooded man liked to stay inside and as a result got on everyone's nerves. I think they were relieved when the time came for school to start. Off to Murree it was and getting ready for the spring term. While lifting beds and mattresses and other things, the old hernia came back, but it was not too bothersome.

One morning, just before boarding opened, one of the bus drivers asked if I wanted to go down to Pindi to pick up the *missahibs* at the rail station. I guess he wanted to talk with me, and on the way down we had some good conversation, with his broken English and me with my Babu English and limited Urdu. We made a great team. The driver went off to do some errands and I went to the photo shop. I met the driver at the location we had agreed on and to the station we went. The train arrived and there we met the *missahibs,* six or seven of them.

They were Kitti Clarke, Glennis Brown, Ellen Brell, Eunice Hill, Margaret Wheeler, and Margaret Cunningham. The one that struck me the most was Margaret. It was not her beauty, hairstyle, or anything like that, but the fact that she did not yak-yak like all the other women. I thought to myself, "These women have traveled on the train together for several days and they still have something to talk about." Miss Cunningham said a few words of pleasantries but maybe she was tired. Anyway, all up the road to Murree these women yakked a blue streak. The driver and I took glances at each other and grinned.

School started and I was in charge of the fourth- through sixth-grade boys. Looking back to my own years in India, I wanted this boarding experience to be a time for them to remember. I also wanted a fine-tuned program with discipline and fun time. As a boarding parent, I wanted them to have a balanced life of love and taking responsibility. The bus arrived and in ran these kids, fresh from a three-month vacation; some of them had just come from Kids' Kamp and they were pent up, ready to hit it.

The one thing I had learned after some years of working with children was that it is best to start out hard-nosed and then work down to a more tolerable level of behavior, and that is what I did. I called it lean and mean. Lights were to be out by a certain time and other things had to be done, like homework and rooms cleaned up before bedtime. We had devotions with reading from a book of adventure, a portion from the Bible, then prayer. I did all the reading and praying at first and then gradually gave the responsibility to some of the older boys.

Infractions were considered by severity. Out-and-out disobedience was a good couple of swats on the rear and then a prayer by me to tell them I loved them and that God loved them. I gave warnings at first and then on the second or third time it was hit the deck, kid. I used a paddle that I made and it hung in plain sight for everyone to see. At first there was some testing and a couple of rear ends were busted, and the message came across that "Unk" was serious but he was fair. For my nephew, Jon Mitchell, I was double-Unk and I told him from the start that I would be hard on him as I did not want to show any favoritism.

For some infractions I used an Army system of "policing"

the place. The boys who did the misdeed had to go around the school property after school and pick up paper and anything that was not biodegradable. There was some complaining about this, but the system worked. I used other forms of punishment also and soon we had a pretty good deal going.

We had some fun times. One of the best was the "chicken fights." The biggest boys carried the smallest ones up on their shoulders and it was hand-to-hand combat, trying to pull down the other two boys. We did that often. Another favorite activity was wrestling matches on the playroom floor after pulling down mattresses. Beds were stripped, of course, only with the permission of whoever's bunk it was. We had strict rules as to weight and size and tried to pit even size boys with one another. We found that some of the smaller boys did quite well with other boys and they sort of grew in stature as we made the matches go up in size and weight.

We took some memorable hikes, too; one in particular was a test for togetherness and teamwork. I told the boys that we were going straight down the hillside to the road below and then hike back on the road, back to Jhika and then to the school. I said that we were to all help one another and that this was to be a group hike. We did well until we got halfway along the road and then boys started to get tired and started to complain that it was too long. We made it, though, and everyone found something in themselves that said, "I did it, even though it was hard." Other hikes were done in the moonlight. We also sometimes went for tea and *samosas* at one of the local tea stalls.

One thing that I brought to MCS was drunken beatles. I found out when I was a kid in India that if a beetle feeds on very ripe bananas or mangoes, it gets drunk and cannot walk straight and will even stand up so that it falls over backward. We would get the Bamboo beetles drunk too and they would fight the Stag beetle. Well, during the monsoon time here came the June Bugs and some Bamboo beetles. I think I found a couple of stag beetles also. It was off to find some bananas and I squashed them with a spoon and put the dish over the hurricane lantern to heat it up. Then I fed it to the beetles and it was on with the fight. For some reason this did not set well with the rest of the staff and I had to squash the project, but Jon Mitchell remembers the event quite well. Then I instituted chestnut fights and we had a round with those. It was Woodstock days all over again!

Often on my Wednesdays off I went down to Pindi to shoot pictures. I usually drove down with Rosie Stewart and she would let me off at one of the bazaars on her way to the U.S. Embassy. I would walk around, talking with shopkeepers and college students who frequented the tea stalls. I would have some tea and a *samosa* and we would have a gab time. I found a photo place that would process my pics and got to be quite friendly with the owner. I must have taken hundreds of pics and maybe that is why I was asked to leave Pakistan. Who knows. Anyway, I had lots of fun taking pics, getting them processed, and then handing a copy to the person in the photo. I never drank so much tea, but it was all good and no one ever bothered me.

One thing I found out very soon was that when I took my day off each week the kids were hard to manage for the next couple of days. Just that short period of being off did something to their behavior. Parenting is a full time job, seven days a week, fifty-two weeks a year, twenty-four hours a day.

One time I saw some girls running around the campus with short shorts on and halter tops, and I yelled at them to cover up and told them they were not allowed to be on campus with such skimpy clothes. They looked at me like I was from another planet. Afterward I thought I was quite boorish for doing such a thing.

Some things were more serious. I remember walking into the chapel one morning and seeing a bouquet of marijuana plants sitting on the school stage. Some of the boys thought it was a great joke. I told Chuck Roub that the school was in deep trouble and that there would be a drug problem in the very near future. I found out later that there were whole bushes of the stuff growing right behind the tea shop across the road from the school.

* * *

One of my responsibilities was to see that all my boys were well enough to go to class. I would go around and if any of the kids were sick it was off to the nurse. There were the usual cheats who tried to fool me and I would take out the thermometer and take the temp and if there was no temp, they did not go to the nurse and it was off to class. One of the German boys in my department became quite sick and I brought him to my room. I put him on the bed and I slept on the floor. Right off, I told the nurse that a doctor should be called, because I thought it best. Well, the boy was in my room for over a week, and I was up every night with wet cloths to cool down his fever, and wash out the upchuck bucket from time to time. Hey, I was not even married and here I was looking after a sick kid that wasn't even mine. Another memorable time was when Alastair Bavington got bit by a monkey and the nurse said he had to have rabies shots. I did not think he got bit, only scratched. He had to have these shots anyway, so it was special treats each time he got a shot—treats for everyone. We sort of made a big deal out of the situation.

I will always remember having early morning prayer with Chuck Roub. And every night I had a time of prayer with my niece, Joy Mitchell, before she went to sleep, and the other little girls insisted I give all of them a kiss as I gave Joy one. I guess they missed their parents quite a bit . . .

Since my responsibilities were mainly in the dorm, I spent most of my time there, sleeping near the boys and eating in the dining room. The other dorm parents ate in the dining room also, next to where the children ate, so that we could watch the children and take turns being monitors. Some of the boys had a problem drinking the milk, which had to be boiled. After it cooled down it had a film on the top and some of the boys just could not get past that film and refused to drink it. One boy, from England, just refused to drink his milk; so I went to his table, dipped my finger in his cup of milk and took the film out and then said, "Drink it." And he did.

Miss Cunningham lived in a basement apartment of the hostel, so she ate meals with the dorm parents. We got to talking, mostly about the boys she was teaching—third- and fourth-graders. The two of us formed a kind of PTA after supper, and we got to do some good evaluating of some of the boys. This helped me to see some of the problems that they had and what could be corrected in the study hall time and the free time afterward. Well, our PTA meetings started to last longer and before you know it things were going pretty good. Somewhere along the line, I was asked to take care of the maintenance of some of the building and to oversee some of the Pakistani workers. Well, that brought me into more contact with Miss Cunningham. On a number of occasions, I had to unplug the toilet in her classroom and do other odd jobs there. This brought us together even more. I thought this very interesting and decided to test this "thing" very closely.

On one of my trips to Pindi I asked Rosie Stewart if she thought that if I asked Miss Cunningham out for a date, she would go with me. "Oh, no. She is too tied up with her kids," said Rosie, "and besides, she is not in the least sociable. Do you think she would even look at you? She has not looked at any of the other single men that I know of and I am sure she is not going to look at you." Then I asked Rosie if she and Inger Gardner would go out to dinner as chaperons with Miss Cunningham and myself if Miss Cunningham would agree to go out on a dinner date. "Fat chance, Mitchell," was the reply. Finally, I got Rosie to agree to go if Miss Cunningham would agree to go. So I asked Miss Cunningham to go to dinner with me, to the Green Hotel, the one out past the school. She said, "Yes, I would love to go," and so on a Wednesday evening we took off in Rosie's VW and the four of us had a lovely evening over dinner.

It got to be that I stayed more and more in the third- and fourth-grade classroom, helping to clean up the room and putting books away, as the semester was coming to a close. Miss Cunningham kept asking for help for this and that. Was romance in the air? For myself, I was not sure. Margaret was forty-five years old—ten years older than me, and that was the outside limit I had set. I had been "in love" several times, even engaged on one occasion and in Vietnam had been on quite a mad love feast for two years, till the girl's father put an end to it, so things were sort of wait-and-see.

I did not want to strike out on this one, so I made sure that we were never alone in any of the rooms, but that other people were there, whether it was the dining room or the classroom. I do not remember if we had decided this, but I made the decision for myself, just to make sure that no one on staff or the student body came to any conclusions, right or wrong. Also there had been a rule come down from the MCS governing body that students could not go out alone as couples, as this was a Muslim country. They had to be circumspect in their actions on campus, as well. We followed the same guidelines set down for the high school kids.

Because of her mother's illness, Margaret was going to the

States during the semester break at the end of May. There were signs that she was quite agitated about this separation, but I was still mulling it over in my mind as to the implications and any decisions that were going to be made. I knew that she was tied to the situation and if there was fault on anyone's part it was my doing, because I instigated the process. Along with a number of others, we went down to the airport in Pindi. There were a good number going at the same time. Everyone said their goodbyes, and up we went to Murree again. I went down to stay with my brother and family for the week between semesters and then it was back up to Murree for the next three months. I still looked after the fourth- through sixth-grade boys and we did the same things that we normally did.

In August I received word that my visa was going to be revoked. I traveled down to Peshawar and to Pindi several times to find out what was wrong and why they were revoking the visa. They kept asking me where I got the visa and I said, "It says on the passport—in Afghanistan." I went to the U.S. Embassy in Islamabad to find out what was going on. I asked to see the head man and out walked one of those short-haired, ivy-league-dressed individuals that grace so many embassies around the world. I asked him what could be done to find out about why my visa was revoked. He asked me who my friends were in the area. When he found out that all the people that I knew were missionaries, he sort of gave a snort and said, "Is that all you could find to make friends with here in Pakistan?" I looked him in the eyes and gave him a piece of my mind: "Let me tell you something, sir. The missionaries here are the only Americans who learn the language well. They are the only ones who really know what is happening here in this country. They are the ones who really get to know the heart of the people and are the ones the people really trust. When there is a natural disaster in-country, the missionaries are the first ones to get there and help the people. Your office and type are the last ones to get there. Your type does not learn the language, nor do you get to know the people. You are busy sitting by your swimming pools and drinking your highballs." He did not look too pleased afterward and when I got back to the States, I surmised I did not make a friend on that occasion.

To make a long story short, my visa was revoked and I had to leave Pakistan. I heard from Ken Old that the order came from Bhutto himself—the old man president. I was a little perturbed about it, and then I made up my mind that I had to do something with this romance. I wrote Margaret that I loved her and that I was coming back to the States soon, and I then sent a telegram for her to meet me in Los Angeles before she went back to Pakistan. I left in such a hurry, and with Margaret on my mind, but those nine months at MCS were the highlight of my years in Asia.

Margaret and I did meet in L.A. and became engaged on September 4, 1973. She then went back to Pakistan and I guess there was a surprise announcement for all the staff and student body that we were engaged. That happened on Halloween, when Joy Mitchell wore a costume made of a heart with an arrow through it and "DM loves MC" lettered across it. I guess no one knew that we were at all interested in each other, even though I sent her an aerogram every day, even though at times she got them in bunches. This goes to prove that the mail did get through in Pakistan.

We were married in Los Angeles eight months later.

Margaret (Cunningham) Mitchell (1963-1974)

My parents were missionaries in South America, and my brothers and sister were born in Argentina and Paraguay. We kids attended the local Argentine school and used Spanish with our friends and classmates. English was too difficult! During World War II, our family returned to the USA where I attended high school. After receiving my B.A. from Sterling College in Kansas, I began teaching fourth grade. I took graduate courses during the summers with the goal of serving the Lord Jesus Christ; I wanted to return to Latin America as a teacher. However, when I applied to the United Presbyterian Mission, I was asked to consider teaching in a school for missionaries' children.

So in 1958 I went to Hope School in Ebolowa, Cameroun, in West Africa. I had nine pupils in grades three through six, including some French, Swiss, and Greek children whose fathers were businessmen dealing in cocoa beans. In the summer of 1961, I returned to the United States by way of Europe, England, and Scotland. A missionary friend and I traveled down the Rhine River. Our little ship had a congenial group of passengers, but one morning we noticed that our fellow passengers were quite nervous. We asked what was happening and they mentioned a wall that was being built in Berlin. Someone had heard a sketchy report over the radio and rumors were circulating as to what it all meant. No one knew.

As a newly-commissioned career missionary, I went to Stony Point, New York, in the fall of 1962. The Missionary Orientation Center there, sponsored by the National Council of Churches, was run by the Methodists and attended by folks from several denominations. While there, I met Alan and Norma Seaman who were getting ready to go to Pakistan with their three kids. Later, I had all four Seaman children in my classes at Murree Christian School: Ruth, Martha, Paul, and Miriam, who was born in Pakistan on my birthday.

Early in January of 1963—the Seamans were still waiting for visas—a group of missionaries from the United Presbyterian Church left New York City by ship. The *Vulcania* had sat in the harbor for many weeks because of a strike. Our missionary group could only take as much luggage as we could carry. Because of the dock strike, no one was around to help us. The ship was extremely cold because it had been unheated all the time it had been anchored in the harbor. We sailed to Naples, Italy, and then took a second ship, the *Victoria,* to Karachi, by way of the Suez Canal and Aden.

It was quite an experience to go by train from Karachi to Rawalpindi. No one had heard of taking a bedroll, drinking water, and food on this twenty-four-hour trip. We were very green. The instructions that we were to have received eventually arrived some time after we did. What a relief to finally reach our destination! Since MCS was closed for the winter break, I did not arrive at Sandes Home until late February. One problem that I faced was who to go to for answers to questions. I was assigned to MCS but supported by the UP mission; I had come to teach missionaries' children but was required to study Urdu. These were areas that I never was able to sort out!

When the school opened in March, I met my class of third- and fourth-graders and found them to be cooperative, alert, above average, and most of them had good work habits. For me, one of the daily hardships was walking down the shortcut from Sandes Home to the school a mile away. The slippery slope was a hazard for me—but not for the elementary school kids! As soon as the bell sounded, and the pupils had congregated by the large tree below Sandes Home, it was a race. When we got to the road at the bottom of the short cut it was much easier to walk, except when we met a convoy of army trucks. As we walked to school, I had a chance to get acquainted with the pupils. Once, a fourth-grade boy told me that his father was coming up to the school office. He was quite excited at the prospect of seeing his dad. I asked him if his father was a CPA (certified public accountant). "Never," he said. "He is TEAM" (meaning from The Evangelical Alliance Mission). Here was an interesting side to missions and denominations. In some cases there was a spirit of competition and, sad to say, not cooperation. I wondered what the Pakistanis thought about this.

I was impressed by the pioneer spirit displayed by the elementary students at MCS. They worked hard at their studies despite a cold, smoky classroom, poor lights, and inadequate books and resource materials. They missed their parents but came to love their houseparents. I came to admire these missionary parents who had taught their children good attitudes. These kids loved the Lord Jesus and despite problems did their very best. Of course, there were difficulties with conflicts between staff members and between boarding and teaching staff, but overall, considering personalities and different backgrounds, I believe the Lord helped us to adjust. Even so, the presence of counseling personnel would have assisted a great deal in reducing these tensions.

*   *   *

Murree in the summer was very beautiful until the monsoon arrived. Who can ever adjust to mold, mud, and dampness? In November of 1963, a staff member rushed in to say, "Someone just shot your president!" We Americans thought that was in poor taste until we found out it was true. John F. Kennedy had been shot in Dallas, Texas. Rumors were everywhere. The high school students produced an enormous sympathy card and many signed it.

A little over a week later, however, a different kind of buzz was in the air. Trunks were everywhere and the words "train party," "vacation," and "home" were constantly being heard. No point in teaching new material—everyone was marking time until the buses arrived and the students and their baggage and picnic lunches and other food parcels were loaded aboard.

I spent the winter in Sialkot, at the Hajipura Girls' School run by the Presbyterian mission. I took Urdu lessons and learned something about missionary work. And so a pattern was established. I became involved with what the single lady missionaries did and prepared lessons for the spring term. Life in a school for Pakistani girls proved to be quite restrictive; I attended some weddings but travel was limited.

The years 1964 and 1965 were years of "bazaar gossip" concerning the looming war between Pakistan and India over Kashmir. Rumors circulated freely that Americans were aiding India. The U.S. consulate recommended that children remain with their parents. A number of mothers remained at Sandes Home to be with their children. "Blackouts" were the order of the day and the MCS bus had to be covered with mud and branches so that enemy planes would not see it. School carried on and the adults had to appear normal, which was a challenge.

The groundbreaking for the new hostel provided a highlight in the midst of this difficult period. Students, teachers, boarding parents, and servants all gathered together at a special service to dedicate the "home away from home" site. One of my pupils wrote home, "I'm OK and I hope you are OK and keep praying for cement." Cement was scarce and plenty would be needed to build the hostel.

I came back to the United States in 1967 for a furlough. I enrolled at Kansas State University, taking courses in how to teach above average children. The program emphasized creative lesson plans that would encourage students to share the traditions, history, music, art, drama, and spiritual heritage of their own countries. We also grappled with how best to test children from different educational backgrounds. It was a challenge and I learned a lot.

When I returned to MCS in the summer of 1968 there were many changes in personnel, and an elementary classroom block had been built, with apartments for the teaching staff on the second floor. That was a big plus. In December of 1971 war broke out again between West Pakistan and India. Several families evacuated. East Pakistan became Bangladesh. This was a terrible defeat for Pakistan, but brought to an end several months of civil strife and atrocities by the West Pakistan army in the eastern province. Several of our students at MCS had parents working in East Pakistan, on the other side of India; the kids were worried about their families and we didn't know what was really going on over there. Once again, the children held up impressively well through a very tense time.

The biggest change in my life came in early 1973 when I met Daniel Mitchell. We were very discreet with our romance because of the Muslim culture. Marrying Daniel was the best plan God had for me and has been truly fulfilling.

21

Bomba

Kilts, Compassion, Fiery Temper

The short sketch below was submitted by Malcolm Murray, '86. The author is unknown.

Suddenly from behind a wall comes an enormous roar. The beast appears, horrible legs covered only by knee-length white shorts and ankle socks. The hairy face, too terrible to look at, eyes alight with burning fire, it moves toward you. No one moves. "Are you ready for P.E., lads?" We all breath again and say, "Yes, Mr. Murray."

We know where Mr. Murray is by his voice, by his famous "Bomba" T-shirt, and of course by his kilt. He even has a story of how, at a tournament, a man whom he had never met before said, "I know you, you're Mr. Murray!" So, there is proof that he can be identified by the particular kilt he wears, but all of the people around Murree recognize him because he is the only man who wears a kilt! (Other people are not so clear: At one interschool convention, it seems that some Kabul or KAS students wondered if MCS was named after Mr. Murray—because he was so loud and pushy.)

In Mr. Murray's classes, one has to have an extremely able sense of hearing: Often his thoughts and words get ahead of his writing, but when a helpful student remarks about the discrepancy between what is seen and what is heard, Mr. Murray just advises to listen to his thoughts and not his words.

Experiments rarely work out as they are meant to, but Mr. Murray never lets this interfere with their educational intent. One time in physics class we were combining several different colors of light with the goal of achieving white light. Of course it didn't work, but we were assured that all we needed was a little imagination and the light would begin to go white.

Like any thrifty Scotsman, he builds his own experiment equipment to save money, but if any problems happen to arise, the class is assured that expensive equipment is actually no different.

One day in senior physics class, Mr. Murray is at the chalk board trying to explain with much effort the phenomenon of the Doppler effect, as witnessed by standing next to the tracks of an oncoming train. The physics are complicated and time drags by. Roy Montgomery, sitting in the front row with Tim DeHart, suddenly shoots up his arm. Now, if it had been a girl, Ian Murray would have stopped right away and acknowledged her, but Roy's arm hangs in the air for a while. Mr. Murray finally stops his monologue to ask impatiently what Roy had on his mind.

"I rode on a train once," Roy says.

Mr. Murray is so flustered, all he can think of to say, after a moment, is "Did you, really?" The class all laughs, grateful for the comic relief. Roy Montgomery has a knack for poking fun at things with an innocence that lets him get away with things others wouldn't dare say.

The Mr. Murray of the class is a different man from the Mr. Murray of the field. He loves doing strenuous exercises, such as leg raises, because he is very fit and the boys aren't, so he can feel free to growl at them. After all, never make a student do what you can't! When he gets bored, he just settles back to watch the boys repeat an exercise over and over again. How humorous exercises can be!

Mr. Murray's contributions to MCS have been numerous: from math teacher to team mascot; he has served as vice principal and advisor to the Photo Club; but he is remembered most as a *friend*.

—with additional comments by Scott Kennedy, '73

* * *

Ian Murray trained as a civil engineer and Isabel as a teacher. Both were brought up in Christian homes and came to know Jesus personally through the work of Scottish Scripture Union school meetings and summer camps. Neither wanted to be foreign missionaries, but while doing his national service Ian felt the Lord's prompting to work overseas and they offered their services to the Church of Scotland.

They didn't need engineers, but were desperate for teachers, so Ian went back to college for teacher training after their marriage in the summer of 1960. The Murrays thought they were bound for Nigeria to teach in a school for nationals there, but were requested to change to a different location—in the wilds of Pakistan, to teach in a school for the children of missionaries, especially to meet the needs of the British and non-Americans. In those days the majority at MCS were from North America.

The Murrays have been on the staff now since they arrived in 1962 with a two-month old daughter.

Ian and Isabel write:

> It has not always been easy and we have had our hard times, but we are thankful that the Lord has blessed and kept us. We raised all three children at MCS and praise God for His goodness to them all. Like all MKs, our kids have gone through many difficulties and have their own stories to tell. We have sometimes failed them as we have failed many of our students, but God forgives and it is only through His grace that we continue to seek to serve Him here. We miss our kids now that they have gone, but all parents do and there is no easy answer and no point in making out that there is.

* * *

In April 1987, the Murrays were traveling to Peshawar on business, on a Friday afternoon after a busy week. About six miles outside Islamabad Ian fell asleep at the wheel. Their little Morris Minor smashed into a road abutment on Isabel's side of the car. While Ian was basically unhurt, physically, Isabel sustained multiple fractures to both legs and a ruptured spleen, which resulted in heavy internal bleeding.

Emergency surgery was performed late that night in Islamabad. Members of the American and British diplomatic community donated fourteen pints of blood. Missionary and embassy personnel cared for Isabel round the clock, under the direction of Mrs. Senove Mitchell (Jonathan Mitchell's mom). Six days later, with a doctor and nurse attending the stretcher, the Murrays flew home to Edinburgh. Pneumonia, jaundice, and the many operations required to put her legs back together kept Isabel in the hospital from April till July; and then again in November and December, she returned for surgery to lengthen and rotate the femur which had not gone quite right due to the long delay in the initial setting because of several factors.

In March 1988 the Murrays returned to MCS, only eleven months after their near-fatal accident. Who knows why God's graciousness prevailed in this case; but Ian and Isabel will never forget the prayer support, gifts, and letters from staff, students, and alumni all over the world. "It was a hard time," Isabel says, looking back,

> but the Lord was very real to us through it all, and a lot of good came out of it—people working together in the MCS community during our absence, things that happened in the hospital in Scotland, the people we met there, and so on. Of course, the accident certainly changed Ian and me. It is a miracle that I am alive and that awareness has affected our relationship with each other, with other people, with life itself.

*   *   *

Jonathan Mitchell, '79

As little kids we were terrified of Mr. Murray. We would sit in our classrooms and listen to him shouting instructions to his tennis students or encouragement to his soccer team. For a little guy he had quite a voice. Inside, we learned in time, he had a heart of butter and gold.

Ian Murray is mostly known for his science and calculus classes, but for me it is his British History class that stands out. He had chosen a fantastic text which brought out the personalities who shaped the history we were studying. It even included "Punch" cartoons from the period. The book filled us in on the Disraeli-Gladstone jokes, which now make for great party pieces. Disraeli had just given a rousing speech that brought the House of Commons to its feet. A member of the opposition, hoping to dampen the response, chose this moment to ask an innocent question. "Sir," he said, "could you please distinguish between your use of 'calamity' and 'catastrophe'?" "Certainly," replied Disraeli. "If Mr. Gladstone were to fall into the Thames River, that would be a calamity. On the other hand, if someone were to pull him out it would constitute a catastrophe." Gladstone, of course, was rather upset at this analogy and plotted to embarrass Disraeli that evening at a public gathering. Disraeli was speaking with the Queen when Gladstone sidled up and said, "I hear, sir, that you can make a joke about any subject. Let us hear a joke about the Queen." "The Queen, sir," replied Disraeli, "is not a subject." Touche! What wit! If only we had a measure of it to use on choice occasions when the girls in our class got out of hand.

I remember one British History exam very well. There had been a BBC production the night before which featured Tchaikovsky's *1812 Overture*. In his enthusiasm, Mr. Murray had recorded it on the school's ancient Wollensak reel-to-reel tape recorder, and he decided to use it as background music for our exam. I can still see him skipping up and down the aisle "*do-dee-do*"ing to himself, much to the distress of those poorly prepared for the test. Sheryl Walsh finally told him to turn it off. He complied, but I heard him muttering his usual "suffering catfish" as he turned it off. This was the same test in which most of the questions referred to William Ewart. Sunil Lall couldn't recall ever hearing of this chap and didn't realize until it was all over that this referred to William Ewart Gladstone.

Mr. Murray earned his nickname in that class. We read of King Ferdinand of Sicily who used to revel in harassing his guests. We read that he was well known for pulling out the chairs from under his guests, and his subjects therefore dubbed him "King Bomba." It occurred to Sunil Lall and me that this was a very suitable name for Mr. Murray. He was rather fond of teasing the girls by untying the cute bows on the backs of their dresses. However, when he nearly undressed Tammy Khan in this fashion the joke was on him. I have never seen him turn so red or apologize so profusely. We saw a tender side of him that time which he was later increasingly unable to hide. Yes, "Bomba" was a great name for him. It not only suited his personality, but it enabled us to express our fondness for him in a way that he would not consider rude. As students we certainly couldn't call him Ian.

Bomba played a large role in our lives at Murree. Not only did he teach British history, physics, chemistry, and other assorted classes, but he did his best to give us some useful exercise in P.E. It invariably rained when he was in charge of P.E., and rather than let us tear up the field he would take us on "mud marches." A "mud march" consisted of him leading us through the woods on a meandering run and telling us to head home when we were several miles out. We would slither down the *kud* trying to take shortcuts, but this was a futile exercise as Bomba would immediately turn the other way leaving us with further to run. We would return from these marches soaked through and covered with mud. Rob Bailey would come up with the most foul descriptions of these exercises, but some of us secretly enjoyed them.

Bomba was also head of the Photo Club. He had made a contact printer out of some clothespins and a kerosene tin which worked wonderfully. We would use his ancient cameras with huge systems of bellows which would fold into a neat little package if you could figure it out. Operating them was a bit like putting together a puzzle ring. These cameras used a large format film so contact prints didn't look too bad. David Heaton and I would stay in the dark room late Friday nights trying to come up with tricky special effects. Our best effects were usually the result of mistakes which we would later try to repeat. I remember once when the paper developer had gotten very cold and wasn't working well. I used an immersion heater to boil some fresh developer and poured it into the tray. The print developed instantly where the developer first landed while the effect wore off towards the edges of the print in a beautiful swirl pattern. I used this trick years later on a print of the Taj Mahal and won a three-state photo contest in Chicago.

Photography became a large part of my life at Murree. Marty Ketcham and I set up a darkroom in a walk-in closet at

Sandes, and I even dropped out of sports my senior year (something unheard of at Murree) to devote all my time to taking pictures of old men in tea shops. We even tried doing color slides. Bomba had brought fifty feet of color slide film back from Scotland made by a company called Barfen (a most creative name) and had the chemistry for it as well. He invited us to try a few rolls. Ketcham and I duly spent an afternoon in Charlie's (a local tea shop) sipping tea and taking pictures of some of the wizened old locals. Bomba had the system set up in his bathroom at home, and we went there the same evening to process the results. They were fantastic, marred only by me accidentally pouring the stop bath down the drain. This was an embarrassing mistake as it made the remaining film useless. With our usual resourcefulness Ketcham and I filled the empty bottle with a mixture of acetic acid and blue food coloring, hoping no one would notice. Virgil Das and Steve Wright were next in line to develop their color film and we knew if the results were poor it could be blamed on their inexperience. No one noticed that anything was wrong, and we emerged with our reputations intact.

I am indebted to Bomba for igniting and nurturing my interest not only in photography, but also in computers, calculus, physics, and auto mechanics, to name only a few.

*   *   *

Years later I had the pleasure of knowing Bomba and his wife Isabel, who patiently put up with his many shenanigans, as close friends. Kate, my beautiful "Limey" wife, and I were working in Islamabad during the 1980s and would often drive to Murree for supper at the "Cockroach Inn" followed by tea at the Murrays. We would warm our toes in front of their fire as we caught up on the local gossip or reminisced of times gone by. Bomba was always in fine form. One night as Isabel was pouring tea for us he gave her a juicy pinch. "Ian!!!" she shouted, glowering at him. "Ah," he chuckled, "I have so much to learn. My wife tells me there is a time and place for everything. I got the right place but the wrong time." Kate and I treasured these moments, and as we returned to Islamabad we would marvel at the rich relationships God had given us.

Relationships like that with the "Bombas" often deepen in times of suffering. In the spring of 1987, before Kate and I were married, Ian and Isabel had been driving to Islamabad and had a near-fatal car accident several miles short of the city. Ian was unhurt but Isabel was dying. Her legs were broken in many places and she was bleeding internally. Late that night they began surgery to save her life. I remember sitting next to Bomba holding his hand when Irv Nygren, our former government teacher at MCS, emerged from the operating room and said, loud enough for us to hear, "Someone had better prepare Ian, it doesn't look like she is going to make it. They can't get a pulse." I squeezed his hand so hard it hurt.

I don't know how long we sat there with everyone milling around us, but Irv came out again to announce that her heart was beating again and her blood pressure was rising. Her spleen had been ruptured. Isa-bel was eventually flown to Scotland where she endured countless surgeries to repair her legs. We didn't know if she would walk again—much less participate in Scottish dancing or run through the woods at Murree. Imagine Kate's and my surprise that summer when Ian and Isabel arrived at our wedding in Birmingham, England. She had only been out of the hospital a week and had just begun to walk. I could see she was in great pain, but, against doctor's orders, she was determined to walk on her own with the aid of a cane. Kate cried when she saw them. Here was real love and loyalty.

The Murrays have been at MCS for more than thirty-four years—and certainly hold the record for longest continuous service. Over sixty now, Isabel still coaches the girls' hockey team, and like Bomba, still leads by example.

22

Graduation*

Jonathan S. Addleton, '75

I was part of only the eleventh class to graduate from Murree Christian School, and yet the traditions associated with graduation already seemed as if they had been around for centuries. A baccalaureate service was scheduled at Holy Trinity Church in Murree, even as it had been held for the three graduates representing the class of '64 eleven years before. The processional music, number 414 in the hymnal, "God of Our Fathers," was the same. In our case, we also had special music— "The Prayer of Saint Francis of Assisi" as rendered by Pat Nye—followed by a sermon, a congregational hymn ("Be Still My Soul") and a recessional ("A Mighty Fortress Is Our God").

After it was all over, we gathered outside for photographs with Ian and Isabel Murray, our class advisors. We also posed for family photographs, an event that two years earlier had gotten my father into so much trouble with one of our supporting churches back in Macon, Georgia: my brother David's hair was too long; my sister Nancy's skirt was too short; and my mother

---

*Taken from the concluding chapter of Jonathan S. Addleton, *Some Far and Distant Place: A Memoir of Pakistan,* © University of Georgia Press, 1996. Used with permission.

wore a pants suit. The church, disturbed at this particular set
of missionaries who did not live up to expectations, dropped
their financial support on account of the photograph.

We felt very self-important that day, overtly religious and
spiritual-minded, as if this really was a special launching out
into the wider world from which we had been so insulated
these past many years. There was a certain pensiveness as
well, a feeling that we were watching an event in slow motion
rather than actually participating in it ourselves. Our parents
had taken us this far. Now we were on our own, spreading
across the globe within the week, strengthened in parting only
by the lingering words of a last sermon, a farewell hymn and a
final prayer.

The gifts we received from other parents and teachers emphasized the spiritual aspect of our departing, often including
as they did a Bible verse to "take with us," along with the obligatory $5 or $10 checks. The Roberts, Australian missionaries
working in Quetta, gave me Deuteronomy 31:8 ("The Lord himself goes at your head"). The Wilders, Presbyterian missionaries working in Lyallpur, gave me Psalms 84:11 ("The Lord
will hold back no good thing"). Liz Legget, the English teacher
from Scotland, passed on an odd verse from the Psalms, Psalm
34:11 ("Come my children, listen to me: I will teach you the fear
of the Lord"). Eva Hewitt, the school librarian, now in her seventies, gave perhaps the most familiar verse of all, Philippians
4:13 ("I can do everything through Christ which strengtheneth
me"). Hoyt and Edna Smith, Methodist missionaries working in
the Punjab who arrived in Pakistan even before independence
in 1947, now nearing retirement, offered a verse from Hebrews
which resonates still, nearly twenty years after the event:

> Remember where you stand: not before the pal-
> pable, blazing fire of Sinai with the darkness,
> gloom and whirlwind, the trumpet-blast and the
> oracular voice
> . . . No, you stand before Mount Zion and the city
> of the living God.

I stood before a mountain, that was for sure; I also imagined I stood before the living God, who knew what lay ahead
even if I did not.

Spiritual themes also dominated the commencement exercises held in the cavernous MCS school auditorium the following week. We marched solemnly, in time to a recorded rendition of "Pomp and Circumstance" and then Don Calderwood gave the invocation. Ellen Christy gave the valedictory address, striving mightily to offer a new twist to themes of parting that already, in the short history of Murree Christian School, were becoming stereotypical—appreciation for all that had been given us; a few back-handed compliments and cynical musings to maintain credibility, to suggest that there had been times when those around us had failed to maintain the high ideals which had been set before us; and a final recognition that, whatever may have happened in the past, we were now on our own, nothing much else could be done for us now.

Ellen, slight and with short hair, spoke softly. She stood on an upside down crate so she could see over the podium and into the audience below. As always, I admired her from afar; she seemed so competent, even as I continued to struggle with my own inarticulateness, my own feelings of emotional inadequacy, my continuing habit of lighting upon the awkward turn of phrase that so often degenerated into a stutter. Chuck Roub responded to the speech with grace and understanding and a few jokes, as he had in so many other commencement exercises over the past decade. Dr. Norval Christy, Ellen's father, a medical missionary from Taxila who specialized in cataracts and had himself restored sight to an estimated 100,000 people, distributed the fifteen diplomas in turn. Then we marched out into the night to the lingering lines of our school hymn, sung so often in Friday chapel services over the past twelve years:

Nestled neath the great Himalayas, far above the plain
Stands the school we love and cherish, more than
earthly gain.

Built upon a firm foundation, in God's hands a tool:
Shaping lives of dedication, Murree Christian School.

There was a reception line outside on the basketball court, then refreshments provided by all the high school mothers. Portraits of the fifteen graduates representing the class of '75 were posted on one wall. At the receiving line, one elderly missionary embraced each mother in turn, repeating the same phrase over and over again. "A fine son, a fine son," he announced gruffly before moving on. "Ma'am, you have a wonderful son."

By late evening, the crowd began to thin and, after a time, only we graduates and our families remained, talking quietly among ourselves. It was over, it was really over—there would never be a night quite like this, not for us anyway, an evening so full of promise and yet so tinged with all the sadness and inadequacies of adolescence. There was so much I wanted to say, so much I longed to do; but, as happened so often, I held back, keeping emotions inside that at this, of all possible nights, should have been on open display for all the world to see. I felt empty when I said my final goodbyes to people amongst whom I had spent almost my entire life, leaving in most cases without so much as a final handshake.

My brother and I walked back to Murree together that last night, along the three miles of winding road to our house at Ospring, just below Kashmir Point, hardly a mile from where I had been born eighteen years before. He had returned for my graduation, after finishing his first two years at Wheaton College. Even his accent had changed, inflected as it was by the latest in student jargon at that particular campus. Almost every sentence seemed to start with a "hey jack this" or "hey jack that," as if to underscore the growing distance that I feared might already be growing up between us.

We talked about his two years in America, about what I might expect to find when we would next meet again, at the Greyhound bus station in downtown Chicago six weeks from now. We couldn't aspire to follow in the footsteps of the missionary children of a previous generation, the Henry Luces who founded magazines, the John Herseys or Herman Hesses who wrote books, the learned scholars and prominent diplomats who grew up overseas, the progeny of missionaries, becoming experts on China and Japan and the Middle East. We were of a different time, representing a life experience that had already moved to the fringes of American society or at least American academia, where notions of a life motivated by love of God or orders from God seemed alien, even threatening.

I would feel the cultural shift in much more personal ways, in the academic community which I would shortly join. "Oh, your father is a missionary," was the usual comment, once it sunk in that such types still existed. "How interesting." The thought behind the expression seemed to be saying something quite different. "Oh, your father is a missionary," it suggested. "That explains everything." "You're grown up now," a professor said to me a few months later, not long after I arrived in Chicago, jumping to conclusions, little realizing the shaky and impermanent ground upon which his own philosophical premises so blithely rested. "You've got to stop believing these things."

Continuing on toward Murree, David and I talked about the trip I was embarking on early the next morning, with Stephen McCurry and Mark Pegors, two classmates who had shared with me in the same high school graduation exercises that very evening. The three of us were going "overland," by bus and train, to Paris. The route—Peshawar, Kabul, Kandahar, Tehran, Tabriz, Istanbul, Belgrade, Vienna, Munich, Amsterdam, and finally Paris—tripped off the tongue like poetry, I could not imagine the turbulence that would mark at least the first half of our itenerary in the decade ahead.

Again, I felt grown-up and self-important, as if setting off on a 10,000-mile journey across the wilds of Asia was a test of manhood. It would take ten days to reach Istanbul, at a cost of $40, all transportation, meals and cheap hotels included. There, waiting for a bus to Vienna, we would be asked to carry a cache of hashish; only Steve's immediate refusal spared us from what might have turned into a lengthy term in a Turkish jail. In Paris, we slept our last night on benches in a park near the Eiffel Tower, almost missing our $200 chartered flight to New York. We were met the next morning at John F. Kennedy Airport, by Dudley Chelchowski who had already graduated from Murree, left for America one year before us, and was now contemplating becoming a policeman.

All this seemed far away on that last night in Pakistan, as far away and incomprehensible as the stars. Ellen. William. Joel. Virginia. John. Nancy. Robert. Stephen. Deborah. Mark. Susan. Elaine. Emily. Margaret. Jonathan. Other names also, the names of our near contemporaries at Murree Christian School, those who had gone ahead and those who would shortly follow after. It was impossible then to imagine the different roads we would take, the choices we would make, the lives that were to come. It would have been a harder parting had we been gifted with a second sight, had we been able to peer into the future and know what would become of us.

David and I walked in silence for a time, words once again proving inadequate for the occasion. Suddenly, just below Rock Edge, at the halfway point between Jhika Gali and the Murree Post Office, my brother David stopped and looked across the mountains. Up the hill, at Rock Edge, was the house where I was born, the grey house with the corrugated tin roof and the thin wooden walls where my parents had lived when they first arrived in Pakistan two decades before. Kashmir was behind the mountains, beneath the Pir Panjal where snow was visible, even in summer, against the moonlight of the cloudless sky, the sky that stretched toward Nanga Parbat in one direction, toward the plains of Punjab and Sind in the other. It was the same sky that David and I had looked up at each night from our rope-slung beds, underneath sagging mosquito nets, on the mud roof of our Ratodero home, my father pointing out the constellations, my mother saying it was time to stop talking, time to be quiet and go to sleep.

It seemed so astonishing, that all this should ever have happened, that all this was about to end, that I was finally leaving Murree and Shikarpur and Ratodero behind, that it was unlikely that I would ever have opportunity to return. We stopped, we gazed up at the night sky, at Orion, at Taurus, at Pleiades, at the expanse of the Milky Way, whole universes improbably shaped and formed, as improbably shaped and formed as we who watched them now. The words that finally came were short and to the point, understated and brief, acquiring meaning only in later years, when I once again recalled the mountains and the sky, a sky that seemed to go on forever, a sky that had not yet been dimmed by the glow of a hundred cities, the lights of a thousand street lamps, the electricity of a million homes. "Look carefully," my brother said, casting a final glance upward at the sky which had sustained us all these years, which gathered round about us even now for this last and final time. "Look carefully," my brother said. "It will be a long time before you see stars shining this brightly again."

23

Coming "Home" (Re-entry)

Darlene Liddle, '87

The plane circled slowly over Chicago's O'Hare International Airport, waiting clearance to land. My eyes widened in dread and apprehension as I saw the colored dots below crawling along the black scars across the countryside. "NO!" my mind screamed. "I don't belong here! Pakistan is my home; or the United Arab Emirates." The dots materialized into fast-moving vehicles, and I clenched my fists. How different from my first arrival in a foreign country. Then, I had skipped excitedly free from the Pan Am 747, eager to do and to see. Now, twelve years and six schools later, I was tired of moving, tired of starting anew. I wanted to be home, and stay home, and my home was surely not here in this little-known land of my birth. I jumped as the tires shrieked and bounced off the runway. Breathing deeply, I thought, "I must have an open attitude," and made an effort to push aside this dismal frame of mind.

It took forever for the plane to taxi up to the terminal, extending the agony of my ambivalence: no easy jump between worlds for me. Finally, the whine of the jet engines stopped. Then, before the silence could soothe me, came the busy clatter and swish of seatbelts unbuckling, bags being zipped and tossed over shoulders, and people shuffling into the aisle. I stumbled into the queue, out the door, and stepped unwillingly into the unknown.

Immediately, I noticed the absence of the protective military officers with their shiny black machine guns, and a brief wave of vulnerability washed over me. The airport was strangely uncrowded, with spotless floors, and the subdued hum of voices held a distinct American accent. Standing in the passport line, I gasped suddenly as I glanced at the long line of airline agents. They could have been one and the same person, so identical did they appear. Each had heavily-shadowed eyes, black spikes of mascara, high-cheeked blush, and blood-red lipstick. Each seemed to be wearing identical wigs of long, curly blond hair, piled up with extra-body mousse, and frozen in place with extra-hold hairspray. As I watched in horror, they smiled engagingly and said, "Have a nice day!" over and over again. But their eyes were hollow and the unsmiling, tedious job of earning a paycheck showed through between each customer. I felt a pang of homesickness, remembering the genuinely friendly faces I had left behind, and the simple life of Pakistan, where individuality had sung strong and clear.

The transit lounge was lined with snack bars and gift shops, and the tantalizing aroma of pretzel and hot dog tickled my nose. My stomach growled, but then I saw the price. One dollar for a pretzel!? Seventeen rupees? Oh, for the inexpensive life of Pakistan with the one-rupee snacks . . . the potatoes and onions and peppers fried in spicy batter, the bags of potato chips, or the soft ice cream cones. I was suddenly hungry for the hot roast chicken, the curries, and the chunks of grilled, red-peppered beef. These potent dishes could fire the mouth with ecstasy, but also blast the eyes and noses of the inexperienced and force them to dive desperately for a drink of cool water . . . With a sigh of resignation, I bought a tasteless hot dog and smothered it with mustard.

During the long ride home, I stared out the window of the big, luxuriously purring car. Vehicles whizzed by on four-lanes- - no, *six* lanes—of blacktop. I had never seen so many different kinds of cars! But the drivers uniformly stared dead ahead, oblivious in their air-conditioned compartments to the surrounding hues of green, and the wide expanses of corn and wheat . . . I was suddenly glad for the narrow, serpentine roads of the Himalayan foothills, which had forced buses and vans to slow down enough to allow passengers to notice and soak in the majesty of God's mountainous handiwork. And I was glad for the many walks I had taken. I remembered the moss-covered walls of closely-fitted stones slanting heavily against the mountainside, the great overhanging boulders, and the half-uprooted pines ready to topple with the next rain. I remembered the cheerful clusters of daisies and buttercups holding tenaciously to the rim of steep emerald slopes on the other side, and the thick pine forests through which an occasional crack exposed, in rugged splendor, the reaches upon reaches of ragged snow-caps. I also remembered the warm pies of smelly manure, all too easy to step into if you forgot to look at the road ahead.

A few days later, just when the scream in my heart was beginning to wind down, I made my first visit to the mall. It was like the airport—except more so. The lights were bright and gaudy, and the word "SALE" shouted from every window. Couples walked by, openly holding hands, and teens stole kisses in the corners. Huge stores, with racks upon racks of clothing—all priced at $19.99—ritualized an automated materialism. I was soon lost in a maze of aisles. I searched frantically for a way of escape and yearned for the unthreatening world of the small shops in Pakistan.

In Murree, the "mall" referred to the main street through town, a winding road where no cars were allowed, walled in on either side by shops of all kinds; and if you knew where to look, you could find almost anything. Restaurants, shoe shops, photo studios, earring shops, hotels, ice cream parlors, fabric stores, tailors, and general purpose stores that sold a more Western variety of goods—nail polish, batteries, canned milk, children's toys, and imported chocolate bars. Narrow openings between buildings frequently concealed varied flights of stairs that led precipitously downward to the lower bazaar. Here, a steep, cobbled-stoned road twisted past the cloth dyers, the many vivid skeins of yarn, the small tea shops, the tiny grocery stores, the butchers' stalls.

Halfway down the main mall, a wide walkway branched off to the right. Entered by a short flight of broad, shallow steps, the covered bazaar also cleverly covered the main route to the bus stations farther down the hill. Nut shops displayed their goods in large straw-woven baskets, fabric merchants flaunted brightly-patterned lengths of silk and satin, and everywhere salesmen vehemently urged shoppers to consider the many intricate wood carvings and brass ornaments. It was the kind of place where, if the time were available, you could spend hours with friends, wandering about in fascination, or where you could immediately find what was needed, if necessary. Yet, in the malls of America, I was lost and soon fled.

*   *   *

I caressed the dark padded cover of my senior year picture album and opened it slowly, painfully. Yet, even as I pleaded with time to move backward, I realized that the past had vanished beyond recall. Those intense high school days of emotional roller-coasters were gone forever, leaving only today and tomorrow. Leafing through my yearbook, I began to say my final farewells, imprinting those sacred memories in the treasure chest of my mind. I looked up, a healing catharsis of tears washing my cheeks; and then I took the yearbook and album from my bedside table, stowed them with finality in my bottom drawer, and reached for a Kleenex.

This "descriptive essay" was written in October 1987 as an English assignment Darlene Liddle's first semester in college. Along with the several books mentioned in the Introduction (Footnote, page 6, see Peter Jordan, Re-entry: Making the Transition from Missions to Life at Home *(YWAM Publishing, 1992) which offers a sympathetic discussion of the issues raised in this chapter and includes some helpful pointers.*

24

More Than Earthly Gain

Results of the 1993 Alumni Survey

In March and April of 1993, I (Paul Seaman) mailed a survey to everyone on the MCS alumni list. It was the first time that a poll of this sort had been taken. The one-page form contained sixteen questions and was designed to be completed in about fifteen minutes.

Most of the questions were simple statistical data: age, sex, national origin, number of years at MCS, etc. Three required some reflection and these, of course, provided the most interesting results: #13—*Overall, would you describe your exper-ience [at MCS] as a happy or unhappy one? Please elaborate if you wish;* #14—*Have you maintained a faith perspective similar to that which was presented at MCS?* and #16—*Other comments.* These questions elicited many striking and insightful statements too diverse to summarize here, except to note two recurring themes: 1) an appreciation for the uniqueness of MCS, with its rich spiritual life, cultural diversity, and intense sense of community that has rarely been found since; and 2) the oft-repeated paradox: "I wouldn't want to live it over again [or, I would never send my kids to boarding school], but I'm glad for the experience and wouldn't trade it for anything in the world."

Of approximately 600 surveys distributed, 162 were completed and sent back within a year of the initial mailing—more than a 25% return, a remarkably high rate for a mail-in poll. Forty of these were from staff or former staff, representing 25% of the total respondents. (With so much research emphasis in the past few decades on MKs and boarding school *students,* it is interesting to note the strong impact MCS had on *staff* as well.) Half of those who completed the survey contributed additional comments or narratives that provided most of the material for this book.

The respondents ranged in age from sixteen to ninety-three (the late Eva Hewitt holding the latter honor). Surveys that were filled out by parents for their adult children, by students still in high school, or by those who graduated after 1992 were not included. The percentages reported in the following paragraphs are calculated from the 120 responses from former *students* only.

Seventy-two percent described their overall experience at MCS as a happy one, 9% felt it was unhappy, and 18% thought it was mixed. It should be noted, with reference to this question in particular, that any self-administered, voluntary survey will have a measure of self-selecting results. It can provide some data, or indicate some characteristics, of *those who responded to the survey,* and not necessarily reflect accurately the whole target group. For example, many MCS alumni who may have had an unhappy experience at MCS, or no longer consider themselves Christians, may have been less likely to return the survey. This factor is impossible to calculate, but suggests that the statistics reported here should be seen as relative and not absolute.

In this spirit, question #14 was admittedly ambiguous: *Have you maintained a faith perspective similar to that which was presented at MCS?* It is assumed, however, that most people understood this to mean "conservative evangelical values"—traditional Christian beliefs with an emphasis on personal salvation, the importance of "witnessing" (saving the world for Jesus), and a literal interpretation of the Bible as God's Word. Sixty-eight percent of the MCS alumni continue to identify themselves this way; 29% do not, but most of these are Christians, "with a broader perspective" now. Ten percent of the alumni surveyed do not identify themselves as Christians. Since 98% of the respondents came from missionary homes this last figure cannot be accounted for by the students who came to MCS from outside the missions community.

(Of the former staff who returned the survey, 95% still ascribe to an MCS-style/evangelical faith, 100% identify themselves as Christians, and 96% describe their time at MCS as happy.)

The age range of alumni respondents was twenty to forty-six; 60% were in their thirties at the time they filled out the survey, 24% in their twenties, and 17% in their forties. Forty-two percent were male, 58% female. The majority of respondents—84%—were at MCS during the Sixties and Seventies; 65% of them were from the United States, 20% from Great Britain, and the others from Europe, Australia, New Zealand and Canada; one person came from Guatemala and two from Pakistan.

The average time at MCS was seven years, while 45% spent nine to twelve years there. Seventy-three percent were there with at least two siblings.

Of those surveyed, 66% have visited MCS at least once since leaving and 26% have worked, or are now working, in Pakistan (this includes as staff at MCS as well as other missionary and non-missionary occupations). Twenty percent currently serve as ministers, missionaries, or their spouses (this figure may be low since some females identified themselves only as "housewives" or "mothers"). Including these, 61% of the respondents have gone into human service occupations. Seventy-two percent are married, 22% single, and 4% divorced.

In order to keep the survey brief and user-friendly, some interesting questions were left unasked, or are simply beyond the scope of this analysis. Survey results are often more instructive, though, in the correlation between answers to different questions than in the simple compilation of individual statistics. For example, is there a connection between those who had a happy experience at MCS and the length of time spent at the school? Or, how much was a positive experience influenced by having brothers and sisters in boarding too, or by what era one was at the school?

Establishing these connections with such a limited sample

group would probably be unreliable. However, some patterns are suggested by recurring statements in question #16, *Other comments*. One: a secure and satisfying home life makes a significant difference to how well a child will adjust to boarding. And two: those who attended MCS in the late-1950s and early-1960s, when the school was just getting started, generally had a much more difficult and unpleasant time than those who came in later years. This is a solid and very encouraging trend.

The early years of MCS were seen as legalistic, and made more harshly so by the insecurity of an inexperienced staff. (Interviews with former staff confirm this view.) Not all the staff believed the same way, but the others were more willing to compromise for the sake of unity and getting on with the job of starting and running the school. Thus, the more adamant conservative denominations set the tone at MCS for many years. The Christian unity among the staff was certainly genuine, though, and is one of the distinctive features of MCS that both alumni and former staff repeatedly mentioned.

The last twenty years have seen a significant increase in the Christian and cultural diversity at MCS—not to mention new buildings and much easier living arrangements. US Americans no longer hold a majority, and in 1993 a Brit was appointed director (formerly principal) of the school for the first time.

*   *   *

The following section presents a sampling of the responses to the question, "Overall, would you describe your experience at MCS as a happy or unhappy one?"

[Female, 47 years old] Happy. Wouldn't trade it for anything—the education was good enough to get me into higher education and the spiritual emphasis and formal Bible classes give me cause to rejoice that I had access to such a good foundation early in life. . . . As a parent I have come to understand what a responsibility it was (and is) for the houseparents and teachers of MCS to have so much influence in the lives of the students—and what it meant to the parents to give up that influence to those teachers and houseparents during much of the year.

[Male, 46 years old] Mixed. Overall I enjoyed my childhood, but I was carrying a lot of resentment against the house rules and the rigid brand of Christianity prevailing during my high school years; most of us did. Some still are bitter.

[F, 41] Very happy. The first couple of years were not so happy largely due to [my sister and I] being the only British children and being seen as different. Once this was overcome, I can only remember very happy times, which have given me a foundation to always look back on. I could write a book on the spiritual struggles since leaving MCS—difficult to say whether the time there has been a help or hindrance where that is concerned.

[F, 40] Unhappy. Inexperienced boarding parents, legalistic rules, unsupervised and unmonitored peer relationships made MCS horrible; hypocritical staff who laid big guilt trips and didn't prepare kids for transition out of MCS. [I continue to have] bad feelings about churches preaching what they don't live—based on MCS experience where you were never quite good enough.

My earliest memory was being left at age six at Marsden and being told that Mother would not be able to come see me if I cried when she left. Also, big guilt messages of how we helped our parents serve God by our being brave and big—God loves happy children, etc.

I still dream about MCS and my dreams are grief-filled. Those years left me deeply wounded.

[M, 40] I learned to hate letter writing at an early age (which vice is yet far from overcome), because of the supervised letters home in boarding each week that forced us to confront our parents' absence.

[F, 38] The pressure to conform to an evangelical faith [was a very unpleasant aspect of MCS]. I had by that time already committed my life to the Lord, but I feel there was undue pressure on us as children to pray in public and give a testimony (I know some imaginative souls who even managed to make one up!). "You must keep a stiff upper lip for Jesus." You were discouraged from telling your parents how you really felt in the fear that you would let God down by dragging them away from "The Work." I grew up hating the Lord, and it took him many years to convince me that he is actually a God of love.

Because I was a very trusting and optimistic child, my memories of MCS are not bitter, but I believe that my experiences contributed toward my extremely low self-esteem and my manipulation by other people throughout my life. For a long time I believed that many of the other kids at school were simply badly brought up, but I've now come to the conclusion that they, like me, were experiencing a lot of trauma being separated from their parents and family lifestyle. I think, in those early days, that the staff were not prepared for what we would be like as a group, and it was often hard to tell that they cared for us at all.

[staff, 1967-71] Jim and I came as very young adults, inexperienced and totally ignorant of children's needs at any deep level. Jim was trained as a teacher but this was his first job. I was a nurse. We found a great deal of love and tolerance; when we look back on all the mistakes we made, we feel very humble—especially when we remember all the kindness we received.

[staff, 1976-78, 81-82] MCS taught me to appreciate an international interdenominational Christian atmosphere. The people were not all perfect, but they were on "The Way."

[staff, 1982-86; age 70] Very happy! Aside from my children, MCS encompassed the happiest days of my life . . . The staff and students comprised the most loving, caring community I've ever seen. I've worked 42 years "away from home" and was never so appreciated nor so enthusiastic about any other job. It was wonderful!

[staff, 1971-77] *Very mixed!* I remember some very good and some really awful times. Sometimes I was very lonely and I found it hard to work, live, socialize, etc., always with the same people. The best thing about MCS were the kids, some of whom gave a lot to me. I have some wonderful memories of them.

[staff, 1973-76] As a teacher, I always felt I learned more

from my students than what I taught them. Having children from ten different countries in my class was a terrific broadening experience. It was also good to see childlike faith in action as we prayed and studied Scripture in class. One neat thing about teaching at MCS was the teamwork I sensed with teachers and parents, though they were physically distanced, and boarding parents. I wish my own children could experience going to a school like MCS. There was a much closer bond than you ever get in a public school here in Canada.

[F, 38] Happy. Unhappy [memories include] seeing my one-year younger sister get hit with a ruler by teacher from England; not learning to dance, not learning to play cards; hearing that my seven-year-old sister got shut in a drawer; and an overly-restrictive Finnish staff person regarding dating.

One of the unfortunate aspects of a religious school is that everybody is forced to abstain from some activities such as dancing and cards because of the beliefs of some. There were probably some inconsistencies in standards set for different students.

[F, 38] Happy, but mostly unhappy. It was a difficult experience being separated from my parents nine months out of the year. My parents were missionaries in the Middle East so we had little contact with them.

[M, 38] Happy. True happiness I would define as a perfect mix of joy and sorrow, which God has expertly blended into my life. Left to order my own circumstances, I would never choose sorrow and would be consequently imbalanced, so my overall feeling for the boarding school experience is gratitude.

[F, 37] Happy. My kids are ten and twelve, and as I live and interact with them each day it seems almost beyond my imagination that I could send them off to boarding school! And yet my time at MCS was generally very positive, and I don't feel any regret or bitterness about those years.

[F, 36] Happy. Being a boarder had its hurts, but looking at the lives of friends in the States, and evaluating what my life could have been, I feel that I had more pluses than minuses. My personal assessment of the problems one hears about concerning boarding schools is that it has to do with how your parents and other significant adults handle it as much as anything. I felt that because I was allowed to feel the negative feelings when they happened, to cry when I needed, to say what I thought, because I never had to be "brave" or live up to anything, that I was able to leave most of the pain (though not all) behind.

[M, 35] I feel that MCS tried to put us in the role of "little missionaries" which was unfair because we hadn't chosen the lifestyle for ourselves.

[F, 35] Unhappy/lonely. There remains an overwhelming sense of rejection, of having been "sent away" to be cared for by someone other than my parents. For nearly two decades I have tried to atone for the unknown trespass that made my parents send me away. Eager to please, extremely compliant, I continue to try to earn the approval and acceptance of parents and authority figures for fear I'll be sent away again.

At thirty-five, it is sometimes difficult for me to acknowledge the needs of a six-year-old in boarding school. But often it is the little girl feelings that surface with such force.

[F, 35] Mixture. Experience of boarding school conjures up a lot of painful and happy memories—although difficult, the experience brought an intensity of closeness to those around you and a bonding that is similar to a war experience or the like.

[F, 35] MCS did let us down rather badly in not advising us about drugs and sex, and how to deal with them in a real-time situation (not just pray). I think this was a serious defect in the school.

[M, 35—*grades 1-4*] Very Happy. It is the school I have the fondest memories of by far; the only sad times I can remember were a few days after leaving home, and the few days before going back home. I greatly appreciate the influence MCS—pupils and staff—had on my life during a very formative period. Although it was the first of four schools, it is the only one I ever still think about now, twenty-five years later.

[M, 30] Freedom given by teachers and houseparents was

fantastic and quite a contrast to one year of English boarding school that followed, which I absolutely hated.

[F, 28] Mixed—valuable. I felt lucky that I had siblings at boarding school, especially my oldest sister. My parents and brother and sisters had a lot of family problems. One sister was mentally/emotionally ill. I felt very guilty for being "spoiled." It was hard to be separated from parents at such an early age. Also, I was mistreated by the older roommates (third graders) and will never forget that. I felt like the ugly duckling (I was picked to play the Ugly Duckling *and* Swan in a school play, though). My fondest memories are of my *Pakistani* friends, and of the traveling we got to do, in Pakistan and abroad.

[I have some fun memories of MCS, but the staff] were much too strict and I would never send my son to such a boarding school. I especially remember the rules about food: "huge" no-thank you helpings and prizes for good manners; lots of stupid rules. It was hard to adjust to life and children in the U.S. I would not trade the experience of living overseas, though.

It has been difficult to have an identity. I was considered so different by U.S. classmates and teased a lot, even though I lived in a fairly cosmopolitan, university town. It was also hard to associate with the well-to-do (doctors and scholars) in the States, and yet to have so little materialistically ourselves.

Still, all in all, living side by side with other cultures and seeing true poverty and war firsthand, along with the travel, was *invaluable*. I feel sad that other people cannot relate to my feelings or experiences. Even my husband is not interested, and my son probably won't be either.

[M, 27] Happy. I found the lack of social skills that would be appropriate to my home culture really difficult when I returned to the U.K. at age fifteen. I had never used a phone, never been in a supermarket, and I didn't know how to dance. So I went through quite severe culture shock. Boarding school gave me experiences I am very glad I had, but also deprived me of others. I wish I had more time with my parents as I see that my relationship with them is not all it could/should be and we all regret that. It's hard to make up time lost like that. Houseparents in Murree were brilliant, but no substitute for the long term stability of knowing your own parents well.

[F, 27] Very happy. My childhood/school days at MCS were the best years of my life in some ways—a great and very positive experience. A time of fun, adventure, learning and a great time for experiencing close friendships with both my peers and houseparents. MCS has had such a profound effect on my life. I had an extremely tough time settling in England because I was so "American" and just so different from people here.

[F, 25] Happy. I probably wouldn't exchange my time at Murree for anything, in terms of learning, development, exposure; but there are regrets—for example, segregation from the Pakistani or non-MCS culture; and that I haven't really kept directly in touch with my peers.

[F, 23] Unhappy. There were moments, even weeks, of great happiness at MCS, but these were against a backdrop of seven years of social rejection which happens to "someone" in almost any institution—but should it happen in a Christian community?
I am a committed evangelical Christian, but have found since returning to [my home country] that there are many more ways of looking at life than TEAM and American Baptists seem to allow.

[F, 20] Happy. Friendships I formed in those early years are still going strong. There were plenty of lonely and unhappy times when I was excluded from a group, made worse by the fact that we lived together, not just saw each other at school.

[M, 20] Happy. In elementary grades, boarding was a very tough experience, being separated from my parents. Due to this my faith was strengthened though. Maybe a boarding school is too tough for the very young (ages 6-9). I found it this way and cannot express in writing the hell I partly went through. Later, I felt deep friendships with teachers and students, independence (as a boy), responsibility (student council), and high academic and spiritual standards that are pillars of my life today. Not only do I gladly look back on many positive experiences, but I feel strongly that God blessed the decision—and the sacrifice—my parents made to send us there. Both negative, harmful and hurtful experiences and the happy, good ones molded us into mature young adults in a manner that I am thankful for.

Boarding school is not an institution of the past, there is also a great future in it! Important foundations which I found helpful: 1) going through school accompanied by teachers and dorm parents who are believers; 2) the academic standard was so good that an easy transition to Germany was possible; 3) the possibility for students to develop talents other than academics and sports (this one could be enhanced—I was so thankful when I finally realized I didn't have to be good at sports to be cool); and 4) the wide spectrum of cultures, languages, denominations, and people was great!

* * *

MCS was the opposite of the Tower of Babel: the staff gathered from the far corners of the Earth and somehow, for God's glory and through God's grace, were mostly able to put aside their human egos and speak with one tongue. Many may suppose that in a conservative evangelical boarding school one could expect a certain uniformity among the staff. In fact, the staff at MCS represented many different cultural backgrounds and nationalities, with widely differing personalities, theological views, levels of education, and leadership styles. It is impressively to the school's credit that the staff nonetheless managed to present a singleness of purpose and a remarkable consistency in their expectations of students.

In spite of their differences, the nearly constant duress of circumstantial hardships, and the ongoing stress of being entrusted—totally—with the responsibility for other people's children, the staff at Murree Christian School provided us with the safety and security of an adult world at peace with itself. In ten years of living in close quarters, I never once saw staff members speak harshly to one another or heard a married couple fight.

In many ways life was probably harder for the staff at MCS than for the students. For those of us who grew up there, at least, what we experienced was normal, it was home. But the staff had to deal with the disorientation of culture shock, sometimes severe health problems, an unaccustomed lack of privacy in such a tiny community, with no real alternatives for fellowship or friendship, and the tension of having to set a good example all the time.

As children, we could not appreciate how inexperienced many of the staff at MCS were, or perceive how much they struggled with their own feelings of inadequacy. Perhaps MCS did not have more than a normal share of emotionally immature or unstable adults; but isolation, insecurity, and fundamentalism are a dangerous combination. A cultural mindset of religious absolutism combined with a strong belief in private sanctification—and unquestioned authority—is a recipe for cultism. Eunice Hill once commented that MCS was "saved by the British"—meaning, I think, that MCS has been largely protected from rigid or parochial thinking by its international and interdenominational character.

This diversity has helped to keep the school accountable, not only for its educational or religious standards but also for the personal behavior of staff members. There have been remarkably few cases where a boarding parent at MCS proved to have an unsafe temper, or otherwise did not show discretion or respect with regard to students—and these situations were dealt with quickly, always with the children's best interest in mind.

In my work with Global Nomads International I have heard horrendous stories of physical and sexual abuse in MK schools—and not just in the distant past, but experienced by people my age. These situations tended to occur in small isolated, single-denomination boarding schools where there were no structures of accountability. I am glad (and a little bit proud) to report that no such stories have been attributed to Murree Christian School.

The damage some of us sustained from growing up at MCS was more subtle. There is not space here to elaborate on the paradoxical inheritance of guilt and arrogance that such an upbringing ingrained in us—and the lifelong emotional, social, and professional consequences of the expectations we were given. I can only highlight a few areas of concern that came up repeatedly in my research and in conversations with other alumni.

Is boarding school by definition a callous institution, especially for the very young, detrimental to children's emotional development and family well-being? There are credible arguments and plenty of personal anecdotes on both sides of this question. Any effort to calibrate the qualitative weight of one experience over another is usually a dubious exercise. What can be accomplished by trying to rate the relative pain of peer rejection to that of rape or the social chaos in Bosnia and Somalia? As one former student put it, "MCS was neither wonderful nor terrible; it was a life." We deal with what we are given and can only hope that we do so constructively and with integrity. Without getting sucked into making erroneous comparisons about the pettiness of our own suffering, a wider perspective on the relevant issues can help avoid both the paralysis of guilt trips and the crippling effects of self-delusion. Developing a wider perspective has, of course, been one of the major purposes of this book—and reflects my own "testimony" in this area.

My heritage as an MK turned out to be quite different from the rootless, maladjusted stereotype I had accepted. The more I examined the distinctive combination of grief, alienation, pride, and nostalgia that I associated with the TCK legacy, the more I noticed that many of these "unique" characteristics were shared by others, including immigrants and refugees. When I became involved with Global Nomads International, I heard the stories of other TCKs whose parents had been in the military or foreign service. For them, changing schools—and countries—ten times in twelve years was not uncommon. Compared to their experience, my childhood at MCS was remarkably stable!

My friend Lois Gilliland, a Christian family therapist in Pasadena, California, with a special ministry to older MKs and TCKs, was sixty-eight years old before she could write about her own experience. When she was eight-and-a-half she was put in a boarding school in Canada run by the Sudan Interior Mission while her parents went off to serve the Lord in Nigeria. She did not see them again for *five years*. (Gowan's Home continued to operate through 1966.) Later, she and her three sisters were sent to Westervelt School for Missionary Children, in South Carolina. When her mother came home after only three years and took them out of boarding Lois was overjoyed. Yet, at the same time, Lois felt guilty for pulling her mother away from the mission field and from her husband who remained in Africa.

Was MCS too strict? Certainly it was far less strict than

most British schools—public or private. And the Catholic schools attended by millions of American children put MCS in pretty broad company. Indeed, the heavy regulation of our daily lives was matched by a remarkable degree of freedom (for boys, at least), especially as we grew older. The rational basis for some of the rules was sometimes not adequately explained and some of the rules seemed to have no basis—other than the symbolic exercise of authority. We complained earnestly, often, and righteously (mostly among ourselves), but basically accepted the status quo. The only times that really elicited rebellion, bitterness, or trauma were when the punishment far exceeded the "crime," and seemed to be prompted not by a need to uphold the system but by anger or even vindictiveness and fear. Fortunately, these occasions were rare and, if I am to be honest, I experienced far more misery from peer abuse than from overly strict staff.

I can remember many summer mornings when I was seven and eight, waiting at the school bus stop near Bexley and experiencing such awful "teasing" that I sometimes fled home in tears before the bus arrived. Why was there no parent or other adult chaperon waiting with us? One former student, commenting on the dangers of too much unsupervised time, compared our experience to that in *Lord of the Flies*.

Margaret W. Long has written an intriguing paper suggesting that MKs may be more susceptible to cults precisely *because of* their strong religious upbringing. MKs are accustomed to being told what to do, they tend to be highly idealistic, and they often have a strong need for meaningful community (a sense of belonging, or home). Combine these factors with the rootlessness MKs often experience from the transition back to their country of origin and, as Long illustrates from personal experience, the danger can be quite real. Drawing on another researcher's study of "totalitarian evangelicalism" (V. M. Doland, 1983), Long notes the possible similarities between cults and evangelical boarding schools.

> Ask yourself these questions: Is order maintained for the purpose of control versus the purpose of doing things in a decent, orderly manner? Do the school's energies mainly have to be spent on controlling? Do you seek to develop uniform behavior that is reflexive? Do you instill the idea

that the individual and his needs are subordinate
to the school, the group, or the family? Do you
have unnecessary rules that are designed to condition the individual to obey? Do you attempt to
evaluate the individual's attitude as well as his
actions? Do you use severe and humiliating punishment for disobedience? Do you discourage
questioning, suggesting, and critical thinking?
Are you isolated from the outside world? Do you
instill the idea that the outside world is evil or
bad?*

From my experience (in the 1960s and 1970s), MCS would
have to answer "yes" to more than half of these questions. Long
emphasizes that just teaching about cults is not enough. This
approach "obscures the fact that most people, especially Christians, who join cults do not do so because of the teachings of the
group, but because their basic needs are met" (p. 381). We studied cults in Bible class at MCS, but even in junior high I found
the materials we were using to be simplistic and self-serving.
They did not address the emotional, psychological, and social
issues involved, but merely offered scriptural "proof texts."
Margaret Long reminds readers that Tim Stone, the second in
command of the Jonestown cult in Guyana, which in 1978 or-
chestrated the mass suicide of 913 people, was a student leader
at Wheaton College and a staunch Baptist (p. 373).

The widespread experience of depression within the missions community—including among MKs—is another issue
that is finally beginning to be acknowledged and, sometimes,
dealt with directly.** Some staff members at MCS were crip-

---

*"The Cult Appeal: Is the MK Susceptible or Immune?" in *Under-
standing and Nurturing the Missionary Family* (Compendium of the
International Conference on Missionary Kids, Quito, Ecuador, 1987,
Vol. 1), eds. Pam Echerd and Alice Arathoon, pp. 372-386.

**See Ruth E. Van Reken, *Letters Never Sent;* Anne Townsend, *Faith
Without Pretending;* and Marjory F. Foyle, *Honorably Wounded:
Stress Among Christian Workers;* also Wayne Muller, *Legacy of the
Heart: The Spiritual Advantages of a Painful Childhood,* an im-
portant work with a distinct ecumenical approach that includes no-
nonsense insights and practical meditations.

pled by depression; not only was their service on the mission field deeply affected but, consequently, they have had to struggle—sometimes for many years—with their very sense of identity as people who were called by God and failed. Beyond recognizing depression as a legitimate illness, recent scientific studies of nutritional and virus-related causes of depression have profound implications for the spiritual self-image of individuals who experience depression—as well as for how their co-workers and employers respond to them.

The missions community in general has begun to address more broadly, with the benefit of the social sciences, a whole range of issues related to missionary service, boarding schools, and MKs. Consequently, there are now many resources available to mission agencies and to adult MKs. The International Conferences on Missionary Kids (ICMKs) held in 1984, 1987, and 1989 are prime examples of this new sensitivity and commitment to holistic support. So is the general credibility now given to the term "Third Culture Kids" as a useful model for understanding the experience of expatriate children, the impact of re-entry, and the causes and consequences of grief as an integral part of the TCK experience. Papers on MK research now appear regularly in scholarly journals, such as a recent article reporting on screening techniques various mission agencies are now using—or ought to use—to ensure quality control in recruiting staff for MK schools.*

Closer to home, Ian and Isabel Murray, with the support of Murree Christian School and their home board, the Church of Scotland, spent four months in 1994 (August-November) interviewing MCS alumni to find out how to better prepare students for life after they return to their countries of origin. The Murrays' "North American Tour" prompted nineteen reunions and enabled them to interview 147 alumni. They also met sixty-two spouses and 123 children, visited with 144 other people connected with MCS, and slept in forty different beds.

While the Murrays' survey had a different emphasis than mine, it is interesting to note the similarity in some of the themes that emerged. A preliminary summary of the Murrays' project included these observations: Many alumni had dif-

---

*Glenn Taylor and David Pollock, "Boarding School Staff: How to Get the Best," *Evangelical Missions Quarterly* 31:2 (January 1995).

ficulty with re-entry—felt they were not adequately prepared for life in the home culture, and with loneliness—partly due to coming from such close relationships at MCS; many alumni feel they are missing a part of their heritage by not having been exposed enough to Pakistani culture; and most alumni say they would come back to Pakistan to work, but many would not want to put their children into boarding.

The Murrays' questionnaire went much further than mine in soliciting specific advice from alumni on what changes the school could make to better prepare current students for re-entry. The fact that such an extensive survey was even conducted—in person—indicates the school's commitment to addressing many of the concerns raised in this chapter.

This can also be seen in the leadership role MCS has taken in providing resources to missionary families who choose to home-school their children. The school facilitates skills workshops and support forums, and staff are available for interviews to counsel parents about educational issues. Each year, home-schooled children are invited to attend day classes at MCS for the month of August.

The spiritual earnestness of Murree Christian School has gained a more earthly application. As its leaders more deeply appreciate the many facets of human wholeness, the words of the school hymn become less abstract:

> There within her halls of learning
> Wisdom's torch burns bright;
> Where indeed her students grasp
> The Good and True and Right.
>
> Teachers, students work united
> Toward this common goal:
> Christ to serve with consecrated
> Body, mind, and soul.

*   *   *

The following three reflections are by Nonie (Lundgren) Wakeman, '65, Roy Montgomery, '73, and Marybeth Tewksbury, '74, respectively.

I gratefully look back on my time at MCS as a rich spiritual heritage. Every time I join a study or discussion group I realize the amount of Bible knowledge I gained through devotional times and Bible classes in those growing up years. I know we didn't always appreciate the enforced "quiet times," chapel, and evening devotions, or the formal Bible classes, but I have seen over and over how much more familiar I am with Scripture than a great many of my peers in the local church. That level of familiarity has proved valuable many times over the years.

It's also amazing to me that even after all these years (thirty since graduation!), whenever I hear or sing certain songs, pictures of MCS friends and places come to mind. "When Morning Guilds the Skies" goes with Sandes Home. We must have sung that one for breakfast "millions" of times. And "What Can Wash Away My Sin?" with Tim Philbrick and his "squeeze box." There are also songs that, at one time, I thought I wouldn't miss if I never heard them again! Like "O Come, O Come Emmanuel," which I associate with St. Denys' chapel. But now those songs evoke memories of experiences that I wouldn't trade for anything.

*   *   *

MCS was kind of an isolated culture unto itself. All new students had to undergo adjustments in order to fit in. The school represented a rich mosaic of nationalities which all blended into a unique culture that was certainly "Western." Of course, Pakistan also is a rich mixture of tongues, classes (in an Islamic republic we wouldn't suggest castes), creeds, tribes, and peoples, all "Eastern." The boarding staff were entirely Westerners, so at times their directives ran at cross-purposes with the scruples of their semi-Eastern children, particularly with those who had a preference for the East.

A couple personal examples I might relate: Being informed that my very best embroidered Pakistani *kapara* was inappropriate for church (I put a foolish bow tie over a Nehru collar and wore it anyway); and being pressured to take a date to that dreadful annual banquet. I hope there weren't too many school girls who misinterpreted respectful distance (my "Eastern" reservations) for arrogant aloofness. At the time, I'm sure I couldn't have explained the difference anyway, so I went along with the excuse offered that I was just too blooming shy.

One conversation that stands out in my mind was in Urdu with a stranger as we walked toward Jhika Gali from Gharial. He was utterly dumbfounded to learn that I had lived most of my life in Murree, yet knew next to no Punjabi. That represents one regret of mine—that I didn't make a greater effort to make local friends. By grades eleven and twelve, this unlegislated apartheid began to bother me so I made some amends—such as eating my lunches at the tea stall rather than the cafeteria, switching from Latin to Urdu classes, choosing a Jhika haircut over the then in school vogue of long hair, and wearing Pakistani clothes more of the time. Urdu lessons with Mr. Bahadur were sheer pleasure. A better-natured, kinder gentleman I have never met.

One fine fellow (a beggarman) that I spent some time talking with almost every day going to and from school had a daily comment for my attire. If I were dressed Eastern, it suited me very nicely, he'd say; or, if Western, very poorly. Once at school, however, quite the opposite opinion would often be subtly expressed. I grew a "soochi" beard (a respectful word for a peach-fuzzish one), which I shaved off prior to graduation—to the great disappointment of my Pakistani friends. If a Pakistani grows his beard it is for religious reasons, and he doesn't turn around and shave it off. Now, how could I explain to them the pressures I was under to do such a thing?

I think I was in my grade ten year in the States when I fully realized what a privilege it was to live in Pakistan. All my glorified notions of the USA were brought down to earth. Likely all "Third Culture Kids" experience an identity crisis wondering where they fit, but on furlough I found where I fit—that is, where I *didn't* fit. That year overseas showed me that whatever an American was, I wasn't one and was unlikely to ever become one. I suppose it sounds odd, but I had always viewed my parents as foreigners in Pakistan, but not myself. In the States, the truth hit me that I was the real foreigner.

One interesting experience from that furlough was meeting an old British military man who had worshipped in the church at Gharial during his tour of duty in India. He was very interested to learn that it had been made over into a school.

It was during that year at "home" that I determined to make the most of my last two high school years. I fully understood that this would likely be my last chance to enjoy Pakistan before I finished out my days in exile elsewhere. Landing back in Karachi, I could have knelt and kissed the tarmac. I knew then for sure that the sights, smells, heat, flies, crowds, noise, and even hostilities were as home to me as hearth and fireside are to others.

So what is my nationality? Jordanian by birth, Scots-Irish/American by parentage, Pakistani at heart, Canadian by choice.

*   *   *

There is always pain and pleasure mingled together in memories. Boarding school was not all happiness. But then, growing up "normally" in the States wouldn't have been all happiness either. Life is painful. I've had to work through some of the hard things. I still have a tendency to postpone dealing with difficult situations because I learned growing up that all I had to do was wait, hold out for three months and the circumstances would change. But I would say that overall I am thankful for the way I was brought up and feel I had a happy childhood.

Apart from one man who used to whip the boys and come into the girls' room when we were dressing, I disliked most having my mother as boarding parent. But that was because she was trying so hard to be fair that she stopped being mother, and that was harder to figure out than having someone else in that position. Those in charge must have realized that man was pretty bad, because he didn't come back after that one time.

The train party was always exciting, whether going to school or coming home. Getting ready for it was rather bleak. In our house it was about the only time the record player was put on (I'm not sure why), so for some time after I associated classical music with goodbyes. The goodbye itself was hidden neatly away in the excitement of meeting friends and getting settled onto the train. The grieving didn't set in until the first night in Murree. Then I had to get over that mountain of pain and get on with living. I suppose all those departures had an effect on me. Always a bit resistant to change, I find it very difficult to handle even now.

So much of one's experience depends on oneself. Not having been particularly good at relating to others, my most painful memories involve other people. My solution was usually to leave them behind while I disappeared into a book, or the beauty of the woods, or something else. . . . Even so, I don't regret the boarding experience. I wouldn't relive it, and I wouldn't give it up for anything.

I think one of the most positive aspects was being part of such a close community where everyone belonged in some way to everyone else; something close to kinship. There was some sort of strength in that, that I have seldom been able to find again. We were mean to one another like normal kids, our families moved away and returned, and we had our cliques and exclusive groups. But we still belonged to a common experience that separated us from the world and made us welcome in each other's homes and lives in some inexplicable way. Anything approaching that sense of belonging I find I have had to work at, and even then, never quite achieved.

25

Hiking the Paper Trail

Evolving in the Eighties

There's not much left that needs to be said, except to fill in the gaps. Most of the material in this book was written by people who were at MCS during the 1960s and 1970s (reflecting who responded to this project) and, therefore, mostly covers that period. To get a sense of MCS life in the years since then, I have had to rely on official publications and internal documents from the school. This has given me a sense of what impression someone from the outside might get of MCS, following only the paper trail.

CONSTANCY AND CHANGE

The Constitution of Murree Christian School states that the primary aim of this association is: "To maintain a school in which a high quality of Christian education may be offered in a Christian atmosphere to children of missionaries and such others as the society may from time to time determine." Precisely what is meant by a Christian education is clearly delineated in the Preamble to the Articles of Association:

240

In as much as the founders of the school purpose to establish an institution in which the historic evangelical faith would form the teaching
basis of the school and guide its general policies,
the following articles of the faith summarizes the
doctrines held in common by the cooperating missions and associations:

A. The Scriptures of the Old and New Testa-
ments as the inspired Word of God, the infallible
and only rule of faith and practice.

B. The deity of our Lord Jesus Christ.

C. The necessity and efficacy of the sub-
stitutionary death of Christ for the sins of the
world and the historic fact of His bodily resurrec-
tion.

D. The presence and power of the Holy Spirit in
the work of regeneration.

E. The consummation of the kingdom in the glorious appearing of the great God and Savior, Jesus Christ.

Note: The PREAMBLE may not be amended.

All board members and staff of the school were and are
still required to sign a statement expressing their agreement
with the doctrines outlined above. While this preamble may
seem curiously dogmatic for an organizational document, it is
worth noting some major doctrines of the "historic evangelical
faith" which are not mentioned, including the Virgin Birth, the
doctrine of the Trinity, and the exact methods or prescriptions
necessary for individual salvation.

More than thirty mission groups from a dozen countries
and denominations have at various times been affiliated with
Murree Christian School. MCS has evolved tremendously since
its sketchy beginnings. Yet, there have been remarkably few
changes to this founding document in the forty years since the
United Presbyterian mission first submitted a draft for approval. The only significant change discernable in the revised Constitution (1990) was that the proportion of non-missionary children allowed to attend the school has been raised from ten per-

cent to twenty-five percent.

The Student Handbook (1989), on the other hand, reflects considerable changes in the regulations and cultural trends at MCS since the 1960s. The usual elective options and extra-curricular activities are listed: music (choir, school band, and private lessons for piano and other instruments); athletics (soccer, field hockey, basketball, track and field, tennis, volleyball, and table tennis); student council; stage productions; photography club; and yearbook staff. Additionally, the curriculum outline now includes computer and art classes. Some traditions have been codified, such as Senior Skip Day; the role of student monitors is carefully delineated; and so is the practical basis ("sensitivity to local culture") for some of the "old-fashioned" and seemingly arbitrary rules, such as the conservative dress code for girls.

The school has added a full-time chaplain (as of 1989) who teaches in the high school as head of Christian Studies, as well as "serving in a pastoral capacity to both staff and students." The annual summer Hobby Show has been replaced by a "Fine Arts Festival."

Conventional playing cards are still forbidden and boarding students are not allowed to attend the cinema. On the other hand, folk dancing—yes, dancing—Scottish, Jewish, and American Square dancing, "for grades 7-12, with parental permission is an accepted social activity; disco dancing and other forms of social dancing are not allowed." Junior and senior high boys may not wear shorts to class and "boys are not allowed to wear earrings because of cultural reasons." (Intriguing, that this last item should be necessary to include—times have changed!) An Ad Hoc Music Committee, which "screens" questionable tapes that students bring to boarding, must now also review and set policy for videotapes as well. (Sadly, the arrival of VCRs in every boarding department has seen the demise of the traditional Saturday Night Movies, one of the few regular activities that united the school—and siblings—in an informal, family-like atmosphere.) And the final, conclusive proof of the school's new, more modern attitude: High school students (grades 10-12) "having written parental permission may *single* date *unchaperoned*" (italics mine).

*   *   *

Perhaps nothing exhibits the modernization of Murree Christian School so much as its student newspaper, *The Akbar*. During the '60s and '70s, this publication managed to get cranked out (literally) only once or twice a year—blotty, mimeographed copy on two or three long sheets of coarse pulp paper. By the 1980s, *The Akbar* was being produced monthly, printed on four pages of oversized "tabloid" paper. The new, four-column format included photos on every page, regular features, and an upcoming events calendar for each month.

News reports now cover cultural conventions, the summer barter sale, the fall carnival, and unusual weather (a record eleven feet of snow during the winter of '81-'82). Staff profiles introduce both new folks and long-termers—including the Pakistani support staff. (The scariest moment in Don Calderwood's time at MCS was in 1965 when India and Pakistan were at war; one night, while he was out checking to see if the school building properly met the "blackout" requirements, a soldier stuck a gun in his back and accused him of spying—till Mr. Calderwood explained himself.) Other articles present new students offering their impressions of MCS; give updates on students whose families are leaving for furlough or welcome returning students back; report on alumni visiting the school; and describe Auntie Eunice Hill's visits to alumni on *her* furloughs. One piece offered "Tourist Tips" for the summer break with information about Khagan, Swat, Gilgit, and Hunza—all only a couple days' journey from Murree.

Regular features include profiles of various countries and fact sheets on the effects of drug use; book reviews; devotionals; and "Dear Flabby," a clever spoof on the well-known advice column. Poems by elementary students appear frequently. "From Days Gone By" offers interesting historical tidbits, such as that the school briefly had Girl Guides and a Boy Scout troop (1962-63) and that in 1983 the school ordered new algebra textbooks (after using the same ones since 1967!). An October 1982 article reported on how the high school art classes drew inspiration from Dr. Betty Edwards' book, *Drawing on the Right Side of the Brain*. In the same issue, a letter to the editor (by Adrian Das) highlighted some familiar complaints:

> When you read articles, you read how good
> Murree Christian School is, and what the De-

velopment Committee is doing for its future. But there are a lot of problems at MCS that seem to get ignored, such as:

FOOD — This is a problem in many boarding schools and institutions like MCS. I realize you are going to say that there are so many people to feed. Well, the Tea Shoppe in Jhika Gali has to feed many more and they prepare excellent food. . . . We have just finished working five long periods and come to a lunch that doesn't taste good. And if you don't eat it, they give it to you for leftovers the next day. Other times we go away hungry.

FACILITIES — . . . Some of the toilets are very dirty from not being able to flush them and many have broken seats. . . . The rooms are so poorly insulated that when the cold comes, it seeps right through the walls and windows and some of us don't even have heaters. The ceiling is leaking again, too. This happens many times, and if you are new to a certain room you won't know where it leaks and your belongings will get wet. In my bathroom, it leaked on a light bulb while it was turned on and the whole thing popped—throwing glass all over the place. . . .

RULES — These have changed drastically. Now we're not allowed to go to Murree on weekdays. Why shouldn't we go if we're back before bedtime? Also senior [high] boys aren't allowed to go to junior boys' rooms without special permission, even to talk to a younger brother. You get into trouble if there is the slightest disturbance in the dorm.

LAUNDRY — Nowadays if you want it cleaned properly, you have to do it yourself. We wash our own jeans because of the strange things that happen to them in the laundry. For instance, one student sent some light tan cords that were brand new and they came back pink. Some socks never show up. Shirts are missing. . .

Why shouldn't something be done to protect our belongings?

A special issue of *The Akbar* is devoted to the winners of the annual Creative Writing Competition and another honors the parting seniors. In July 1982, Stephen Gordon wrote the following "Last Impressions," a remarkably nostalgic piece for someone who had not yet left the place:

> Many of the students here at MCS have had the privilege of growing up in Pakistan. A few of the students were born here, others came when they were still in diapers. I was one of the latter.
>
> I arrived in Pakistan in 1967. Four years later, Pakistan and India engaged in war and from those days I have many memories: evacuation to Shikarpur in the middle of the night with our Land-Rover being covered in mud and filled with fourteen people; jumping into bomb shelters whenever the siren sounded; watching the Indian fighters and bombers scream overhead to wreak destruction upon all the nearby industry; gazing down, down, down into the craters which misguided bombs created; collecting bomb fragments from the nearby fields; and last of all, the good news of surrender and the end of all the bloodshed.
>
> MCS came into my life a couple of months later. Spring '72 was my first term in boarding. Nate Irwin and Paul Johnson were amongst the "big boys" that I remember from those days. . . . Seventh grade brought me to Sandes, and the mystique of that wonderful place will remain with me forever. Jhika was another one of my early high school discoveries, and from that day till this, I must have drunk at least a million chais!
>
> A full moon, the sky a kaleidoscope of stars, and the silent watch bring back to me many unforgettable memories. My first boar hunt was with Andrew Wilder, Tom Roberts, and John Lotze. Since then "Blizzard" and I have spent many

a happy hour pig-digging. . . . Thank you Pakistan, for the best childhood any human being could ask for, and thank you for teaching me the many lessons I've learned.

Adieu, my friend, adieu!

*   *   *

Like any small business, a small school has a high overhead of fixed costs, such as housing and staffing requirements, and is dramatically effected by even relatively small changes in the "market" (number of students). Thus, throughout the years, the MCS Principal's Reports indicate a continual struggle with the same major issues: shortages of water, staff, and space, and the complications resulting from a student body whose numbers fluctuated from year to year. Between 1964 (the first graduating class) and 1994 the student population averaged 144, with a low of 115 in 1985 and a high of 180 in 1990. When the student body increases, so does the staff; but when the student body decreases, the staff size tends to remain high.

In a report to the board of directors in June 1986, MCS principal Stewart W. Georgia describes two of the problems related to enrollment:

> A. Classes tend to have uneven numbers of boys and girls. . . . We have tried to get parent cooperation in producing even numbers of boys and girls for each class, but so far without tremendous success!
>
> B. Classes vary in size from 5 to 21. When a large class or two large classes in a row move through the school year after year, it causes a bulge in departments. At the present time the bulge is in the Jr. High boys. This will move into the Sr. High department as each year goes by. . . . Depending on where the bulge might come, we would need more houseparents to cope with the increased numbers, and to continue having the spiritual input, which a smaller group enhances. This would mean additional staff housing.

An increase in elementary students, he goes on to say, would necessitate another teacher and another classroom.

Of course, there was already a shortage of classrooms and teachers. In this same 1986 report, Georgia proposes building more classrooms in the play area underneath the elementary school block and above the stage area in the main school. The first suggestion was realized just a year later and the renovation of the stage area was completed in 1993. Both projects included new library rooms for the elementary school and the high school. In 1992, the roof of the main hostel was raised to facilitate a better technical shop and home economics room.

In his 1987 Principal's Report, Georgia highlights some of the spiritual and social activities at the school: "Beyond having Bible in each class, chapel every Friday, and the Sunday services, other events are being used. Did you know," he asks readers,

> that by the end of sixth grade each student should have memorized the following chapters: Exodus 10, Psalm 139, Matthew 5-7, John 14-15, Romans 13, I Corinthians 13, Philippians 2, Hebrews 11, and James 3? The elementary students are progressively studying character traits such as boldness, contentment, gratefulness, and forgiveness. The junior and senior high have had a [particularly meaningful] Spiritual Emphasis weekend.

At the 1987 interschool Cultural Convention (held in Delhi, India) MCS brought home seven first prizes, three second and three third. That year MCS students learned about career opportunities from representatives of Occidental Oil, the U.S. Drug Enforcement Agency, and the U.S. State Depart-ment.

In 1988, the Senior High Student Council sponsored an all-school campaign called "It's Yours" to make students understand that Pakistan is their adopted country and to encourage them to treat its people rightly. "A five-minute spot in chapel each week is bringing this across and a theme song has been written," Georgia reports.

That year, the school had 165 students and 45 expatriate staff (boarding, teaching, and support staff, including spouses); national staff (including drivers, night watchmen, maintenance workers, sweepers, and cooks) represented another forty. Alumni statistics indicated that nine out of ten MCS graduates go on to higher education, two-thirds of them to Christian institutions.

A report by the business administrator listed nineteen major expense items from the past two years. These included two new Toyota Coasters (large minivans), which replaced the school bus; installation of a seventy-kilovolt diesel generator capable of lighting the whole school compound during the frequent blackouts; resurfacing the very steep road up to Sandes Home (the high school boys' hostel); several new classrooms; three new water tanks; a new multi-purpose recreational court behind Sandes ("Mr. Murray is now enjoying a tennis facility close to home."); new basketball uniforms for boys and girls, and part of the expenses involved in sending nineteen students and four staff to the inter-school Cultural Convention and Basketball Tournament in Delhi.

Also in the Principal's Report for 1988, Stewart Georgia offers a telling comment on one factor affecting MCS's perennial space problems: "Staff and students bring with them an affluence today which was unusual over twenty years ago when the hostel was designed. It is strongly felt that changes need to be made to provide adequate living space for both staff and students." Most missionaries no longer considered housing eight to ten children in one bedroom to be an acceptable option.

With admirable candor, Mr. Georgia goes on to discuss the constraints of working with a deficit budget and the difficulty of having to constantly choose between equally demanding needs. He points out that MCS's commitment to keeping the school almost exclusively for missionaries' children contributes to its financial problems. Non-mission expatriate children pay a tuition that is *twelve times* as high as that charged for mission-affiliated students. Further,

> The schools in SAISA (South Asia Inter-School Association) demand twenty-six times our tuition. The only way MCS can compete and still win the basketball championship, major awards in the ('87) Cultural Convention, and to produce "commended" scholars is to have staff who are dedicated, sacrificial, and frugal, who give freely of their time and energy, are sensitive to each

other and care for students, and who look to him who is invisible and to a reward in the future.

Yet to keep good staff an invisible budget will not do nor will an invisible living space. . . . Education in these days is not cheap. Staff housing and academic hardware are expensive. We will never have nor do we desire a physical plant and academic hardware such as our international schools have, but not to provide what is needed is being exceedingly short-sighted.

The following items are excerpted from a Principal's Letter to "Friends of MCS" dated June 1989:

SPIRITUALLY — We have struggled and been encouraged, with students who have burnt their tapes of music which were keeping them from a close walk with the Lord; with staff who say, "Thank the Lord and those who have prayed with me for the change which you have seen," and parents who say, "My child has grown and matured spiritually."

SPORTS — In the fall of 1988, the girls won the SAISA Basketball convention for the third straight year, undefeated. Considering the size of the schools we compete against, this is an accomplishment to be proud about. The boys also won the Sportsmanship trophy, which shows we are winning in more ways than one.

CULTURAL CONVENTION IN KARACHI — saw the MCS Debate Team, Holly Fogleboch and Amy Jo Inniger, sweep every debate without a loss. Andre Munzinger was selected as the best male actor and best couple actor in the Instant Rapport.

STAFFING — Since January 1987, the board has requested the following positions: teachers

for special education and English as a second
language (ESL), a piano instructor and a librarian. As of this summer, only the latter two have
been filled. We must remember that each new
person on staff requires a new dwelling. Staff
turnover is a concern. This July/August we will
have fifteen leaving of whom four will return after furlough. We will have thirteen new people
coming. [An accompanying chart shows that
more than fifty percent of the current staff had
been at MCS less than one year.]

When Fall Boarding opens, Eunice Hill will be
the only boarding parent who was present in the
hostel a year before. This highlights the continuing problem of recruitment of long-term
boarding staff. The Middle Girls Department has
been most ill-affected with as many as fourteen
changes of houseparent over the last five or six
years.

JHIKA GALI* — The south side of Jhika has
been demolished. New retaining walls built back
further will provide a wider road so the traffic
jams should be less frequent. The new buildings
will probably necessitate building a new image of
Jhika in your mind.

From November 1991:

DELHI SPORTS TOURNAMENT — Thirty-two
students and staff are eagerly awaiting the arrival of November 21 when they will board a
flight for Delhi. There they will play against other international school teams from Pakistan, India, Nepal, Bangladesh and Sri Lanka. A trip to
Agra to see the Taj Mahal should prove educa-

---

*A crossroads bazaar which clung precariously to the narrow saddle
between the hill of Murree town and the hill on which Sandes Home
and MCS are located.

tional. The hours spent on visas (for India and re-entry into Pakistan), police papers, extensions of stay, etc., are running into weeks of man power-er.

DISCIPLINE — This semester has seen one student leave and eight suspended for a week. Now we see relationships healed and re-established. We have seen forgiveness and attitudes change. The Lord has been gracious. We just wish there was an easier way.

In a letter to parents the same month, Stewart Georgia offers no details on this dark drama, but sets it in a broader context:

This has been one of the most traumatic semesters the school has had for some time. Some staff have been sick, staff have doubled up on teaching loads to cover all needs, inappropriate words have been voiced and wrong actions have been taken. We are thankful that the Lord promises in Psalms 66:12 to take us *through* the water and *through* the fire out into a wealthy place.

And keeping trials in perspective he closes with this note:

AUTUMN IN MURREE — Do you remember? The yellow leaves of the Horse Chestnut trees as they come floating down? Gathering chestnuts and playing conkers? Viewing the snow caps in the distance? Watching the snow caps march closer until they descend upon us? Breaking the ice on the puddles on the road? Adding layer to layer as the temperature drops? We are thankful for the natural beauty of Murree; and we are thankful for better heaters in school—less fumes and more even heat. We now have more on order from Germany.

In July 1992 he wrote:

ASHE WING — The old Ashe Wing at Sandes is

no more. The two quarters from the turn of the century are now six single/couple accommodations in a modern building that many marvel could be built in Murree.

NILD — We are sending Mr. and Mrs. Barry Lock to the National Institute of Learning Disabilities seminar at the Black Forest Academy in Germany [sponsored by Norfolk Christian School in Virginia, USA]. We look forward to being better able to help students who have learning disabilities.

This semester has seen students mending relations, working together and reaching out both to one another and to our Pakistani community. Some of the older girls have gone to make friends with the girls at St. Denys' in Murree, our boys helped keep a house from slipping down the hillside, and the little kids have talked with national staff and prayed for their needs. We are encouraged.

BUILDING REPORT [excerpt]: Due to the encroachment on school land by various locals it was deemed necessary to clearly demarcate the boundary of the school land. . . . so a three-foot-high stone wall was built with a six-foot high chainlink fence on top. At the most vulnerable spot on the compound, 120 running feet of this has been erected and other boundary fencing has been repaired. We hope to add to this next year as part of our land is still being used as a local toilet and grazing ground for cattle!

In 1992, in spite of the school's acquisition of several computers four years earlier, Principal's Reports were still being cut on stencils. A "Dear Parents" letter from that summer (which included a list of books missing from the elementary school library with a plea to return them), ended with this item:

ON THE LIGHTER SIDE — In our staff application we ask the following question: "You allow your boarding student to buy tea from the shop across the street but other staff won't give this privilege to their students. You feel justified because this helps to establish a helpful atmosphere, but other staff feel you are undermining their rapport. For the sake of unity, would you feel obligated to conform to their regulations?"

One applicant after answering the question put this P.S. to his letter: "In Wichita they deal with metal detectors to catch firearms in junior high and high school, gangs getting by with drive-by shootings for entertainment and drugs and pregnancies in seventh and eighth grade. Discussing drinking tea in class seems a bit trite, from this point of view, unless, of course, you are deciding between allowing chai or green tea."

FROM ONE DEGREE OF GLORY TO ANOTHER

In 1955, E. H. Glassman submitted a "Proposal for the Murree School for Missionaries' Children." This remarkably prophetic document addresses all of the major issues that had kept the idea of such a school "in committee" for several years. (See Paul Pulliam's account in chapter 4.) In three brief pages, Glassman provides a complete plan of action that was, in fact, the means by which Murree Christian School became a reality. Four paragraphs from his report are excerpted below:

How much of a school does this proposal envision? To decide at this time how many grades the school will cover is hardly possible or necessary. . . . If we are going to refrain from starting even a high school department until it can be done on the grandiose scale that some millionaire foundation would do it, or even until it can exactly duplicate the facilities available at Woodstock, we shall never start at all.

It is now admitted by members of both our own mission and other interested groups that the only practical way of getting a school started is for some group to take the initiative and start it, with provision for others to come in to it later on mutually agreeable terms. Under the circumstances, the U. P. Mission is the most likely candidate for this task, both because it already has adaptable property at its disposal and because it has financial resources not available to most of the other groups, no matter how great their interest might be in such a school.

We should also be prepared as a mission to face up to the fact that such a project as this cannot succeed unless some <u>person</u> is set aside for the task who will push it through to success. . . . It will take more than a committee to start the school—it will necessitate a person with a vision for it.

. . . would not the wisest and most financially conservative plan be to go ahead with the use of this church? Perhaps the Lord is asking us, as he did a very reluctant Moses, "What is that in thine hand?" (Exodus 4:2). And perhaps he will take the seemingly insignificant and inadequate thing, already in our hand, to accomplish his purpose.

In his Director's Report to the school board almost forty years later, Phil Billing outlines his educational philosophy— one that perhaps offers good advice for life in general:

Change is here to stay and it is the school which develops flexible structures and adaptable management arrangements to empower its staff and students that may not only survive but flourish.

MCS has the advantage of being removed from the chaos. In a sense we can look on from a safe distance, see how the national scenarios [educational trends and debates] develop and then choose our strategies accordingly. We need not adopt all or any of the changes we perceive in our home countries. But it is essential that we screen the environment thoroughly and that we plan for change that will better equip our students as they return to their turbulent and competitive environments. We need to take the best of what we see and discover how to implement it here. . . .

Of course, MCS is not only a school, it is a boarding school where students spend two thirds of their day in the care of boarding parents. How inconsistent it would be to address issues of change and development in the classroom and not extend our thinking to the boarding departments. Thinking about child development and child care is very much in the public arena in our home countries—often thrown into the limelight, unfortunately, by unsavory incidents involving adults and children in institutions. Gender issues; sexuality; religious posture; the media; equality; physical, emotional, and sexual abuse; and ethnicity are all high on the agenda. As a Christian school we need to examine our response and practices. How can we be proactive in the care and nurture of our young people? How can we better prepare them for a world increasingly hostile to Christian values? How can we best use our personnel and environment to give our students a positive and lasting experience in which they can remain steadfast?

As we confront the challenge of change it is my hope to stimulate and promote in our staff and older students a <u>personal vision</u> of what they can contribute to the school and community. Staff and students need to genuinely own changes if they are to be implemented with enthusiasm. Further behind the teaching of a class or the care of a child must lie a <u>moral purpose</u> rooted in a living relationship with God.

Of course, our efforts to develop the school will be in vain if student enrollment remains minimal. And perhaps our vision of the future of MCS should include Afghanistan and the Republics of Central Asia, possible networking of information and expertise. The possibilities seem endless; realizing that any of them will require the harnessing of trust, creativity, and hard work.

Christians in my opinion should be at the cutting edge of positive change, for they are those who under God's good hand are themselves being changed from one degree of glory to another.

26

Afterwords

A PHILOSOPHY OF TEA

Timothy DeHart, '73

Brook Bond Supreme, in the red box with yellow leaves on it, is my favorite kind of tea. The top of the box always seems to get folded with the flaps going this way and that. Inside is the wrinkled foil bag, and the aroma of good Pakistani tea. Why does it smell so special? It's not just the tea, but the countless memories its aroma brings back. As I prepared another batch of steaming chai at my class's twenty-year reunion and watched the dark leaves swirling around, some vaporous thoughts began to condense, forming some perspective on all the issues raised by this event.

I've had all kinds of chai over the years, from the semi-transparent variety served by tea shops trying to stretch the shrinking rupee to cups of "a-special" tea with a bit of real cream. *Dude-patti,* made mostly with fresh buffalo milk has its own savor, as did the tea with fresh ginger root enjoyed once in Gilgit. I remember too the time we were out camping in high school and ran out of sugar. "Just put in some salt instead" was a local's advice, but its tang was far from the "perfect ten." Tea with other spices has its own charm, whether anise, black pepper, cardamom or cinnamon. One fellow was rather proud of his concoction of chai made with some instant coffee mixed in with it! Then there was the taste of chai made with evaporated milk, back before the ubiquitous "milk-pak" was available, used in areas where fresh milk was in short supply. And chai made over a wood fire inarguably has its own unique character.

Chai construction has been a hobby of mine from as far back as I can remember but only within the last couple of years have I settled on a personal favorite. The tea flavor tastes best when the leaves are added right after the boiling water (with sugar already added) has been taken off the stove. While the tea is steeping for its five minutes or so, the milk is heated to boiling. The freshly steeped tea and the hot milk are then combined in the pot for the perfect cup of tea. I say "perfect" while at the same time recognizing that each time, no matter how I measure or guess, I think, "Maybe that would have been better with a little more (or a bit less) sugar," or, "Those tea leaves have been sitting around for a long time, wouldn't that have tasted better with a fresh batch?" or, "This Shop-N-Save milk will do, but oh, for the taste of some fresh buffalo milk!" Perhaps, on second thought, I have never had the *perfect* cup of tea.

Nothing in my experience is more intertwined with memories of Pakistan than chai. It is a symbol of the fellowship, hospitality, sweetness and flavor of the Pakistan I know and love. At times, the rich and creamy pull of nostalgia is so strong that I would give my proverbial right arm to make the past real again. There are other memories, like indifferently thin or bitter tea, that bring no urge for a revisitation.

How then do I deal with memories? To say "I had a cup of bitter tea once, and I want no part of it again!" is just as naive as to say "Tea is great stuff, always sweet and creamy, and just the right zippy taste." I know that when I process memories, as when I make tea, it is not my intention to duplicate the bitter (though some victims of my more unsuccessful chai experiments may wonder otherwise). Rather, drawing from the best of the past, my intent is to better the future. Yet, this does not give closure to the past, for this is an incomplete philosophy of tea.

In a larger sense, to understand tea is to go back beyond the leaves and the bush and see them as a microcosm, a glimpse of the Creator through his creation. I'm sure it didn't escape the divine perspective that this simple plant would provide so much pleasure to so many. A belief in the goodness of God is consistent with the Scriptures when they tell us that he "richly provides us with everything for our enjoyment."

To reflect on the imagination utilized in the preparation of this "brew" is fascinating as well. "No two the same" may refer to fingerprints, the owners of fingerprints, or even cups of tea, and I have come to recognize that the infinite variety of creation is a stamp of the divine. The amazing creativity of humankind is an undeniable statement that we are indeed made in the image of God.

Most importantly, my thirst for the perfect cup of tea has its parallels too. The best that I can know of life on this earth only serves to reinforce a subliminal knowledge that I will never taste perfection here. But the very thirst of my soul for perfection—for completion, fulfillment, satisfaction, peace—points to the existence of Perfection. Something deep within me yearns to know its creator—to know him fully. Is this not the ultimate search for roots?

Does "bad tea" mean that Perfection is compromised? Does it make my pursuit of the perfect cup a fruitless quest? My heart honestly cries out for its identity in the Perfect, but at the same time I recognize that I share responsibility for the poor cup of tea and the compromised world of which it is a picture. I am answerable for the rebellion—the corruption—that has changed the Edenic garden into our modern world.

Until my name is called, and I come to know Perfection in a perfect way, I must deal with the constraints of this flawed mirror. My understanding of God as both Creator and one working to reestablish rapport with a corrupted creation, leads me to believe that no foul cup escapes his knowledge. Rather, as with saints of every era, the more profound my experience with pain, the greater the potential for a deepened relationship with the one who knows no corruption. If bitter tea means that better tea must exist, then each unsatisfactory cup whets my appetite for the perfect one.

NO MORE GOODBYES*

Elaine Roub, '75

It was the mountains—those majestic, emerald-clad reminders of eternity—that told me I was home again. Riding up the back of the Himalayan foothills toward Murree, I soaked in the aura of my surroundings: monsoon mists crept over the valleys that fell away beside us as we travelled the winding, narrow blacktop behind the smelly exhausts of gaudily painted diesel trucks. Norway Pines across the valley became a luscious velvet carpet, interwoven with tiny patches of clay red and tinroof silver.

In the hour and a half it took us to travel forty miles of mountain road, I reflected on the journey of my life. Looking back, I might see only the mists of too many goodbyes and new beginnings. Looking inward, would I find more than the mishmash of cultures, confusing images of who I am—like that gaudily painted truck? As a "Third Culture Kid," the child of missionaries, I could not feel quite all American, nor did I really belong to Pakistan. Instead, I was part of the "MK culture," a group of missionary kids who grew up together at a small but multi-cultural boarding school. Long ago we had said our goodbyes to one another and gone our separate ways across the world, not realizing how much we would continue to have in common. Now we share the same sense of confusion when someone asks, "Where are you from?" Or when society insists that we label ourselves either this or that.

But saying goodbye does not mean forgetting. Leaving home does not mean "home" leaves you. My culture is still a part of me, even when those individuals representing it have long ago left my life. And now, I had returned to Pakistan—to my "home" culture—after ten years away. I was not a child anymore; but I saw the mountains, and I was reminded of my roots.

In those mountains I had been born to a missionary couple living in rented summer housing. Shortly after my birth, my fa-

---

*Adapted from an article first published in *Impact,* May 1987, originally titled "Heritage of the Himalayas." Used with permission from the author.

ther took a position as principal of the new school for missionaries children. And so the Himalayas became the backdrop for a stage upon which I played my role for eighteen years. On center stage was Murree Christian School—with about 150 students in all twelve grades. Most of our parents were career missionaries who had committed their lives to God's service in Pakistan. Consequently, basically the same group of children who entered first grade with trepidation and wonder sat on a platform together twelve years later, dressed in blue gowns and caps and facing an unfamiliar world with hearts full of uncertainty.

And in between the first year and the twelfth, a multitude of common experiences marched across the stages of our lives, building our culture around us and within us.

Close community living, either in boarding or on tightly-knit missionary compounds, taught us the meaning of the observation that "no man is an island." "Island" thinking was impossible. Instead, we learned the joys and sacrifices of living in a melting pot. Our extended family went far beyond grandmas and grandpas to houseparents, neighbors, teachers, and the co-workers of our parents. We adopted the British habit of calling any familiar adult "auntie" or "uncle," reinforcing this sense of kinship.

In stepping beyond our cultural boundaries to befriend other missionary kids of many different nationalities and languages, we discovered in one another the blessed roughness of sandpaper. Combine almost any Britisher's reserved, cautious approach to new experiences with the flamboyant, "go-for-it" style of most Americans, and you come up with a hybrid who still thinks high school graduation ceremonies are ridiculous, but is no longer repelled by the American propensity to give standing ovations at any excuse. Toss together the stereotyped but nonetheless fiery temper of an Irish school boy with the quiet, stubborn plodding of his German roommate and the result is a mellow determination to conquer life's obstacles regardless of what anyone says. This began a life-long polishing process for each of our characters.

Like any children, we Third Culture Kids created our own forms of entertainment. Our games were not flavored by Saturday morning TV cartoons, because we didn't have television on Saturday morning or any other day of the week. Instead, we used chalk to draw out a Western town on the tennis court, complete with saloon and a bank to be robbed. Countless hours were spent chasing the "bad guys" through real woods and over bubbling streams. Complete cities were built for our "dinky" toys in a four-foot square sandbox. And a rope swing over an imaginary cavern behind the hostel provided the perfect scenario for runaway orphans. We were never confined to a nineteen-inch stage upon which others played out roles; in our games, we were the stars, with a mix of make believe and marvelous natural surroundings for a stage.

As we grew older, we widened our stage to make room for weekend camping trips, mountain climbs, and walks to the nearest village for a cup of sweet hot chai. We shared drama and music, "small town" gossip, tears and laughter. Oh yes, the laughter—years later we would meet again, or see each other in another MK whom we'd never known, but who had shared our culture on another continent. And in the laughter that comes easily to people who know each other well, we would forget the painful goodbyes that had separated our lives.

In unison we had flipped the tassels on our blue caps from one side to the other. Together we had turned and filed off the stage—not just the platform on which we'd made our graduation speeches, but the stage upon which we had lived our lives.

Another culture stood in the wings of that stage: Pakistan, a Muslim country with an Eastern way of thinking. It was a country in which we were ever treated as guests in spite of the fact that some of us had spent most of our lives there. Only rarely did MKs come to establish authentic friendships with their Pakistani brothers or sisters. Most of us were on the outside looking in. Yet, that view of our host culture standing in the wings of our stage reminded us again that we live on a shared planet. When we returned to our home countries to observe supermarket aisles crammed with forty different breakfast cereal choices, we remembered ragged children leading their blind uncles, hands extended for alms.

A young woman sitting on a street in Pakistan with her deformed baby on a rag in front of her was still a part of me as I looked at half a steak and a buttery baked potato left unfinished in an American restaurant. That young woman would never be a waitress watching food go in the garbage can. Yet, here she was, a part of this waitress. Unbeknownst to her, she'd come out from the wings and her culture with her, and together we stood on my stage; together we were outsiders looking in on my "home" culture.

But today, as we rounded the final bend of the road leading home, I looked once more at the mountains, and I was no longer an outsider. Today I was home. Those majestic Himalayas which had for so long surrounded my life were still there, as they had always been. While I had gone away to play new roles in other theaters, these mountains had remained in place, the backdrop for my first stage. And though their faces changed a little with the passing seasons, they never moved.

I thought I had come back for final goodbyes to the country and the culture that I'd loved. But today the mountains quietly reminded me that home is not a single stage, it's not the first, second, or even the third culture I somehow feel a part of. Today I knew that I had traveled 11,000 miles from home in America not to say goodbye to the stage I'd left ten years before, but to say that "home" had never left me, and there was no longer any need for goodbyes.

27

Their Country (A Second Look)

*Pakistan, Missionaries,
and the Legacy of Colonialism*

How much did we really know about this place we called home? Today, when people find out I grew up in Pakistan they almost always comment on what a rich cross-cultural experience it must have been. Indeed. But privately I suspect that growing up in the tiny, insular community of an evangelical boarding school, in the *foreign* subculture of missionaries, shaped me far more than its context in a poor, Islamic country in Asia. In fact, this is one reason we are described as Third Culture Kids and not "bi-cultural kids." Despite the presumption that we lived closer to the *real* Pakistan, and our tendency to feel superior to the "embassy arrogance" of Foreign Service types, we clearly had more in common with them than with "our Pakistani brothers and sisters."

Because of the somewhat primitive living conditions, most foreigners in Pakistan, including missionaries, have domestic help (as do most upper class Pakistanis). Our parents worried that we might become spoiled and develop a "servant complex." The lost opportunities were far greater than this temporary danger. My childhood playmate during the long winter holidays was Javed, the eldest son of our family's cook. Today he writes

263

me letters in excellent English (not a requirement for his city hospital job). The *spoken* Urdu I can remember is so barely tourist-passable I am ashamed to practice it with the Pakistanis I meet here in the States.

At most essential levels, what we experienced was not as much cross-cultural interaction as it was two cultures living side by side, watching each other. And this proximity did not necessarily cultivate understanding. In contrast to the poverty of most Pakistanis, even economically lower-middle class missionaries from the West seemed immeasurably wealthy. With our superior education and privileges it was hard not to feel superior. After all, the Pakistanis we had the most direct contact with were servants and beggars. And self-contained communities (like MCS), despite their claims and best intentions, will often foster a sense of righteousness and entitlement.

During the late-1960s many high school students at MCS displayed a near-colonial contempt toward Pakistanis and Pakistan in general. To be fair, this probably had less to do with latent racism than with the normal adolescent tendency to reinforce the group's "in" status by putting down outsiders. But this bad attitude presented a very difficult situation for a school whose primary purpose was to teach and exhibit Christian love. Ian Murray was the one who agitated to have local students admitted to MCS, and to start a scholarship fund for them. Since the 1970s, five to eight percent of MCS students have come from Christian Pakistani families and the problem has largely dissipated.

To further increase Pakistani participation, Murray points out, would be extremely difficult for such a small school. A much larger institution like Woodstock School in India can handle the added staffing and cross-cultural demands that such a change would require. MCS cannot, for example, take in Muslim students without then taking the responsibility of providing for their religious education. This would require changing the ethos of the school, something the board is not willing to do—and would give the government a lever on MCS. It would be more feasible to hire more Pakistani staff, but, Mr. Murray asks, "do we want to lure the top Pakistani Christian teachers away from the failing Pakistani educational system?"

In fact, there were, and are, as many Pakistani support staff at MCS as expatriate faculty and boarding personnel, and most of them long-term employees—familiar faces on a daily basis year after year. What did we know of even these people? Allahdad, the school's conscientious (and sometimes mischievous) chief bus driver for more than twenty years, drove a jeep for a British general during World War II, in the North Africa campaign and on into Italy. James Mull, the earnest but unappreciated Urdu teacher at MCS during the early seventies is now the Executive Secretary of the Pakistan Bible Correspondence School and (according to Paul Pulliam) is one of the country's outstanding Christian leaders.

As a young college student, Samuel Barkat tutored missionaries at the Murree Language School. He went on to become dean of a prestigious Christian college in New York and today serves as a vice president and Director of Multi-Ethnic Ministry for Inter-Varsity Christian Fellowship. Khan Zaman came from a noble clan of Pathans. Maybe he wasn't such a great cook, but he had a great heart for small children. One of his daughters, Zeb Zaman, is currently the highly respected principal of Kinnaird High School in Lahore.

To speak only of those we knew overlooks most of what we missed. While scoffing at Pakistan's attempts to mimic Western cinema (and its attendant cultural fashions) we missed the dignity and spiritual depth of Eastern poetry. The Sufi tradition of Islamic mysticism is nowhere expressed better than in the Qawwali singers of Pakistan. The metaphorical mixing of sexual desire and religious ecstacy in their lyrics is a theme many American soul singers would recognize. Nusrat Fateh Ali Khan, the Marvin Gaye of South Asia, is considered by many to be one of the two or three greatest living vocal artists in the world.

Few areas of the globe can boast a richer blend of cultural influences, now muted by the imposition of Islamic fundamentalism. Yet, this too is a situation Christians should recognize from their own religious history. And missionary kids might sympathize with Pakistan's constant struggle to integrate conflicting cultural identities.

Recently, I had dinner with a former classmate from Murree Christian School. We had not seen each other for more than twenty years. Steve is now a health care administrator in the mountainous frontier agency of Gilgit, a rugged tribal region in northern Pakistan known for its beauty and for its isolation

We met in Washington, D.C., where I now live and where the parents of his Pakistani wife make their home. Steve and Zeba Rasmussen are a classic cross-cultural couple: He is an American raised in Pakistan; she is a Pakistani raised in the United States. (They are both employed by a private Pakistani institution, not a mission board. The pioneering work of the Agha Khan University Hospital's health extension program does, however, seem infused with a missionary spirit.) When the meal was over Steve handed me a business card with his Gilgit address on it—including a fax number.

"They have fax machines in Gilgit now?" I asked.

"Sure," he said casually. "Lots of people have cable T.V., too. You can buy a satellite dish for 2,000 rupees [about $150]. Times have changed."

Indeed. But mostly I was thinking what a great chapter title this concept would make.

FAXING TO GILGIT

Pakistan is a "third culture *country*". While it has been both cradle and crossroads to some of the world's greatest civilizations, it has full ownership in none of them. It's sense of belonging is with other nations that share its chosen identity— Islam. For three thousand years Pakistan has been in a nearly constant state of transition—resisting, submitting, and adapting to the various armies and influences that have swept through it. Its modern form, established in 1947, is an artificial construct. The world's most populous Islamic republic is also one of the purist, with a population that is more than ninety-seven percent Muslim. Yet, in its first twenty-five years, Pakistan had ten different governments, fought three wars with India, and saw the amputation of its largest province, when East Pakistan became Bangladesh in 1971.

Often lost in the shuffle of history, Pakistan is a country in between, straddled between the turbulent Middle East and exotic India; between strategic location and cultural displacement. Yet, Pakistan's rich heritage is the result of how it has adapted to its many conquerors while somehow retaining its own identity, accommodating while remaining proudly independent. Today, representatives from nine of the world's twelve great religious traditions mingle in the marketplaces of the Indian subcontinent: Hindu, Islamic, Christian, Sikh, Parsee (Zoroastrian), Buddhist, Jewish, Jain, and the animism still widely practiced in the various tribal groups. However, Pakistan's strict and often oppressive religious identity has limited its appreciation of this diversity.

The Indus River, which runs the length of Pakistan like a spine, tells the story of this land's global currents, starting at the foot of the Murree Hills. On the Potowar Plateau between the ancient city Taxila and the new capital Islamabad, the Soan Pebble culture developed 500,000 years ago, and left behind some of the earliest artifacts of human existence anywhere in Asia. Enigmatic rock drawings indicate that Neolythic tribes in this area were studying the stars two thousand years before Stonehenge. Further south, in Baluchistan, near the border of Afghanistan, are remains of crude urban settlements 8,000 years old, predating the first Egyptian dynasties.

Just two hundred miles north of the Arabian Sea, in an obscure corner of the Sind's Thar Desert, is Moenjodaro, the City of the Dead. Together with Harappa, a sister city further up the Indus in the Punjab, these windswept ruins confirm the existence of a sophisticated prehistoric culture older and larger than the agrarian settlements of ancient Mesopotamia. The Indus Valley Civilization was a remarkably uniform federation that included most of what is now Pakistan and parts of Afghanistan and India. The advanced urban planning, political divisions, social refinement, and art of Moenjodaro are unprecedented. Five hundred years before the pharaohs built the Great Pyramids along the Nile, Moenjodaro had flush toilets on the second floors of graceful brick residences on streets laid out in a grid pattern typical of modern cities; it had an underground sewage system and the first known ritual burial grounds.

The only recent discovery of Moenjodaro, early in this century, proved to be one of the greatest archeological revelations of all time. More than a thousand years before the Babylonian Empire began to spread out from the Tigris and Euphrates, the Indus Valley Civilization had a standardized system of weights and measures and a pictorial language that has yet to be deciphered. A network of cities specializing in the mass production of glazed pottery, stoneware, woolen cloth, or other handicrafts indicate a complex and impressively efficient system of trade and cultural continuity. Then, after flourishing for over a thousand years this great society simply vanished. With the end of prehistoric times—that is, before written records were available—Pakistan's history seems to have literally started all over again.

When the Aryans arrived from southern Russia and Turkistan in 1500 B.C. the Indus Valley Civilization had all but disintegrated. Although the Aryans left little archeological evidence, their conquests are described in a collection of religious hymns known as the *Rig-Veda*. Written in an early form of Sanskrit, it is the oldest such document in the world.

In 500 B.C. the Persian emperor Cyrus the Great invaded the area, followed by Alexander the Great a hundred years later. But Alexander's troops refused to cross the Indus River into the heartland of India. They were exhausted and homesick after ten long years of campaigning. Half of Alexander's army sailed down the Indus to the coast or straggled with him back across the great deserts of Iran. But some of his generals chose to stay, establishing their own little kingdoms and bringing the influence of Greek philosophy and art to the region.

Others went north toward Kashmir where, in the mountains of Gilgit and Hunza, they met the fiercest resistance they had ever encountered. After several inconclusive battles, they too either withdrew or settled in the area, and their Mediterranean genes are still passed along in the blue eyes and fair complexion of many tribal people in northern Pakistan today.

Further south, the Hindu principalities that had united under Chandragupta to repel Alexander formed the basis of the first Indian empire. Chandragupta's grandson, Ashoka, expanded this empire, but in his later years became disheartened by the great human toll of his bloody campaigns and converted to Buddhism. Buddhism became the official religion of Gandhara, his northern kingdom, which had its capital at Taxila—less than fifty miles from Murree. Ashoka had his philosophical thoughts inscribed on stone pillars beside the main roads, including a series of edicts governing civic behavior and the first known conservation laws.

In the sixth century, A.D., while their cousin Attila was sacking Rome, the White Huns pillaged the Persian Empire. They overran northern India with characteristic vindictiveness, destroying both Hindu and Buddhist temples wherever they went. The glorious Gandharan culture was forever lost and India was plunged into its own Dark Ages.

Early in the eighth century Muslim invaders from Iraq and Syria encountered little organized resistance. Contrary to what is often taught, the Islamic conquerors did not make converts "by the sword," at least not in South Asia. They were ferocious in battle, but once political dominion was established, Islam proved to be a benign religion and low-caste Hindus were often willing converts to the egalitarian tenants of Mohammedanism. For almost a thousand years much of the subcontinent remained under Muslim rule, with various dynasties (mostly of Mongolian and Turkish descent) battling, ascending, and being overthrown. Bubar the Tiger followed Tamurlane the Earth Shaker. In 1526, Bubar took Delhi and became the first of the great Mogul emperors whose dominion would extend from the Persian border in the west to the Bay of Bengal, and from the Himalayas to the Indian Ocean. It was the richest empire the world had ever seen and it lasted just two hundred years, until the British—the last foreigners to subjugate the region—began mapping the Indian subcontinent for Queen Victoria.

Bubar's grandson was Akbar the Great. And his grandson was Shaw Jahan who built the Taj Mahal, as well as the Red Fort of Delhi and the Shalamar Gardens in Lahore. Shaw Jahan's son, Aurangzeb, who died in 1707, added the Badshahi Mosque (then the world's largest) to Lahore's splendor. It was a magnificent denial of an empire already crumbling. Yet, in the minds of many people, the archetectural stamp of Islam would remain the subcontinent's most potent symbol.

* * *

In 1947, when the British began dismantling their empire, India was divided in order to provide a safe haven for its large Muslim minority. As a result of the often arbitrary way the borders were drawn to create the new state of Pakistan, millions of Hindus and Muslims discovered that their ancestral homes were suddenly in the wrong nation. They became refugees in their own country, uprooted by invisible rules they did not comprehend and could not control, and told that an unfamiliar place should now be called home.

Pakistan is still straddled between worlds. Though it is the planet's ninth most populous nation, it has often played the pawn in superpower games. In the 1950s and early 1960s, the United States had an air base in northern Pakistan, near Peshawar—part of a "mutual defense pact" that was a thinly-disguised front for CIA operations. It was from here that Gary Powers's now-famous U2 spy plane took off, later to be shot down over the Soviet Union. Part of the fallout from the resulting scandal was that the air base was permanently shut down. Pakistan's feigned ignorance and indignation had a very real concern at its source, one that revealed its delicate place in a world overshadowed by restless giants. With the Soviet Union so close on its northern borders, Pakistan could not afford to antagonize the Russian bear; on the other hand, with the Soviets aggressive track record in Europe and Asia, Pakistan could not afford to leave itself vulnerable. Murree Christian School benefited from the crisis, however, receiving donations of furniture and supplies from the closing American base just in time for the opening of the new boarding hostel in 1965. The most notable of these were a large number of triple-deck steel-framed bunk beds from the USAF barracks.

By the late-1960s Pakistan commanded one of the largest armies in Asia and was among the largest recipients of U.S. military aid in the world—ostensibly to protect itself from a possible Communist invasion from either Russia or China. But Pakistan's real fear was of India, its blood enemy since "Partition," the division of India into two states when the British left. During the 1965 war over Kashmir both sides used U.S. war planes against each other. When India signed a mutual defense agreement with the Soviet Union, Pakistan promptly signed one with China. During the Bangladesh war in December 1971 the United States came very close to sparking a nuclear confrontation with the Soviet Union when, in a replay of the Cuban Missile Crisis, it sent the Seventh Fleet into the Bay of Bengal in an unsuccessful attempt to intimidate India.

Although Pakistan is part of the South East Asia Treaty Organization (SEATO), sponsored by the United States and other Western democracies, it tries to maintain its political balance by being an equal opportunity economic aid recipient. The Americans and the Russians jointly built the Mangla Dam, the world's largest until the Americans and a European consortium built Tarbela Dam, also in Pakistan. In a joint venture with the People's Republic of China, Pakistan built the Karakoram Highway through the Himalayan mountains, linking the two nations by the same routes of the ancient Silk Road. China has long been Pakistan's largest trading partner; the fountain pens, rulers, and paint kits used at MCS were invariably "Made in China."

Today, Western-style democracy—perhaps crucial to modernization—fits awkwardly on a country founded on religious dogma. Pakistan stumbles uneasily between the need to preserve tradition and the need for competitive economic development. This conflict can be seen in Murree, whose quaint isolation is being rapidly paved over as the area is aggressively developed for its tourist revenue. With new roads, easy year-round access has led to a real estate boom in the 1990s, including the recent construction of Pakistan's first resort conference center, the Pearl Continental Hotel, where rooms go for $200 a night.

The cost of living in Murree is very high compared with many other parts of Pakistan. As development continues, and Jhika Gali becomes a satellite of Murree, land prices have soared. This has created tremendous hardships for local residents, including many employees of Murree Christian School. The school provides a retirement fund for its national staff and housing for some of them, but there are no easy solutions to the growing economic pressures.

UPON THIS ROCK ... AND SOME SYNCRONICITY

Long before the age of jet planes and satellites, global uplinks and downloading modems, of VCRs in every desert village and fax machines in Gilgit, events in one part of the world had consequences in another. If they occurred a little more slowly, the results were no less profound. A fascinating example of this is the effect that building the Great Wall of China in the last centuries before Christ had a few centuries later on subsequent invasions of India—five thousand miles away—by Mongol tribes forced to look elsewhere for raiding grounds. Similarly, one of the greatest events to effect the destiny of modern India occurred on the other side of the globe.

The controversies of historic revisionism surrounding Christopher Columbus cannot diminish the incredible impact of his voyages in 1492, and those by subsequent explorers which conclusively demonstrated that the world was, in fact, round. No other event in history has instigated such radical transformations—scientific, political, social, psychologic, religious—in the way the world is perceived and experienced. The changes in lifestyle and perspective between the rural, localized societies of two hundred years ago and today's urban environments seem relatively minor compared with the jump from medieval to modern. The rapid changes that have taken place in the late-twentieth century—the global village brought about by television, computers, and other electronic technology—only begin to suggest the consequences of Columbus's voyages. It was a switch from a two-dimensional to a three-dimensional world, literally from a flat consciousness to a global one.

The Protestant Reformation—and all the subsequent social and theological transformations which that word implies—was partly the result of the human consciousness being so profoundly shaken by this totally new sense of reality. The individual mind—as well as the institutional one—was suddenly confronted with unlimited possibilities. The world was no longer an "either/or" proposition, but presented an infinite number of options—and the freedom to dream without limits.

India's pivotal, if offstage, role in this historic moment—and all its subsequent consequences—is worth noting. After all, it was the search for a shorter sea route to India by the Spanish and Portuguese that stimulated the voyages of Columbus and Vasco da Gama—and changed world history. It is an irony of history that the Indus River, the major geographic feature around which Muslim Pakistan was formed, should be the source from which India is named. Because of geographic misconceptions and navigational error, the name of this river, in a country obscure to most Westerners, is honored around the globe—from Indonesia to the West Indies to the "Indians" of North and South America.

Changing ideas about the nature of the universe eventually led to political revolutions, most notably in America and France. They also affected Christian concepts of evangelism. New knowledge of the world led to new understandings of what it meant to "go into *all the world* and preach the gospel." Two other events with historic consequences contributed significantly to stimulating the momentum of global evangelism: First, the Industrial Revolution of the eighteenth century; and second, the spiritual revival a hundred years later known as the Second Great Awakening.

The invention of the steam engine, the foundation of the Industrial Revolution, led to the creation of a multitude of machines and factories and the production of electricity, changing the face of urban society. Locomotive engines and steam ships revolutionized transportation, dramatically reducing the time and cost of travel—to anywhere in the world. Safer and more accessible to a much greater number of people, travel was no longer limited to great explorers and great armies.

This was also the era of religious crusades, of great tent meetings in the United States and Great Britain and great preachers such as Charles Finney, Henry Ward Beecher and Dwight Moody. The Evangelical Movement as we know it today—Billy Graham, Campus Crusade for Christ, the Moral Majority—grew out of this period, an age of nondenominational and interdenominational religious societies for social reform and missionary work, including temperance unions and the YMCA. The Industrial Revolution gave the means for global missionary work, the Second Great Awakening provided the motivation. It is against this backdrop that the story of Western missionaries in India—and later Pakistan—can be more fully appreciated.

Actually, the notion of Europeans bringing Christianity to India is something of a misnomer. Soon after the first Portuguese sailors and traders arrived on the southwestern coast of India in 1498 they found a Christian community already in existence there, in what is now the Indian state of Kerela. It was a small group, about 100,000, but one that claimed an unbroken heritage back to Saint Thomas, one of the original twelve disciples of Jesus. Known as the Thomas Christians, their tradition asserts that Saint Thomas himself came to India in the first century A.D. While there is no historic evidence to prove this assertion, neither is there any to deny it. As Bishop Stephen Neill points out, there was active trading between the Roman Empire and India from before the time of Christ, and if Thomas had gone to Egypt he could easily have boarded a ship there for India.*

Historical literature does suggest that there may be some basis for this tradition and there are archeological remains of

*Stephen Neill, *A History of Christianity in India,* vol. 1, pp. 16-17.

Roman communities in India from at least the third century A.D. The presence of stone crosses found in South India dating from around 600 A.D. unequivocally demonstrates the existence of Christianity in India from at least that time—almost a thousand years before the first European missionaries arrived.

At the beginning of the nineteenth century—when the first Protestant missionary work began in earnest—there was little to show for three hundred years of Roman Catholic presence in India. In all that time not a single translation of the Bible, or even the New Testament, had been completed. This was due, in part, to the Roman Catholic tendency to "Europeanize" their converts, rather than to learn their language and customs. It is easy in hindsight to view their methods as quaint or counterproductive, but the limited impact of these early Christian efforts should not reflect on the dedication of the Catholic missionaries who faced nearly insurmountable obstacles. Problems of papal authority with its cumbersome and competitive bureaucracy; the wars and religious turmoil in Europe during this period (including the dissolution of the Jesuit Order in 1773 for three decades!); severe isolation in a harsh tropical climate, the hostility of their fellow expatriates—not of the local inhabitants; and the sheer overwhelming numbers involved in the task, were some of the hardships the early Catholic missionaries faced.

The first Protestant missionaries to India, Bartholomew Ziegenbalg and Henry Plutschau, were German Lutherans directly sponsored by the King of Denmark. They arrived at Tranquebar, about 150 miles south of Madras, in 1706. They, too, were not wanted. The colonists felt that their efforts to evangelize the local people would be disruptive.

Ziegenbalg quickly realized that education had to be an integral part of missionary work—both directions. Missionaries must learn the language and thoroughly understand the customs of the Indian people. And educational institutions must be provided not just for the sake of knowledge, but so that Indians could read the Bible themselves in their own language, and also acquire the leadership skills to minister to their own people.

Thus, several decades before the arrival of William Carey, considered to be the great pioneer of modern missionary work, the essential elements of effective evangelism on which he would build were already taking shape: 1) foremost, to preach the gospel at every opportunity; 2) to learn the local language and customs; 3) to translate the Scriptures as quickly as possible into the local language; 4) to establish educational institutions, not merely for their own sake, but for the training of indigenous Christian leaders, and 5) to establish as soon as possible a national church administered by local leadership. These five components would remain the primary guide for missionary work, later expanded to include such "service ministries" as medical and agriculture missions.

In 1793 William Carey, representing the newly-formed Baptist Missionary Society, arrived in Calcutta, the stronghold of the British East India Company in West Bengal. But he too was not welcomed. Consequently, Britain's most famous religious envoy to India began his service in Serampour, a Danish Crown colony just south of Calcutta. He was soon joined by Joshua Marshman, a school master, and William Ward, a printer. These three men formed one of the most famous partnerships in Christian history, a symbolic union of evangelism, education, and literacy/translation—the cornerstones on which all future missionary work would build.

The world missionary movement was given new zeal when the fervor of the Second Evangelical Awakening crossed the Atlantic from America to Britain in the late-1850s. Hundreds of new missionaries came to India in the nineteenth century, a period that has been called the golden era of Christian missions.

Alexander Duff, of the Church of Scotland, arrived in India in 1830. His contribution was an emphasis on reaching the cultured sections of Indian society through higher education in English. And so the long tradition of English-medium schools in India began—again, with the resistance of the British. But Duff's concept proved very successful and soon missionary-sponsored colleges offering a European education began to multiply throughout India.

Until the 1830s almost all the Protestant work in India was carried out by the English societies—the Church Missionary Society (CMS), the London Missionary Society, the Wesleyan Methodists—but soon many nations were involved. The American Presbyterians began work in the Punjab in 1833, and Forman Christian College in Lahore is named for one of their early missionaries. Soon the Lutheran appeared in South India and the Methodist came to the United Provinces of North-central India in the 1850s. At the same time CMS expanded its work into Northern India—to Amritsar, the capital of the Sikh kingdom, and on to Peshawar on the north-west frontier, bordering Afghanistan.

In less than a hundred years the work of Christian missionaries had spread from small strongholds along the coasts of India to almost every part of the subcontinent. If the image of a conquering army comes to mind, it should be noted that in 1851 there were less than 600 missionaries, including wives, in a country of 150 million. There were altogether less than 100,000 Indian Christians, including Roman Catholics.

It was in the middle of this heady momentum of the gospel witness that the Indian Mutiny occurred in 1857, with its decidedly anti-Christian, not just anti-British, fury. The rapid expansion of Western missionary efforts unfortunately coincided with the rapid evolution of the British East India Company from a purely trading enterprise to an imperial power. To regulate this commercial establishment that had now spread its control over the entire subcontinent, more and more administrative—and military—apparatus of the British government also spread across India, theoretically with no political power except over its own subjects and within the "leased" territories of the British East India Company. Of course, the Indians could not be expected to tell the difference as more and more of their country came under control of the British. And the parallel expansion of missionary work gave rise to rumors that plans were being made to forcibly convert the whole population to Christianity.

In fact, the British officials of the East India Company were a barrier to missionary work. All this changed after the events of 1857 (which Indians and Pakistanis refer to as the First War of Independence). The British government disbanded the East India Company and dropped all pretense of a merely commercial investment. The Empire was now here to stay. In an effort of conciliation, one of the first laws enacted by the new British government was to establish the freedom of religions and to declare a policy of impartiality toward all faiths. The ironic consequence of this was that the Christian missionaries found themselves in a much more friendly environment that they have ever had before. They were now able to pursue their evangelical efforts, free from the harassment and limitations previously put on them by the Company.

A major influx of single women missionaries in the 1870s

opened the door for the first time to effective, widespread ministry and service among Indian women and children. For the first time orphanages and schools were established for girls. Two women from the American Methodist Church were instrumental in these efforts. "They were Miss Isabella Thoburn, later to found the first college for women in all Asia, and Dr. Clara A. Swain, first woman medical missionary of any society and founder of the the first hospital for women in Asia."*

While the Protestant and Roman Catholic missions often operated as if the other didn't exist, the spirit of ecumenical cooperation among Protestants has a long tradition. Protestant missions in India were characterized by cooperation and by a commitment to developing a national church. From early on there has been an understanding, later backed up by conferences and official agreements, that one mission would not attempt to do work in an area where another mission was already established. This principle of "comity" has largely enabled India to avoid much of the painful competitiveness and infighting that has plagued some other mission fields.

After India and Pakistan became independent in 1947 the churches briefly attempted to maintain church unity across the new borders, but most local denominational bodies and their foreign mission boards soon created separate churches or divisions for both countries. However, in less than two decades the movement for church union saw the merging of several denominations into the Church of Pakistan.

* * *

There are many misconceptions about missionaries, propagated by those with an opposing agenda, and made easier by many people's ignorance of history. In our haste to shed the naivete of some of the more offensive or grandiose myths that were part of the evangelical indoctrination of our childhood, some of us too readily shouldered the even greater burden of White Man's Guilt without much critical scrutiny of its mythology either. Most of the time, however, history is neither visionary nor conspiratorial; it is reactive. The growth of mis-

*James K. Mathews, *South of the Himalayas: One Hundred Years of Methodism in India and Pakistan,* p. 82.

sions in parallel to the expansion of colonialism must be evaluated keeping this principle in mind.

Much of history is the unintended consequences of actions or efforts with quite different motivations from the actual results. The voyages of Columbus and the American Revolution are prime examples of this. So is the history of British expansion in India.

When the British East India Company was founded in 1600 its intentions were purely money-making; only gradually and often by happenstance did it become a military and political power. The company made at least token allegiance to the Indian rulers and did not interfere in local politics. Its warehouses were fortified and a company militia established to protect its goods and employees from bandits. The company began making mutual protection alliances with native princes and its fortified settlements evolved into powerful commercial centers. When the Mogul Emperor Jahangir granted the company trading rights for all of Bengal in 1651 the die was cast. The French began establishing their own trading settlements in South India, giving the British further reason to expand their company army, and when Europe went to war in 1740 the British attacked the French in India—with both sides using mostly native troops.

Ten years later the French withdrew from the subcontinent, ceding the trading rights of all the areas that had been under their control to the British East India Company, which now commanded a seasoned army of local troops known as Sepoys. With the Mogul empire disintegrating, the company continued to expand its "trading" territory with impunity, no longer bothering to solicit sanctions from their Indian hosts. In 1756 the ruler of Bengal had had enough and attacked Fort William in Calcutta. The fort was taken and 146 British prisoners, one of them a woman, were crammed into a cellar room in the fort no bigger than an average living room. In the morning 123 of them were dead and the "Black Hole of Calcutta" entered the history books.

Given the barbaric treatment a defeated enemy could usually expect in those days, the incident—probably unintended, anyhow—was hardly noteworthy. But it was seen as an offense to the British Crown. Sir Robert Clive was dispatched to avenge this atrocity and defeated the Nawab of Dacca at the Battle of Plassey in 1757. Calcutta now belonged to the company, which meant all of Bengal as well. Warren Hastings became the first governor general of Bengal in 1772 and proceeded to institutionalize British law and civic services. The East India Company quickly became the most powerful force in India and over the next one hundred years expanded its holdings over most of the subcontinent. The boundaries of the subcontinent—every region, state, and rajdom—were surveyed and mapped for the first time. Railroads were built. Hastings was replaced by a succession of governors general with ever greater powers, including Lord Cornwalis who, on another continent, had only recently surrendered to George Washington. It became more and more difficult to distinguish between the company's commercial enterprise and Britain's imperialistic designs. In 1848 the British took the Punjab from the Sikhs and all of India was theirs—still unofficially. It was the largest domain ever controlled by a private corporation.

Long before the word communism was invented, the British worried about the Russian bear threatening from the north. And this too shaped the destiny of Pakistan as the British pushed their territory past the Punjab and into the tribal areas of the far northwest, all the way to Peshawar and the Khyber Pass, creating a buffer zone between the two empires—and the future northern borders of Pakistan.

The Sepoy Mutiny of 1857 was the last cry of defiance when, precipitated by a variety of tensions, Indian troops in the British army rose up against their English officers, sometimes massacring whole families and burning down their communities as well. The British were even more ruthless in their suppression of this rebellion, planting the seeds for the Indian independence movement to come.

Shortly after the Indian rebellion the British government found the East India Company to be corrupt and revoked its charter. The company was disbanded, and the British empire conveniently inherited, ready-made, its "Jewel in the Crown." They now ruled the entire area that today is collectively referred to as South Asia: Pakistan, India, Nepal, Bangladesh, and Sri Lanka (formerly Ceylon). The pride the British took in bringing civilization to greater India—roads, railroads, schools, and a uniform civil service—was matched only by the contempt they brought to their "White Man's Burden." Whereas the early adventurers, merchants, and settlers had adapted to many of the local ways and customs, the new English ruling class dis-

tanced themselves from everything Indian. Abhorring any as-
sociating with "wogs"—"Westernized oriental gentlemen"—the
British withdrew into artificial and isolated communities built
in a wistful and sometimes ludicrous attempt to replicate the
society of jolly old England. Thus began the British Raj. And in
ninety years it was all over. Like the mythical Wild West in
America, this well-documented and over-pondered period has
lasted much longer in legend than in history.

British cynicism and arrogance reached its height with a
scheme—by the governor general—to dismantle the Taj Mahal
and sell its marble back in England. The plan was abandoned
at the last minute only because an earlier shipment of marble,
taken from the Red Fort in Delhi, failed to sell.

Mahatma Gandhi and Jawaharlal Nehru spear-headed the
"Free India" movement in the 1930s and 1940s, while at the
same time Mohammed Ali Jinnah insisted on a separate, independent homeland for India's twenty million Muslims, to be
called "Pakistan"—Land of the Pure. Eventually, both the Indian National Congress and the British government capitulat-
ed to this demand, and the resulting partition of India in 1947
is one of the most painful legacies of colonialism—and foresha-
dowed the consequences of ethnically-dominated politics. Ten
million people moved across the new borders in the largest—
and certainly most abrupt—migration in human history. Half a
million died in bloody religious riots and ethnic massacres.

In 1971, only twenty-four years later, the civil strife in
East Pakistan resulted in equally heartbreaking numbers, pre-
cipitating the birth of Bangladesh.

MONKEY ON THE MISSIONARY'S BACK

The legacy of colonialism has shaped much of the late-
twentieth century debate about Western missionary activity—
and, indeed, shaped much of the political, philosophical and so-
ciological assumptions that form the basis for understanding
world evangelism into the next century. Yet, there are many
misconceptions about missionaries, propagated by those with
an opposing agenda and made easier by many people's ignorance of history. In our haste to shed the naivete of some of the
more preposterous or grandiose myths that were part of our evangelical indoctrination, some of us too readily shouldered the
even greater burden of White Man's Guilt without much crit-

ical scrutiny of its mythology either.

For many people, the very word "missionary" brings to mind Victorian times and morals: pith-helmeted explorers and sexually-repressed school teachers. The "missionary" is often equated with "colonialism" and the arrogant efforts to dismantle native cultures—whether in Africa, Asia, or America. Today, "imperialism" is used exclusively in a pejorative sense, implying reproach, yet we continue to celebrate the Greek and Roman empires as the cradles of our now lamentably declining Western civilization. Further this righteous condemnation always seems to be applied only to *Western* imperialism, while equally impressive dominations by Chinese, Russian, Japanese, and Islamic civilizations are conveniently lost to modern history.

The experience of colonialism and the forms it took were quite different in India than in Africa or Latin America.* (And it was different again, of course, for the "resident" colonies of North America, Australia, and New Zealand.) India was a huge geographic area under a single European power whose political role had evolved from an economic relationship—trading settlements—with little interest in subjugation or political control for its own sake. The "acquisitive" colonialism that developed in Africa was the result of several competing European powers there. And in Latin America, where the Roman Catholic kingdoms of Spain and Portugal dominated, the history of the church was almost completely and inseparably in the service of the Crown.

It is important to distinguish three major types of imperialism: political, economic, and cultural. While mission agencies certainly have an economic impact on the areas in which they work, missionaries are most frequently accused of promoting or participating in cultural imperialism. Unfortunately, there is almost universal agreement in our time that this is the most destructive and most residually hated form.

In fairness to the missionaries of previous centuries, we should distinguish good motives from often undeniably neg-

---

*See Brian Stanley, *The Bible and the Flag: Protestant Missions and British Imperialism in the Nineteenth and Twentieth Centuries,* esp. pp. 25, 16. This is an particularly good discussion of colonialism and missionaries--a fair, thorough and scholarly work.

ative consequences. Missionaries, like everyone of us, are creatures of their times. We can fairly judge them as to the extent to which they "bore witness," or stood prophetically for good against the prevailing values and practices of their time, by those very values and assumptions—not by late-twentieth century hindsight and ethical standards. Nearly all the framers of the American Constitution were slave-holders; yet, we do not say that this invalidates their achievement—or the positive legacy of that historic document. Similarly, the "cultural imperialism" of missionaries should not negate either the sincerity of their faith or the positive legacy of the good works they have accomplished.

A careful and fair-minded examination of Indian history during the relevant period—roughly, the 350 years between 1600 and 1947—belies many of the myths about missionaries and colonialism. Not only is the relationship between the expansion of missionary work and the rise of imperialism far too complex for such partisan labels, but the whole history if full of more ironies than a dozen nineteenth century "social" novels. It is interesting to note, for example, that the myth of "the materialist West and the spiritual East" was invented by an Indian intellectual with an anti-colonialist agenda.*

Missionaries were not the vanguard of colonialism; in fact, the opposite was usually the case. Certainly this was so in India. European traders had settlements in India many decades before any missionaries came. And even then, religious persons were sent for the spiritual care of the settlers, not to evangelize the local population. In fact, as has been shown earlier, the British East India Company resented the missionaries and in some cases had laws forbidding their work among the local population. Evangelizing and educating Indians may have "Westernized" them somewhat, but it also enabled them to respond to the foreigners on an equal footing and gave rise to an articulate national movement.

While British rule unquestionably had its shameful aspects and brutal moments, it was far less barbaric and its justice far more impartial than any previous regime. For almost two hundred years—ninety years, officially—the British raj

---

*Stephen Neill, *The Story of the Christian Church in India and Pakistan,* p. 126.

brought to India a complete unity and a continuous peace that the subcontinent had never seen before. Foreign oppressors? Missionaries brought not only spirital solace but social change, liberating low-caste Hindus from a dehumanizing state. Before the arrival of European Christians, outcastes—both male and female—were forbidden from wearing any clothing above the waist, as an indication of their low social status. Missionaries were instrumental in what was called the "upper cloth movement." Similarly, the employment practices of the indigo plantations in northern India amounted to slave labor. Christian missionaries lobbied successfully—after the introduction of British rule—for better working conditions.

In South India, at least, the local inhabitants saw the British as liberators from the Muslim oppressors, and during the uprising of 1857 southern India was noticeably unresponsive and unaffected. The Moghul empire itself was a foreign dynasty imposed on India. By the time the British took over, that empire had already sunk irretrievably into corruption and political decay. India was fast descending again into the bloody chaos of feuding feifdoms.

The relative merits of Western civilization that the British gave India—education, railroads, a unified civil service—can be debated against their commercial exploitation of the country's natural resources. But the fact remains that the vast diversity of India today under a single federal government would not have been possible—in any democratic form—without the structures developed by the British. India's stability, its growing middle class, and its current significance as a global power is directly linked to these imposed changes—changes that without Western "interference" are unlikely to have occurred, certainly not in the short period in which they were achieved.

British rule, especially after 1858, brought the natural geographic area of the Indian subcontinent under one political administration for the first time, with a breadth and thoroughness that had never been accomplished even at the height of the Moghul Empire. The unbroken peace for more than eighty years facilitated many other morally conscious—not exploitative—developments: 1) a *unified civil service,* reorganized on the basis of competition, not patronage resulted in new standards of honesty and efficiency; 2) a vast *network of railroads* throughout the continent that was built not only between military and industrial centers, but laid out to ensure rapid access of grain to famine-prone areas; 3) this, and the implementation of a *national famine code,* virtually eliminated the recurring specter of mass starvation; and 4) the largest and most *sophisticated irrigation system* in the world led to a much greater and more efficient cultivation of the land, so that as early as the 1880s overpopulation became a potential problem for the first time.*

These achievements may be downplayed by Indian and Pakistani intellectuals with a Western education (often from missionary-sponsored schools) and politicized by Western ideas of democracy and nationalism, but to the vast majority of Indians, accustomed to continual political turmoil and natural calamities, the benefits of British rule were self-evident.

Christian missionary organizations were the first to establish Western-style schools and universities in India, for Indians. The primary impetus for this was to provide a theological education for Indian pastors at an equivalent academic level to that of their missionary counterparts, with a view to creating an Indian Church with local leadership. This effort expanded into the many missionary-run English-medium private schools throughout India. Though at first resistant to the idea of educating Indians, the British colonial government eventually started such schools of its own, to create an educated Indian middle class from which to fill the administrative infrastructure of the Indian Civil Service.

Indeed, the British goal of an autonomous India, within the British Empire, preceded the Indian National Movement is obscured by the mythology surrounding Mahatma Gandhi and the non-violent civil disobedience campaigns of his Independence Movement. The legacy of British colonialism is ambiguous, its balance for good remains controversial. It seems clear, however, that a total condemnation of colonialism can only be made in ignorance of history—and of the situations in subject nations that preceded European control.

In any discussion of Columbus, colonialism, missionaries—

*See Stephen Neill, *The Story of the Christian Church in India and Pakistan,* chs. V and VII, esp. pp. 90ff and 128ff. Neill argued that "the savior of India was the railway," providing the foundation of a rapid transportation system that facilitated the commercial and industrial development of modern India.

or memories—our modern tendency is to try to separate the myth from the reality. But this obsession obscures the very real ways we are often shaped by our myths more than by so-called objective reality. So it is important, not to discard our myths, but to understand how our emotional associations have shaped not only our values but even what we remember.

Missionary work as we think of it today, in all its variety and connotations, has taken shape only in the last hundred-and-fifty years. Many of the sponsoring agencies our parents worked for did not come into existence until after 1857, some not until after the Second World War. At that time the United States replaced Great Britain not only as the leading world power, but the dominant force in missions, with American missionaries for the first time outnumbering—and far outnumbering—British missionaries in India and Pakistan. The modern missionary tradition that my parents and their colleagues joined in the 1950s and 1960s, and the way they experienced it, lasted only a few decades—as the age of nationalism has quickly evolved into an era of internationalism.

The ongoing changes in the nature of Christian missions have been difficult both for national churches and missionary organizations. What does the community of faith look like at the end of the twentieth century? What methods of proclaiming the Gospel are relevant, reconciling, and redemptive in a time of interdependence and transcultural movements? These questions have given rise to "Third World" (that is, non-Western) approaches to theology, such as the liberation theologies of Latin America and Africa. The end of the "frontier" approach to missions has brought a new understanding of evangelism, different from the traditional dynamic of Western missionaries from developed nations going to the "underdeveloped" nations of the three-fourths world. Today, evangelism is seen not only as a partnership between missionaries and local leadership, but the "mission field" itself is viewed in both directions, with Christian workers from Asia, Latin America, and Africa coming to the mission fields of the industrialized West. The Kydon (the United Church of Japan), for example, has a large agency specifically for sending missionaries to America and Europe. In fact, the United States now *receives* more missionaries than any country in the world other than Brazil.

*   *   *

Eleven years after leaving Pakistan my mother, Norma K.
Seaman, wrote this poem:

Pakistan, Oh, Pakistan! How I miss you!
When I read in depth of you,
   see pictures which recall treasured memories,
     meet your sons . . .
I miss you so!
Tears well up, my heart aches—
   aches to return to you.
How I love you, Pakistan, Oh, Pakistan!

Is this what grief is like?
Is this the pain of the bereaved?
Oh, Pakistan, I am bereft of you.
How did I come to love you so?
How can a foreigner, after dwelling with you only
   nine short years,
    feel so longingly for you?

Pakistan, my Pakistan!
But I can't call you mine—you belong to the universe.
You always were. You always will be.
My arms reach around you—
   you and the whole subcontinent,
    for you are really one, one organism
     with many beautiful parts.

When can I come to you?
When will my sweat mix with yours?
When will I climb your mountains
   and feast my eyes on your grandeur?
When will my tongue taste your wheat and corn
   ground on the mill of your weary backs?
When will my feet feel your earth,
   the mud-paste made from perspiring toes
    on dusty roads?

Pakistan, Oh, Pakistan!
Where are your green fields, cool in the dusk

after a long sweltering day?
Where are your rivers, so dangerously swift
   at their mouths,
   so desperately needed at the last canal capillary?

Pakistan, Oh, Pakistan! I hear
   your groaning, the groaning of the masses unsatisfied
   in body or soul,
Yet so patient, lulled by the fate of the ages.
Pakistan, Oh, Pakistan—"land of the pure."
May I be pure in the very soul of me,
Worthy to return and serve you.

How can I ever repay you?
You gave me so much—
You gave me the enrichment of a whole new world
A world of warmth and draining heat,
A world of hills and unknown vistas,
A glimpse of antiquity and competitive struggle,
A world of darkness, yet light glistening
   brighter in that grim backdrop,
A world of created beauty—
   the rose blooming in the desert,
   the skilled artistry from practiced hands,
though the mind may never have met the three R's,
A world of love and devotion.

You taught me so much, beloved Pakistan.
You taught me that to be is better than to do.
You taught me that time is flexible, not
   slavish.
That life can go on after tragedy,
That goals can be reached if we wait,
   and work, and wait.

Pakistan, Oh, Pakistan!
My arms reach out to you,
   but they are too short.

I will wait, and work, and wait.

For Further Reading

Sources to Footnotes and
Other References in the Text

Addleton, Jonathan. *Some Far and Distant Place: A Pakistan Memoir.* Athens, GA, and London: University of Georgia Press (forthcoming 1997).

Austin, Clyde N. *Cross-Cultural Reentry: A Book of Readings.* Abilene, TX: Abilene Christian University, 1986.

———. *Cross-Cultural Reentry: An Annotated Bibliography.* Abilene, TX: Abilene Christian University, 1983 (available from the author at ACU Station, Box 7000, Abilene, TX 79699, USA).

Canadian School in West China. Brockman Brace, ed. Toronto: N.P., 1974.

Craig, Hazel Innes. *Under the Old School Topee.* London: BAC-SA/Chameleon Press, 1990.

Echerd, Pam and Alice Arathoon, eds. *Understanding and Nurturing the Missionary Family,* Compendium of the Inter-

290 FAR ABOVE THE PLAIN

national Conference on Missionary Kids, Quito, Ecuador, *1987,* Vol. I. Pasadena, CA: William Carey Library, 1989 (P.O. Box 40129, Pasadena, CA 91114).

Foyle, Marjory F. *Honourably Wounded: Stress Among Christian Workers.* Eastbourne, E. Sussex, England: MARC/ Kingsway, 1987.

———. *Overcoming Missionary Stress.* Wheaton, IL: Evangelical Missions Information Service, 1987 (EMIS, Box 794, Wheaton, IL 60189, USA; or MARC Europe, Cosmos House, 6 Homesdale Rd., Bromley, Kent BR2 9EX, U.K.).

Insight Guides: Pakistan. Tony Halliday, editor. Hong Kong: APA Publications, 1992. A tourist guidebook with several good historical and cultural essays.

Jordan, Peter. *Re-Entry: Making the Transition From Missions To Life at Home.* Seattle, WA: YWAM Publishing, 1992 (Youth With A Mission, P.O. Box 55787, Seattle, WA 98155, USA; telephone (206) 771-1153).

Kids of the Kingdom:A Working Bibliography on Missionary Kids. Compiled by Mary P. Schimmels. Wheaton, IL: Billy Graham Center Library/Evangelical Missions Information Service, 1991 (EMIS, Box 794, Wheaton, IL 60189, USA).

Mathews, James K. *South of the Himalayas: One Hundred Years of Methodism in India and Pakistan.* Nashville, TN: Parthenon Press, 1955.

McCluskey, Karen Curnow, ed. *Notes from a Traveling Childhood.* Washington, D.C.: Foreign Service Youth Foundation, 1994.

Miller, Sheila. *Pigtails, Petticoats and the Old School Tie.* Seven Oaks, Kent, England: OMF Books, 1981 (available from EMIS—see *Kids of the Kingdom*).

Muller, Wayne. *Legacy of the Heart: The Spiritual Advantages of a Painful Childhood.* New York/London: Fireside/Simon & Schuster, 1992.

Neill, Stephen. *A History of Christianity in India* (2 vols., through 1858). Cambridge/London/New York: Cambridge University Press, 1984, 1985.

——. *A History of Christian Missions* (rev.). Middlesex/New York: Penguin, 1986.

——. *The Story of the Christian Church in India and Pakistan*. Grand Rapids, MI: Eerdmans, 1970.

Pollock, David and Ruth E. Van Reken. *Growing Up Between Worlds: The Third Culture Experience*. Yarmouth, Maine: Intercultural Press, forthcoming 1997.

Sovik, Gertrude and Charlotte Martinson Gronseth. *The Rooster Crows Again: The Story of American School Kikungshan*. Northfield, MN: Private, 1985 (see *Kids of the Kingdom*).

Smith, Carolyn D. *The Absentee American: Repatriates' Perspectives on America*. New York: Aletheia Publications, 1991.

Smith, Carolyn D., ed. *Strangers at Home*. New York: Aletheia Publications, 1996.

Spectrum Guide to Pakistan. By CAMERAPIX; Susan Williams and Jack Crowther, editors. Edison, NJ, USA: Hunter Publishing, Inc., 1989. An excellent introduction to Pakistan with many color photographs.

Stanley, Brian. *The Bible and the Flag: Protestant Missions and British Imperialism in the Nineteenth and Twentieth Centuries*. Leicester, England: Apollos/InterVarsity Press, 1990.

Townsend, Anne. *Faith Without Pretending*. London: Hodder and Stoughton, 1990.

Van Reken, Ruth E. *Letters Never Sent*. Indianapolis, IN, 1987 (LETTERS, 8124 N. Lincoln Blvd., Indianapolis, IN 46240, USA; tel. 317-251-4933).

The Contributors

Listed on these two pages are the names of the eighty-two people who provided narrative material that was used as a resource for this book, whether or not it received a separate entry in the text. The number after each name indicates class year at MCS. Names with no year given are staff, former staff, parents or other missionaries. Thank you for sharing the vision and for trusting me to handle your memories with care. I am honored to be part of this community.   —PAS

David Addleton, '73
Jonathan Addleton, '75
Brigid (Anderson) Murphy, '68
Joanna Arnold, '91
Susan (Arnold) Herbert, '85
Robert Bailey, '78
Malcolm Bavington, '81
Richard Bingham, '64
Ralph Brown
Don and Evelyn Calderwood
Leslie (Christy) Valencourt, '73
Esther Corcoran, '79
Margaret (Cunningham) Mitchell
Helen (Mrs. Paul) Davidson

Agnes (Mrs. Carl) Davis
Charles Davis, '67
David Davis, '64
Marie (Dalton) Lehman, '74
Timothy DeHart, '73
Graham Duncan, '76
Sharon Erb, '75
Ruth Feldmann, '74
Judi (Fidge) Cox, '84
Mark Flowers, '78
Julie Friesen, '89
Inger Gardner
Joe Haas, '67
Judy Haas McKeehan, '65

Glen Hamm, '73
Wayne Hildebrand
Eunice Hill
David Hover, '75
Alison (Mrs. Jim) Hunter
Amy Jo Inniger, '89
Patty (Irwin) McGarvey, '73
Carolina Koole, '84
Don Lotze, '65
John Lotze, '80
Winona (Lundgren) Wakeman, '65
Paul Lundgren, Sr.
George McMillan
Michael Meadowcroft, '76
Helen Miller Price
Janet Miller, '64
Daniel Mitchell
John Mitchell, '81
Jonathan Mitchell, '79
Bruce Montgomery, '66
Roy Montgomery, '73
Marjorie Montgomery
Sabine Munzinger, '87
Isabel and Ian Murray
Andy Norris, '91
Deborah (Nygren) Willow, '75

Ruth (Nygren) Keller, '77
Irv Nygren
Ken Old
Tim Old, '76
Wendy (Olsen) Bates, '71
Kem Philbrick, '74
Tim Philbrick, '65
Paul Pulliam
Gene Purdy
Rick Ralston, '77
Steve Rasmussen, '74
Becky (Roub) Treb, '71
Elaine Roub, '75
Charles Roub
Debby Rupe
Joel Ryther, '72
Miriam (Seaman) Mullins, '82
Ruth (Seaman) Freeman, '74
Rachel (Steeves) Fairchild
Rosemary Stewart
Margaret (Tebbe) Spoelman, '75
Marybeth Tewksbury, '74
Cindy Webster Trulson, '74
Ella Young, '68
Janet (Young) Puddy, '71
John Young, '73

Acknowledgments

My warm thanks to David Addleton, Ruth Van Reken, Jonathan Addleton, Rob Bailey, and Sara Taber for your encouragement and faith from the beginning; to Chuck Roub, Don and Evelyn Calderwood, and especially Isabel Murray for cooperating so patiently with my numerous requests; to Margaret Spoelman, Dave Wickstrom, Beth Dekkers, and Ruth Keller; and to many folks who generously read early drafts—your help was invaluable. My deepest appreciation goes also to David Shaver and Jone Bosch at William Carey Library for graciously making a commitment to this book, in spite of an already crowded publication schedule. Thank you, Rosalie, companion of my heart, for tolerating my many mental absenses and yet being always available to offer suggestions or provide insights when things got tough.

Financial support for this project came from the Presbyterian Church (USA), the General Board of Global Ministries of the United Methodist Church, Associate Reformed Presbyterian Church, Church Missionary Society of Australia, Church Missionary Society (England), Conservative Baptist Foreign Mission Society (now CB International), Finnish Evangelical Lutheran Mission, Pentecostal Foreign Mission (Norway), SIM

International, and TEAM (The Evangelical Alliance Mission). Many alumni and other friends of MCS made individual contributions. Thank you all for helping to make this book possible.

NOTE

Murree Christian School neither commissioned nor endorsed this book. *Far Above the Plain* is intended as a companion volume to *Paper Airplanes in the Himalayas: Reconstructing a Missionary Childhood* (forthcoming 1997), Paul Seaman's more personal memoir about growing up at MCS and the resulting legacy of being a global nomad. *Paper Airplanes in the Himalayas* also features additional reminiscings and reflections by other alumni, including David Addleton, Rob Bailey, Carol (Patzold) Berg, Judi (Fidge) Cox, Glen Hamm, Amy Jo Inniger, Darlene Liddle, Patty (Irwin) McGarvey, John Mitchell, Jonathan Mitchell, Roy Montgomery, Tim Philbrick, Elaine Roub, Leslie (Christy) Valencourt, Deborah (Nygren) Willow, and John Young.

Glossary

bijilee   electricity

bishti   water carrier

burka   an outer garment worn by strict Muslim women when going out in public; usually made of black or white cotton cloth, it covers the body from head to toe—essentially, like a big upside-down bag with a double veil or screened eye-holes

CB, CBFMS   Conservative Baptist Foreign Mission Society

chai   tea; local tea already mixed with milk and sugar

chapatti   round unleavened flatbread, like tortillas; also *roti*

chappal   sandal

charpoy/charpai   wood-framed bed, usually woven with rope

chowkidar   watchman, caretaker

darzi/dhersi   tailor

deputation   when missionaries, while on home leave, report to and raise money from their supporting churches; usually involves a great deal of travel

dhobi   laundry, laundry person

furlough   home leave, usually three months every two to three years; sometimes extended to a year to facilitate educational needs. Changed to *"home assignment"* in the 1980s to more accurately reflect that this time is usually anything but a vacation (see *deputation*)

jalabe   orange, pretzel-shaped deep fried sugar candy

kud   a very steep slope or drop off, as in "over the kud"

kucha   poorly-made, weak, slapped together (opposite of *pukka*)

mem'sahib   term of respect for a married woman

missahib   a single woman, usually addressed to Westerners

MK-CART/CORE   Missionary Kid Consultation and Resource Team/Committee on Research and Endowment, a project that grew out of the International Conferences on Missionary Kids (ICMK), held in 1984, 1987, and 1989

mullah   Islamic holy man, teacher

pataka   fire-cracker

pugri   headcloth, turban

pukka   solid, firm, well-made, reliable (can refer to agreements and relationships as well as things, though *kucha* is rarely used this way)

raj   rule; esp., the British Raj, which officially lasted from 1857 to 1947

roti   bread, esp. local flatbread

somosa   triangular-shaped, deep fried pastry filled with vegetables or ground beef

TCK   Third Culture Kid; also global nomad: anyone who has spent childhood years in a country other than that of their parents' origin because of a parent's occupation (such as foreign service, military, international business, voluntary agency, or missionary organization)

TEAM   The Evangelical Alliance Mission

tikka   small pieces of charbroiled meat, a shishkabob

tonga   horse buggy

UP   United Presbyterian Church, now Presbyterian Church (USA)

wallah   vendor, or person of a particular trade, as in tonga-*wallah*, ice cream-*wallah*, etc.

Photo by Chip Aldridge

Paul Asbury Seaman is former president of Global Nomads Washington Area and a associate editor of *Global Nomads Perspectives*. For the last nine years he has worked at the Churches' Center for Theology and Public Policy in Washington, D.C. A disk jockey and contra dancer, Seaman is currently writing a novel about the 1971 civil war in East Pakistan.

Paul Seaman can be contacted through the William Carey Library or

    c/o Ruth Freeman
    R.D. 1, 80 Van de Bogart Road
    Willseyville, NY 13864
    U.S.A.
    tel. 607-272-2478